MUSIC IN THE

CHILD'S EDUCATION

ROBERT B. SMITH

UNIVERSITY OF ILLINOIS

THE RONALD PRESS COMPANY • NEW YORK

Library of Congress Catalog Card Number: 78–110557
PRINTED IN THE UNITED STATES OF AMERICA

To my mother and father, who believed
so strongly in the early development
of musical capacities

PREFACE

This book is designed to provide college students preparing to teach at the elementary school or preschool level with a practical approach to presenting an effective and comprehensive music program. Because of the many detailed teaching suggestions for vocal, rhythmic, listening, and other elements of a program, the book is also a useful source for the practicing general classroom teacher. The emphasis throughout on a structural sequence of musical growth makes it a helpful tool in developing programs suitable for a wide variety of situations.

In the selection and organization of the materials there have been two prime considerations. First, the child's musical capacities and needs have been considered from his earliest experiences with music to the completion of elementary school. Secondly, each activity and example of music literature has been chosen with careful regard to the total scope of the general music education program and with the purpose of guiding the child's musical growth.

The consistent underlying theme of the text is that *every* child has musical capacities. The content is carefully organized to show how each of these capacities may be developed in a sequential program of musical activities through classroom group instruction. The author has, at all times, taken into consideration the child's level of development and his previous experiences with music as he structured each stage of musical growth by means of challenging and worthwhile activities.

Detailed longitudinal studies have provided the description of children's musical capacities and the musical activities which should be introduced to develop these capacities. The author has participated in research projects with groups between the ages of three and twelve. Several thousand individual vocal tests have been analyzed over a period of ten years in a testing and training program involving every preschool and elementary school grade level. The remainder of the text is also based on the results obtained from factual research projects. Varied approaches to rhythm, listening, and music reading development have been carefully tested in the classroom. Suggestions for music in special education programs are also the result of research studies. References at the ends of chapters suggest suitable materials for each type of activity described and guide the reader to literature on important recent developments in music education.

The author is indebted to several people for their contributions to the preparation of this book. Catherine McHugh, Professor of Music at Southern Illinois University, is responsible for my introduction to this field. She contributed many constructive criticisms which were always presented in terms of the child's musical needs within the total scope of a comprehensive general music program.

Other educators have influenced the direction, content, and scope of the text. Dr. Charles Leonhard of the University of Illinois has provided the most direct contribution through his personal guidance and his pervasive influence in the field of music education. Cecil Shaffer, elementary school principal in Urbana, Illinois, spent many hours evaluating each page in terms of practical application in elementary classrooms.

Finally, thanks are due to the thousands of children whom the author has taught. They have shown through their joy in participating that there should indeed be music for every child.

Robert B. Smith

Urbana, Illinois
    February, 1970

CONTENTS

MUSIC IN THE
CHILD'S EDUCATION

I

MUSIC IN CHILDHOOD EDUCATION

Music resounds through the corridors of the typical elementary school from the beginning to the close of the school day. Indeed, music is often heard before and after school as groups meet for additional choral and instrumental activities. Music comes from every classroom as patriotic songs begin the day's activities. Exuberant musical sounds herald a break in classroom routine as children use singing for relaxation and a needed change of pace. Various activities provide the child with recreation through song or physical movement. The reasons for introducing musical activities are as varied as the activities themselves.

Music correlates well with other subject-matter areas. Songs and other activities are included to heighten the child's awareness of another culture or of a period in history. The special relation of certain types of music to other parts of the curriculum is often presented as a justification for the place of music in the school.

Holidays and other special occasions are celebrated through song. Mankind has always used music to celebrate important events. This tradition is continued in the child's education as holidays and other special events are made more meaningful through music.

These reasons for including music in the daily school schedule, however, are not sufficient. Teachers may find other activities that will help the child relax. The child will participate in many other recreational activities. The study of other cultures and periods of history may proceed without the element of music. The school day is becoming more and more crowded. New math, new science, and many other curriculum innovations require a larger portion of the daily schedule. A music program that is defended or justified for these reasons may be easily replaced by other subjects or dropped from the curriculum.

Music in the child's education must be explained and justified in musical terms. Every child has musical capacities which should be developed as he participates in a daily school music program. Every child should become aware of the vast heritage of music literature which is a living element in our culture. Every child should realize the enduring value of music as he receives a general education.

THE PLACE OF MUSIC

One major purpose of education is to develop capacities that are common to all children. These common capacities or educational potentials must be those which can be developed through group instruction. They are the ones that will lead to further growth and to a greater understanding of a specific educational area.

Every child has musical capacities which can be developed through group instruction. All children have needs that may be defined in musical terms and satisfied through musical activities. The subject of music should therefore be included in the child's general education.

The Child's Capacities and Needs

The child's *aesthetic capacities and needs* are often neglected in his general education. Yet, many decisions made by older children and adults are aesthetic choices ranging from the selection of a phonograph recording to the design of an article of clothing. While other areas of education may contain an aesthetic element, those areas that emphasize aesthetic sensitivity will provide the child with a more comprehensive basis for the development of aesthetic judgment. Music, with its rich aesthetic component, provides inexhaustible opportunities for aesthetic growth.

Young children do not enter classrooms with fixed and definite musical tastes. Their preferences in music develop as a result of the quality and the quantity of experiences they have with many types of music. The older child who prefers to listen to music of enduring quality, rather than the latest trivial favorite, shows that he has been involved in many experiences that have developed his aesthetic sensitivity and selectivity.

Classroom experiences with music may hinder the child's aesthetic growth rather than help it. Teachers of the youngest children must realize that an untuned piano, a poor record player, or a singing example that is neither expressive nor accurate will interfere with a child's aesthetic development.

The child's *physical capacities* will also enable him to develop basic musical skills. Every child can become a tuneful singer, respond to rhythmic pulsations, and learn to listen attentively to music. Activities that will help all children develop these musical capacities should form the nucleus of the preschool and elementary school music program.

Singing, rhythmic, and listening activities should begin as soon as the young child enters a classroom. Preschool and primary grade children acquire the basic musical skills with almost unconscious ease and develop a basis for later experiences with music. Older children will reach a readiness level for more complex and varied activities after they have developed their basic physical capacities. Later successful experiences with music depend to a large extent upon the younger child's development of musical concepts, skills, and attitudes.

The child's *emotional capacities and needs* can be developed and fulfilled through music. The young child who responds actively to the excitement of a martial pulse or quietly to the soothing sound of a lullaby is developing his emotional capacities and fulfilling his need for a rich variety of expressive experiences. The older child will continue to develop these capacities as he responds to more complex selections and performs music with more subtle expressive nuances.

Some aspects of music will help develop the child's *intellectual capacities* at any level of his musical growth. The young child will respond intellectually as he begins to understand the meaning of musical symbols. The older child is stimulated intellectually as he becomes aware of musical form, styles of composition, and many other elements which are involved in the performance or the understanding of a complex musical creation. He will also become more absorbed intellectually as he becomes more proficient in recognizing and reproducing a large vocabulary of melodic and rhythmic notation symbols.

The World of Music

Music provides aesthetic experiences and academic challenges for every child. The music repertoire is vast, ranging from simple folk melodies to complex compositions involving hundreds of instruments and voices. Children will respond to and comprehend the many styles and types of music included in this repertoire if they participate in a structured and sequential music program that stresses both aesthetic and academic growth.

A large heritage of music has been passed on from generation to generation for many centuries. The musical masterpieces of the western world form the nucleus of this heritage. Ethnic music of other cultures is an important part of the music repertoire. Jazz and serious contemporary stylistic developments provide important additions to this accumulation of musical works. Children should have many opportunities to become acquainted with musical styles ranging from the music of tribal cultures to the most recent contemporary experiments. Activities that will help children become aware of their musical heritage should be selected with great care to progress from the familiar to the unfamiliar and from simple to complex forms and styles.

CONCEPT DEVELOPMENT

Musical concepts are often mentioned as educators plan musical activities for children. The teacher is often left in a state of frustration, however, as he seeks for a definition of the term "concept." The term is widely used in recent music education literature, but seldom is an attempt made to explain just what a concept is.

A concept is *not* an aspect of music itself. It is, instead, an important part of the child's growing awareness and understanding of the many elements that are combined to make music. The child's concept of an aspect of music is directly related to a specific musical element. He must develop concepts of melodic direction, rhythmic pulsation, form and structure, harmonic progression, and the expressive meaning of music if he is to participate successfully in sequential musical activities.

The child should be constantly forming concepts about music at any level of his education. He will show the formation of these concepts by expressing his understanding in a manner consistent with his physical, intellectual, and emotional stages of development.

The young child shows in a direct way that he is forming concepts about music. His conceptual understanding of melodic direction will be expressed by the accuracy of his singing, by the physical motions he makes, and by his verbal identification of such melodic elements as highness–lowness. His developing conceptualization of rhythmic pulsation and tempo changes will be evident as he responds to music with his body.

The older child will demonstrate his musical conceptualizations in more varied and subtle ways. He will show that he understands the functions of melodic elements in listening activities as well as in singing activities. His performance of added harmonic parts will indicate a more subtle awareness of harmonic elements. As he selects appropriate accompaniments for songs and identifies form contrasts in listening activities he also displays a wide range of concepts about music.

These few examples are not intended to show the entire repertoire of musical concepts children will develop through participation in music activities. Neither should teachers conclude that younger children will always conceptualize on one level while older children will show a higher level of conceptualization. Increased sensitivity is as dependent upon experience as it is upon maturation. A concept is the child's definition or interpretation of a musical element, expressed in musical imagery consistent with his level of maturation and with his previous experience. The young child who is showing simple concepts through tuneful singing or expressive movement is demonstrating concept formation as fully as the older child who is creating a musical composition or analyzing a complex recording.

This is an important point that should be kept in mind as teachers plan activities to aid the child in acquiring necessary concepts about music.

THE MUSIC PROGRAM

An effective music program should begin as soon as the young child enters school. Young children should have developed the basic musical skills and acquired basic concepts about music by the second- or third-grade level. Successful achievement and continuing interest in music will depend to a large extent upon the presentation of an effective early childhood music program.

A report of the Tanglewood Symposium shows the concern music educators feel for the musical development of the young child. The need to reassess current practices in early childhood music programs was defined as a critical issue:

> *Music has played a less significant role than it should in the lives of children, aged three through eight.*
> We recommend that MENC, recognizing the unrealized potentials of education in general and particularly of music in the lives of children from the ages of three to eight, (a) establish a commission that would cooperate with recognized leaders in the field of early childhood education and of Head Start and of other programs to develop a systematic plan of action and content for the effective use of music; (b) apprise college and university music departments of the necessity to work closely with experts in early childhood education to prepare music education students to teach music to three- to eight-year-old children from all economic, social, and cultural backgrounds; and (c) charge its Music Education Research Council with the responsibility of defining areas of research related to the use of music for this age group.[1]

The term "early childhood," which appears frequently throughout this text, is consistent with the age range defined in the report of the

[1] Report of the Tanglewood Symposium, "Music in American Society," *Music Educators Journal*, 54, no. 3 (November 1967), 73.

Tanglewood Symposium. Early childhood music programs should be implemented in nursery school, kindergarten, and primary-grade classrooms.

Music in Early Childhood

Children in preschool and in primary-grade classrooms have many common characteristics. They are ready to acquire the basic social and conceptual learnings necessary for further development. They also have approximately the same musical potential and should participate in similar music programs. Extreme differences in program planning will be necessary only if primary-grade children have already been enrolled in an outstanding preschool music program.

A music program planned to meet the needs of these children should emphasize the basic music skills. Children must learn to listen attentively, sing tunefully, and respond to rhythmic pulsations before they acquire more complex musical learnings and responses. The child will also build a vocabulary of basic musical concepts as he develops these important skills.

Children will acquire much more than the basic performing and listening skills during these important formative years. They will begin to develop musical independence and learn to use musical elements in flexible and creative ways. They will form positive attitudes toward music and begin to develop continuing musical habits.

Specific behavioral objectives must be set for the early childhood music program. All children should reach the following levels of achievement after participating in an effective program. Every child should:

> Sing tunefully and acquire a repertoire of songs which he performs with a pleasant tone quality.
>
> Develop sensitivity to rhythmic pulsations and display an awareness of the form and content of rhythmically stimulating compositions.
>
> Show that he has developed the habit of attentive listening through performance, through his identification of instrumental and vocal timbres,[2] and by his preference for performances of superior musical quality.
>
> Use the elements of music in an original manner to show that he is developing creative facility.
>
> Perform without aid from the teacher or other children to demonstrate his musical independence.
>
> Acquire basic concepts about music which are necessary for continuing musical development.

[2] Students and classroom teachers may not be familiar with some of the music terms used throughout the text. A Glossary is included at the end of the book.

Show by his increased interest and participation that he has developed positive attitudes toward music and continuing musical habits.

All children should reach these objectives between the approximate ages of three and eight, although the speed with which different children develop these musical skills, concepts, attitudes, and habits will vary a great deal. Some children seem to be born singing, while others match tones with almost painful slowness. Some children are graceful and imaginative when they first enter rhythmic activities, others appear to be extremely awkward, and a few withdraw from active participation.

These extreme differences should not lead teachers to the false assumption that some young children benefit from musical activities while others do not. All young children have musical capacities, and all should have the opportunity to develop this potential.

Music for Older Children

Children in the approximate age range from nine to twelve have characteristics and potentials that provide them with the opportunity to master musical activities that are beyond the capacities of the younger child. Older children in the elementary school have developed the ability to participate in more complex learning situations. They can work independently and have become self-critical. These and other characteristics will enable the teacher to plan educational activities that are generally not possible with younger children.

A program for older children must be challenging and varied. The child who has reached the levels of achievement listed above has developed a readiness for more complex musical learnings. He can develop a singing range and a voice quality that are suitable for performances of beauty and sensitivity. His physical coordination will make it possible for the teacher to present more complex rhythmic activities, and he is ready to begin the study of musical instruments. His ability to conceptualize may be applied to the analysis of music, and he will be more interested in factual aspects of music study. The child's expanded capacities and interests should be developed as completely as possible during this important period of musical growth. The possibilities of the music program for the older child will be limited only by the training of the teacher and by the amount of time music occupies in the school day.

The following specific objectives should be achieved by the older child in elementary school. He should:

Sing accurately over a wide vocal range with a consistent and musical tone quality.

Maintain an independent vocal part and read melodic notation.

Make more sensitive and complex rhythmic and expressive responses than younger children.

Read and write rhythmic notation.

Identify many instrumental tone colors and show that he has become discriminating in his evaluation of musical performances.

Identify a variety of musical forms as he listens to selections representing many periods and styles of composition.

Create and notate original compositions as he demonstrates his increasing knowledge of form and notation.

Harmonize melodies easily by playing chordal accompaniments on the autoharp, the piano, or other social instruments.

The classroom teacher or music specialist may add other objectives to this list. Those presented above should be regarded as a nucleus that will lead to a comprehensive and varied music program suited to the capacities and needs of all older children.

THE TEACHER'S ROLE

Teachers must be consciously and constantly aware of several important factors if a planned activity is to succeed. The classroom environment must be conducive to learning, and motivation that will lead to the most effective learning should be developed in every teaching–learning situation. Other aspects of the total learning situation are equally important. A teacher's attitude is a crucial element affecting the child's acceptance or rejection.

Learning and Motivation

The teacher may assume that a child is learning only when he is involved in an activity selected to teach a desired behavior or skill. This is a false assumption. The child is learning constantly, and his incidental learnings may interfere seriously with his participation in a planned learning situation.

Children's incidental learnings are often a crucial part of their educational growth. The child entering an early childhood classroom may feel quite hesitant about participating in group activities at first. He may be reinforced in his attempts to withdraw if the teacher provides him with too much individual attention during this period of adjustment to school. His first negative response, reinforced by the reward of teacher attention, may lead him to respond to any new situation in the same way. The success of the music program will be seriously impeded by behavior of this sort.

The teacher must be constantly aware of the total learning situation to present effective musical activities. The child must receive musical satisfaction and personal approval if the program is to be effective and lead to musical learning. Skill development and other aspects of music must become truly satisfying if the child is to want to repeat the experiences he has had and begin to develop musical habits.

Motivation is a crucial factor in any educational environment. The child must reach the point where he is eager to participate in any new activity if he is to develop his musical potential. The teacher who shows the excitement of a new activity will draw the child into willing participation. Teachers who continue to repeat activities on a level that is too easy for children may, on the other hand, discover that their pupils begin to lose interest in the music program. Children are motivated by a challenging new activity when they discover that a familiar element is present in the new situation. They also want to experience success as quickly as possible. The teacher must, therefore, find a balance between activities that are too simple and those that may be frustrating.

The Teacher's Attitude

Classroom teachers must be aware of their own feelings about music, since their positive or negative reactions may seriously affect both the child's attitude and the success of the music program. Teachers who feel that Bach's compositions are dull or those of Stravinsky ugly will either project these feelings to children or neglect listening activities. Young children like both baroque and contemporary music and should have many opportunities to become acquainted with a variety of musical styles. Teachers who feel that compositions of some particular stylistic period or periods are musically uninteresting are simply indicating a lack of previous listening experiences and should overcome these limitations.

The above example is only one of the many ways in which the teacher's attitude may affect the music program in a negative manner. Teachers who do not sing well, who are unable to read music easily, who have had little or no experience with the creative possibilities of music may show negative attitudes toward these important parts of the music program. All these feelings of uneasiness or inadequacy may be removed by additional training. Teachers should feel a personal responsibility to evaluate their own musical deficiencies and attempt to overcome them.

Classroom teachers, music specialists, and administrators should fully understand the crucial part the teacher's attitude plays in determining the success or failure of a music program. An extremely negative attitude on the part of a classroom teacher may lead the child to the false conclusion that music is unpleasant, boring, and lifeless. The teacher's positive attitude, based on confidence and musical competence, will help the child discover that music is a fascinating and joyful experience.

Classroom Environment

The child's physical environment should be conducive to successful learning and musical accomplishment. The space and the equipment provided for the music program will contribute a great deal to the success or failure of the program at any level.

Any classroom should be adequate in size, be furnished with necessary equipment, and have adequate lighting and ventilation. Music activities often require additional facilities in terms of both space and equipment. Many music specialists have a special room set aside for music activities. This room has equipment that is necessary for the music program and that may not be available in classrooms. The special music teacher should not feel, however, that all music should take place in this one room. There are many times when the child needs additional space to move. A school community room or gym may be needed when an expressive movement activity will be limited seriously by lack of space in the music room.

The music specialist or classroom teacher should introduce as many aspects of the music program as possible in the regular classroom. Children will realize that music is a basic part of their daily life if the subject is presented there. They may, on the other hand, consider music to be isolated and unimportant if they always go to a special music room for these activities. Parents often report that their children do not sing at home, and the explanation is that "we just sing when we go to the music room."

Specific equipment appropriate for different levels and facets of the music program is described in the following chapters. One basic characteristic is common to all of these descriptions. The child should hear and see examples of the finest quality as he develops his musical capacities. Outmoded equipment in poor operating condition will detract seriously from the effectiveness of the music program at any level.

PROGRAM EVALUATION

Evaluation is often neglected in the preschool and elementary school music program. Teachers who set specific musical objectives and plan a sequential program of activities to help children attain the objectives must realize that the success of the program is dependent upon this important additional factor. Evaluation procedures must be applied as the teacher determines the effectiveness of specific activities and changes or adapts the program to suit the children's progress.

The total evaluation process consists of three major stages:

Specific objectives are defined to describe the musical behaviors the child will develop.

A sequence of musical activities is selected and presented to aid the child in attaining each objective.

Evaluation procedures are applied periodically to determine the extent to which the child is reaching an objective. The results of this evaluation help the teacher plan other activities directly related to the program objectives.

The third stage of the evaluation process will seem obvious and necessary to classroom teachers and administrators. Testing and other measurement devices are considered to be an integral part of other curriculum areas. Elementary music educators tend to be less aware of the importance of specific evaluation procedures. Effective preschool and elementary school music programs are possible only if appropriate evaluation procedures are applied to determine the effectiveness of the music program at any grade level.

The evaluation process is emphasized throughout this text. The importance of specific evaluative measures is stressed and procedures are suggested.

SUMMARY

Music should be a daily part of the preschool and elementary school curriculum. Every child has musical potentials which should be developed as fully as possible at these levels. Early experiences with music are important to the child's future growth, since a large part of his later musical development will depend upon successful early experiences.

An effective music program should include much more than simple recreational music activities. The child has aesthetic, physical, emotional, and intellectual capacities and needs which may be expressed in musical terms. A structured program of music activities will develop these capacities, meet these needs, and introduce the child to a fascinating heritage of enduring musical compositions.

The child's music education should be planned as carefully as any other part of the curriculum. The music program must have specific objectives, and activities must be selected in direct relation to these objectives. The role of learning and of teacher attitude must be carefully considered. The progress of the program should be periodically evaluated with careful attention to the child's musical development.

"Music for every child and every child for music" is an important goal for music education. This phrase becomes meaningful to the child and to the teacher if an effective and challenging music program is fully developed at the preschool and elementary school grade levels.

QUESTIONS AND PROJECTS

1. Organize a discussion of the place of music in preschool and elementary school education. Prepare for the discussion by surveying current practices in the preschool-elementary school curriculum. The following sources are recommended:

   NEA Journal   Elementary School Journal
   Childhood Education   Young Children

2. Scan several issues of a professional journal (the *Music Educators Journal* is an excellent source) to discover the critical issues and new trends in elementary school music education.
3. Discuss the unique functions of music in the education of children.
4. How should the music program be related to other phases of education in the arts? How should music relate to the total school curriculum?

REFERENCES

Recommended Readings

Broudy, Harry S. "Educational Theory and the Music Curriculum." In *Perspectives in Music Education: Source Book III*, pp. 173–84. Washington, D.C.: Music Educators National Conference, 1966.

Broudy, Harry S. "A Realistic Philosophy of Music Education." In *Basic Concepts in Music Education*, 57th Yearbook of the National Society for the Study of Education, edited by Nelson B. Henry, chap. 3. Chicago: University of Chicago Press, 1958.

Bruner, Jerome S. *The Process of Education*. Cambridge, Mass.: Harvard University Press, 1962.

Colwell, Richard. *Music Achievement Test Manual*. Chicago: Follett Educational Corp., 1968.

Gary, Charles L., ed. *The Study of Music in the Elementary School: A Conceptual Approach*. Washington, D.C.: Music Educators National Conference, 1967.

Gordon, Edwin. "Testing Today." In *The Musical Aptitude Profile*, Bulletin 11. Boston: Houghton Mifflin Co., 1965.

Hartsell, O. M. *Teaching Music in the Elementary School: Opinion and Comment*. Washington, D.C.: Association for Supervision and Curriculum Development, National Education Association, 1963.

Leonhard, Charles. "Evaluation in Music Education." In *Basic Concepts in Music Education*, 57th Yearbook of the National Society for the Study of Education, edited by Nelson B. Henry, chap. 13. Chicago: University of Chicago Press, 1958.

Leonhard, Charles, and House, Robert W. *Foundations and Principles of Music Education*. New York: McGraw-Hill Book Co., 1959.

Lundin, Robert W. *An Objective Psychology of Music*, 2d ed., chap. 12, "The Measurement of Musical Behavior: The Nature of Tests." New York: The Ronald Press Co., 1967.

"Music in American Society," Tanglewood Symposium Report. *Music Educators Journal* 54, no. 3 (November 1967):49–80.

Palisca, Claude V., ed. *Music in Our Schools: A Search for Improvement*. Washington, D.C.: Office of Education, United States Department of Health, Education, and Welfare, 1964.

2

THE EARLY CHILDHOOD
VOCAL PROGRAM

Singing should be a happy experience in the young child's life. Some children seem to have been born with the desire to sing and the ability to sing well. Other children sing very poorly, and the teacher may notice a few who seem to show no interest in singing activities at the beginning of the year. These extreme differences in singing ability and interest may lead teachers to the assumption that some children are able to sing well while others are deficient in this respect. This is not true. The differences will be overcome after children participate in an effective early childhood singing program. While some children will always sing with a more pleasant tone quality and learn songs more quickly in a wider range, the child who begins the year as a poor singer will improve greatly in accuracy, range, and quality. Every child *can* learn to sing!

SINGING DEVELOPMENT

Since 1958 the author has been engaged in collecting information concerning children's vocal capacities and the effects of early group training. The results of this longitudinal study, which have been reported at two national meetings of the Music Educators National Conference,[1] provide the factual basis for the early childhood vocal

[1] Robert B. Smith, "The Effect of Nursery School Group Vocal Training on Kindergarten and First Grade Singing Ability" (presented at the national MENC meeting in Chicago, March 1962); "The Effect of Group Nursery School Training on Later Achievement and Interest in Music: A Ten-Year Report" (presented at the national MENC meeting in Seattle, March 1968).

program described here. One research article has described the beginnings of this project.[2]

Directional Stage

The child begins to sing in a *directional* manner. His attempts to sing move up and down in the approximate outline of the melody, but he seldom matches any tones. Some children pass quickly through the directional singing stage at a very young age, while many other children are still directional or beginning singers in the primary grades.

There are two general categories of directional singers. Children in the first category display a relatively wide and flexible vocal range although they seldom match tones when they first attempt to sing. The teacher who is conscious of their vocal needs will help them pass through the directional stage rather quickly and begin to match tones.

Children in the second category have a much smaller beginning range. They seem to be able to produce only a few adjacent tones with slight changes in pitch level. In the past these children have been called monotones, black birds, nonsingers, and other epithets. None of these terms adequately describes the plight of children in the second directional singing category. They are able to sing only a few tones at first, and they need to hear tones in this small range if they are to begin to sing with any chance of success.

Limited-Range Stage

There are beginning singers in practically all nursery school, kindergarten, and primary-grade classrooms as the school year begins. These children will start the year as directional singers and will become tuneful in a small *limited range* of three to four tones if they have repeated opportunities to match tones within their capabilities. Three-year-olds often produce tones first between d' and g'.[3] Children between the ages of four and eight are generally more successful in a slightly lower range between c' and f'. A few children first sing tunefully in a range lower or higher than those just described. The most common range for limited-range singers, however, consists of three to four tones between c' and g', as follows:

[2] Smith, "The Effect of Group Vocal Training on the Singing Ability of Nursery School Children," *Journal of Research in Music Education*, 9, no. 2 (Fall 1963).

[3] The system for indicating the exact location of tones applied throughout this text is as follows: Tones in the range from Middle C up to third-line B (treble staff) are designated as c'-b'. Higher tones, beginning with third-space C, are identified as c"-f". Tones in the octave immediately below Middle C are shown as b, a, and g.

Example 2–1

BYE-LO [4]

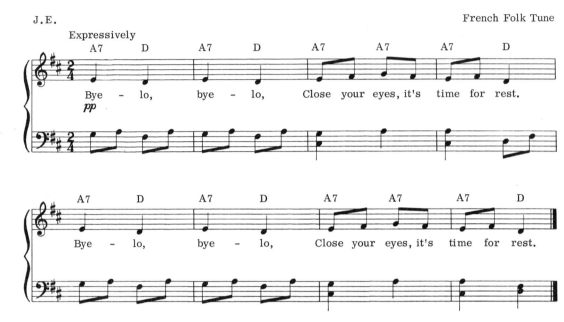

J.E.   French Folk Tune

Teachers must select songs with great care to provide singing activities that will help the limited-range singer. Two types of songs should be selected and repeated frequently at the beginning of the school year. The first type has a total range of only three to four adjacent tones. "Bye-Lo," a French lullaby, is an example (Example 2–1). One other limited-range song is in the Appendix (page 247). The teacher will discover that songs of this type are difficult to find, and songs in a second category should be selected to help beginning singers become tuneful. These are songs with *limited-range patterns,* which are much more numerous. Songs of this type vary in difficulty and in total range, but they have one common characteristic: a limited-range pattern is repeated several times. "Look Around the Room" is a typical example (Example 2–2). The song has a total range from c-sharp' to a'. A pattern from d' to f-sharp' is repeated.

This is an ideal song to introduce at the beginning of the school year. Children will delight in repeating the song time after time as they participate in the following activities:

The teacher may introduce the song first to help children get acquainted with one another. As they sing to each child in the classroom, they

[4] From *Discovering Music Together—Early Childhood* by Robert B. Smith and Charles Leonhard. Copyright © 1968 by Follett Educational Corporation. Reprinted by permission of the publisher.

Example 2–2

LOOK AROUND THE ROOM [5]

C.L.   American Camp Song

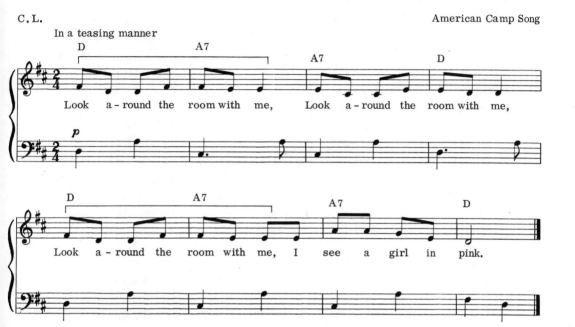

will become conscious of the names of other children and learn to take turns.

Other repetitions of the song will help the teacher discover how well children understand the verbal labels for colors and articles of clothing.

The song may be repeated on other days as a guessing game involving equipment in the classroom. One child will select something to sing about, and after he has sung other children will try to identify the object.

There are many songs of this type. Teachers will find them easily as they analyze a song to discover repeated melody patterns with a total range of three to four adjacent tones. "Riding in a Buggy" (page 279) and "Sing with Me" (page 253) are outstanding examples in this text. A number of other songs in the Appendix also have repeated patterns in this narrow but important vocal range.

Songs with limited-range patterns will be of great benefit to the beginning singer and will also interest the child with previous singing experience. Teachers should begin to emphasize a different type of

[5] *Ibid.*

song, however, when the majority of children in the classroom sing accurately within a limited range.

Lower-Range Stage

Children who have developed limited-range accuracy have reached a level of readiness for expanding their vocal range. Three-year-olds develop a *lower range* from c-sharp' to a'. A few children in this age range sing tones below c-sharp', but for many this is a physical impossibility. Approximately one third of the children in a three-year-old classroom will be able to sing tones higher than a'.

Older children develop a wider lower range. Children between the ages of four and eight are able to sing in a six-tone range between c' and a'. They then add adjacent tones and become accurate in an *extended lower range* spanning an octave from b to b'.

Three-year-old singers with limited-range singing ability will develop lower-range accuracy easily as they sing a repertoire of songs similar to "I Got a Letter" (page 249) and "Who's That?" (page 251). Songs of this type have a range from d' to a'. These simple and repetitious songs should not be considered the exclusive property of children in nursery school. Primary-grade children will also enjoy singing them.

Older children in early childhood classrooms will develop a wider lower range as they learn to sing songs similar to "Little Bird" (page 257) and "I See a Girl" (page 255).[6] The repeated melody patterns within a range from c' to a' are ideal for range expansion.

Children between the approximate ages of five and eight will develop an extended lower range after they have learned to sing a repertoire of songs similar to those described above. Many children in kindergarten and primary-grade classrooms develop a range between b and b' before they are able to sing higher tones, and they pitch songs in this range during solo performances in preference to higher octave ranges.

The teacher should introduce songs similar to "Ha, Ha, Thisaway" (page 263) and "The Allee Allee O" (page 265) to help the child develop an extended lower range. Other songs with an octave range and a higher tessitura should be added to this repertoire, but in most cases they will need to be transposed. Recent research results show that this lower range is important to the vocal development of the young child. Boys, in particular, benefit greatly from opportunities to sing lower tones.

As teachers add songs with the tone b to the classroom singing repertoire, they have the opportunity to help one type of poor singer.

[6] These and the remaining songs mentioned in this chapter are included in the Appendix.

A few children in practically every early childhood classroom seem to have extremely low voices. The most effective way to help these children is to introduce songs with melody patterns that begin low and move upward with scalestep motion. Some extended lower-range songs have such patterns. Other songs with a wider range ("*Savez-vous?*" page 275, is an example) will help these poor singers begin to match tones. Children who sing only a few very low tones are generally imitating a low adult voice. Very seldom do children sing extremely low tones just because they are physically unable to sing higher ones.

All young singers pass through these stages of singing development and develop limited-range and lower-range tunefulness. Lower-range songs and songs with limited-range patterns should, therefore, form the major part of the early childhood song repertoire.

Upper-Range Stage

Children are much less consistent in their vocal development when they attempt to sing in a higher range. The young child who sings lower tones easily and accurately may be completely unable to sing *upper-range* melody patterns. This higher range includes tones above a' for the three-year-old and above a' or b' for older children in early childhood classrooms. Three-year-old children are seldom successful when they attempt to sing these tones. Although a few three-year-olds sing higher tones when they enter nursery school, approximately two-thirds of those in a classroom at this age level are unable to sing upper-range tones.

Children in the age range from four to seven will sing higher tones more easily, but as many as half of the children in first-grade classrooms find upper-range patterns difficult to sing. Ability to control the physical apparatus necessary to produce these tones generally improves by the second- or third-grade level. Songs with upper-range patterns should therefore form a relatively small part of the early childhood song repertoire. They may be grouped into three distinct categories:

1. Lower-range tones are emphasized in the first category, and only one or two isolated upper-range patterns are included. The upper-range patterns are separated from the lower by several tones. This enables the young child to place higher tones more easily when he first attempts to sing them. "Sandy Land" (page 269) is a typical example. There are three lower-range phrases and one higher phrase which begins on c" and moves downward:

La - dies, fare thee   well.

The space of several tones between higher and lower patterns is extremely important when children first attempt to sing upper-range tones. When the higher pattern begins well above the lower patterns children are more apt to use their smaller folds to produce these tones. Much of the difficulty the young child experiences in attempting to sing higher tones seems to be caused by lack of physical control when he must stop using his larger folds and attempts the transition to the necessary use of the smaller.

"Going to Boston" (page 271) is another song typical of the first category. The stanza is entirely in the lower range and appropriate for any young child with previous singing experience. The refrain is almost entirely in the upper range and begins several tones higher than the stanza.

2. A second type of song should be introduced after children have learned to sing several songs in the first category. These melodies begin with lower-range tones and move upward gradually to c" or d". "Three Pirates" (page 277) is representative of this category. The second phrase has the type of melodic motion typical of songs in this category:

Three pi - rates came to   Lon - don town, Yo   Ho _____,   Yo   Ho _____,

Continued practice with melody patterns of this type will help children make a smooth transition between lower and upper tones. They will gradually acquire the ability to begin using their smaller vocal folds.

3. Since many children in early childhood classrooms will be unable to sing higher tones regardless of their experience with songs in the first two categories, songs in the third category should form a very small portion of the preschool and first-grade repertoire. These melodies begin high and move constantly from higher to lower tones. "When the Train Comes Along" (page 281) is an example. The first phrase begins on d":

When the train comes   a - long__, When the   train comes   a - long__,

Combinations of Patterns

All children pass through these stages of vocal development. The songs for young children included in the Appendix have therefore been arranged in the order in which children will be able to sing them. Teachers must not, however, expect all children to reach a certain stage of development or to sing each song at the same time and with the same degree of facility.

Since there will seldom be a time when all children in a classroom sing with equal facility, the classroom repertoire should not consist entirely of songs in one specific range. Some children will be singing well in a wide range, while others are slowly learning to match limited-range tones.

Some melodies include patterns that are suitable for all levels of vocal development. "Hoosen Johnny" (page 273) is an example. The beginning singer will be able to sing this phrase:

Children who have developed lower-range facility will add another pattern to the one above:

The young singer with upper-range accuracy will also be able to sing this phrase:

The Appendix contains several other melodies that have range patterns suitable for all stages of vocal development. "Riding in a Buggy" (page 279), "Three Pirates" (page 277), and "Going Down to Cairo" (page 283) are songs of this type.

SONG SELECTION

The songs described above have been carefully selected to help children develop their vocal capacities to the fullest. Early childhood teachers have many other reasons as well for choosing songs for classroom singing activities. Some are introduced to help children celebrate special events and holidays. Others are selected to enrich another unit or a subject-matter area. Some are introduced solely for recreational purposes.

Melodies appropriate for children to sing must be chosen with care, regardless of any other purpose the teacher has in mind. The following points should be used as selection criteria:

Songs should be selected that will continue to appeal to children after many repetitions. Those composed to cater to the supposed interests of young children are seldom this interesting. Folk songs are often much better choices for early childhood singing activities. They have been passed on from generation to generation because of their inherent interest. Many folk songs will become part of the child's permanent song repertoire.

Songs for young children should have melodic phrase repetition. Children gradually add tones and intervals to their singing vocabulary by hearing and singing them several times. The folk song offers many ideal examples of this type of melody. Repetition of melodic phrases is characteristic of most folk music.

The texts should have repeated word phrases to enable the child to listen to the melody without being distracted by difficult word combinations. Folk songs also have this characteristic. The songs for young children included in the Appendix have simple, repeated word phrases.

The range of the song is of critical importance. A teacher may select a song according to the points previously defined and still present the child with an impossible and frustrating experience. The melody *must* be in the most appropriate range for the child's stage of vocal development.

The early childhood song repertoire should be as varied as possible. Many folk songs are fast, loud, and highly rhythmic. Teachers should select singing material that will provide contrasts in mood, tempo, and harmony. Lullabies help provide a contrast of mood. "Bye O, My Baby" (page 267) is a Scottish lullaby with a calm, slow tempo and a sustained melodic line. Teachers may provide a different type of musical contrast by presenting songs in a minor key. "It Rained a Mist" (page 259) is often sung in a major key. It is even more effective in a minor tonality.

The points for song selection listed above should be considered in choosing any song for the classroom. Children respond in a very positive way to songs with these characteristics. They will choose them time after time in preference to those of poorer musical quality.

RELATED ACTIVITIES

The importance of singing as a daily activity in early childhood classrooms cannot be stressed too much. Singing activities should not, however, be the entire focal point of the music program. Other aspects of a comprehensive program are described in detail later in this text.

There are, in addition, some musical activities that should be considered in terms of their direct relationship to the vocal program. Children may become aware of many aspects of music as they learn to sing. Melody and rhythm instruments provide them with the opportunity to expand a singing activity into a more comprehensive music-learning situation. They will become more aware of melodic and rhythmic movement as they are involved in prereading activities. Their vocabulary of musical concepts will be expanded as singing serves as a focal point for exploring and understanding a variety of musical elements.

The Use of Instruments

The place of musical instruments in the classroom is described in detail in Chapter 8. A few specific examples are included here to suggest instrumental activities that will enrich the singing program.

Simple melody instruments are invaluable additions to singing activities. Bells of different types should be introduced to help the child explore music through this tonal and visual medium. Resonator bell sets, chromatic melody bells, and sets of step bells are appropriate for these activities. Perhaps the most useful and musical are resonator bells, since each bell may be handled separately, and the playing surface is larger and easy for the child to strike.

The child must become aware of varied elements of music if he is to develop singing ability. He must become aware of the rise and fall of the melodic line and the distance between tones. This awareness will be enhanced and accelerated as he plays bells while he sings. His kinesthetic, visual, and aural senses will combine to aid his vocal development through this use of simple instruments.

Beginning singers should be encouraged to play bells while they sing. Limited-range patterns contain no more than three to four adjacent tones which the child will play with ease. The selection by the teacher of appropriate resonator bells further simplifies the playing-singing situation. Children who find and play patterns, and who sing at the same time, generally improve rapidly in their ability to sing. Bells and other simple melody instruments are also a helpful addition to the singing program when the child begins to expand his singing range. He will learn to sing upper-range tones more easily if he finds these tones on bells or at the piano while he sings.

Children will become aware of other musical elements and develop additional concepts about music as they experiment with bells. Their awareness of the harmonic element will be increased as they accompany songs with simple bell parts. Songs that are harmonized with two chords may be accompanied by a single bell tone. The two songs included in this chapter are examples. Both "Bye-Lo" (page 18) and "Look Around the Room" (page 19) are in D Major. Each song may be harmonized with the I (D) and the V_7 (A_7) chords. Both chords have a common tone of A. Every child in the classroom will enjoy playing an accompaniment on this bell while the others song.

Activities of this sort should be a frequent part of the singing program. Children should later discover that the accompaniment will be more varied if the D bell is used for the I chord. These activities may be easily transferred to the autoharp and to the piano keyboard. A number of songs with two-chord accompaniments are listed at the end of Chapter 8. Others may be found in the Appendix.

Children who experiment with melody instruments to discover harmonic accompaniments are also developing a readiness for part-singing. Successful part-singing requires careful listening to other melody lines as well as the one the child is singing. Many of the instrumental activities described in Chapter 8 and in the Appendix will prepare the primary-grade child for this activity.

Other instruments should be added to the vocal program to expand the child's perception and knowledge of music. Carefully selected *rhythm instruments* will enrich singing activities, make children aware of rhythmic elements, and increase their sensitivity to tone color. The child's playing of rhythm instruments should always be directed into musical channels. Hitting a drum aimlessly may provide him with a happy play activity, but no musical purpose is served.

Children should be helped to find basic metrical and rhythmic patterns as they experiment with rhythm instruments while they sing. They will discover that some melodies have underlying patterns of two or four pulsations, while others have three. They will also discover that the length of melody tones is often quite different from the basic meter.

Children should also become aware of the accompaniment possibilities of rhythm instruments and add them to song performances whenever they heighten the musical effect. They will find great satisfaction in these accompaniments. They will also develop an increased awareness of tone color and simple orchestration which they will transfer to listening situations.

Rhythm instruments should be carefully chosen for the classroom, and the following points should be considered:

The instrument should be introduced only if the child has developed sufficient physical coordination. Triangles, small cymbals, and other instruments are often frustrating to many young children. This is particularly true in preschool classrooms.

The instrument should have a musical sound. Many mass-produced rhythm instruments are not adequate when this basis is used to select instruments. A few carefully selected instruments with a variety of tone-color possibilities are far preferable to large quantities of cheap drums, rhythm sticks, and eyecatching gimmicks which produce an unmusical sound.

Melody and rhythm instruments suited to the child's physical and musical abilities may be added to the basic singing program in countless ways. Their introduction and continued use will be limited only by the teacher's experience and creative imagination.

Prereading Activities

Other activities correlated with the basic singing program will help the child's vocal development. Children may be prepared for a basic understanding of notation through experiments with melody and rhythm instruments.

Primary-grade children should have repeated opportunities to discover the basic rudiments of music notation. They should develop an awareness of melodic and rhythmic patterns which will help them begin to understand the relationship between sound and symbol. They develop an awareness of tonal direction as they play melody instruments. They develop a vocabulary of metrical and rhythmic patterns by playing rhythm instruments.

Other activities should be introduced after a period of experimenting with instruments. Children should become acquainted with melodic hand signals and line notation. These melodic prereading activities will accelerate vocal development. They also serve as an important bridge between a singing performance and an understanding of the symbols of melodic notation.

Hand signals are used quite often and almost unconsciously by many teachers. The teacher shows the outline of the melody with appropriate hand motions as children begin to sing a new song or practice a difficult section. Children should be encouraged to imitate these motions. They will feel melodic direction more precisely, and they will develop concepts of melodic movement as they use hand signals. Practice of this type will lead them to the point where they are ready to understand and to read line notation.

Line notation should be introduced to help children further understand both melodic and rhythmic notation. This type of basic notation is more precise than hand signals, since both the lengths of notes and the direction of the melody are displayed on a chalk or flannel board. The following notation for a folk song ("Hop, Old Squirrel," page 247) is an example:

The example has characteristics similar to those of hand signals. The rise and fall are also similar to actual pitch notation, and rhythmic note lengths are more accurately depicted.

The activities suggested here are not the only ones appropriate for the younger child. Some teachers introduce an additional harmonic element in classroom singing activities by singing another part at phrase endings. The child becomes aware of harmonic possibilities in this manner and is actually learning to sing his part against another.

Some of the correlated activities described are appropriate for every young child. Nursery-school and kindergarten children will enjoy experimenting with simple instruments and will have developed sufficient physical coordination to make such activities musically satisfying. The preschool child is also ready to imitate and initiate hand signals. Other activities are more appropriate for the primary-grade child. Some primary-grade children will also be ready for the music-reading activities described in Chapters 3 and 5.

THE TEACHER'S ROLE

Some children learn to sing so easily that the beginning stages of singing development are almost unnoticeable. Other children in a classroom make such slow vocal progress that the teacher may decide they will *never* learn to sing. The teaching procedures described below are as appropriate for the child who sings well as they are for the beginning singer. Every child should become a tuneful singer if these approaches are introduced in the classroom.

Motivation

"I have a few shy children who do not sing with us" or "Some of my boys will not sing! What shall I do?" are typical comments teachers make at the beginning of the school year. These remarks indicate a serious musical problem. The child who tends to withdraw from an activity at the beginning of the year may continue to do so unless he receives quick and perceptive guidance from the teacher.

The shyest child will begin to participate in singing activities when the teacher introduces songs that feature names, colors, and clothing. "Look Around the Room" (page 19) is an ideal choice. "I See a Girl" (page 255) and "Who's That?" (page 251) are equally effective. These three folk songs are appropriate as school opens for another reason. All three have narrow vocal ranges, and two of the songs have limited-range patterns.

Songs of a different type will also help the teacher actively involve each child in singing. The teacher may suggest that children sing one part and that the teacher will sing another. "I Got a Letter" (page 249) is an example. The short, repeated pattern, "Oh yes, Oh yes," may be designated as the part the children are to sing. The child who tends to withdraw from active participation at the beginning of the year will respond and feel quite important as he joins other children in singing *their* part of this song.

Repetition

Some children make little vocal progress in spite of the fact that they participate in daily singing activities. One major reason for this lack of progress is the fact that too many songs are introduced, sung a few times, and then replaced by others. Repetition is an important factor in a successful singing program. Songs must be repeated frequently to give children opportunity after opportunity to hear and sing the same tones and phrases.

Teachers must remember that some children develop vocal ability very slowly, and repeated practice is necessary if they are to learn to sing. Interesting and worthwhile songs must be introduced if they are to be repeated many times during a semester or a school year.

Repetition of a melody does not necessarily mean repetition of the same text each time the song is performed. Teachers who understand the importance of repeating a song many times may suggest the creation of new words. Children are thus encouraged to be creative while they sing.

Many folk songs have accumulated verses in this way. A glance at one of these shows the different texts that have been added to the same melody. Four verses of "Sandy Land" are included in the Appendix (page 269). The verses describe work, travel, and a special event. Children may compose new verses to a familiar melody in a similar way. Teachers who encourage this creative approach will find that folk melodies may be adapted with word changes to celebrate holidays and other special occasions. This approach will benefit the child in several ways. He will have frequent opportunities to practice familiar melody patterns. He will also begin to use words and music in a flexible and imaginative manner. The folk melody which has been adapted to suit a special occasion or a holiday will often prove to be a better musical choice than the many songs of dubious quality that have been composed for these events.

Consistency

Songs should be repeated in the same key as often as possible. This is particularly important when a new song is first introduced and practiced. Children will not acquire the vocabulary of tones they need to become accurate singers if they do not have frequent opportunities to sing melodies in exactly the same tonality. This technique is important when introducing new songs to groups at any level of vocal development. It is particularly important for beginning singers, for children who are beginning to expand their vocal range, and for those who learn to sing very slowly.

Children who are beginning to progress from directional singing to limited-range tunefulness have a very small group of tones in which they can become tuneful. The teacher who presents a new song to help these children might select a song with limited-range patterns similar to "Sing with Me" (page 253). The child will learn to sing the limited-range pattern if it is always presented in the same key. The song will not help him learn to match tones in a limited range, however, if the teacher continues to repeat the song on subsequent days but does not repeat it in the same tonality. Teachers who sing without some "tuning-up" help from a piano or other accompaniment instrument may be performing in an impossible range for the beginning singer (and for tuneful children as well!).

Informal vocal teaching presentations in which teachers do not give themselves a beginning pitch or use some type of accompaniment often lead to a singing group in which a large number of children simply "drone" along or stop trying because they have never had repeated opportunities to hear phrases in the most appropriate beginning range.

Flexibility

Teachers should provide an atmosphere in which the child will feel free to experiment with different ways of singing. An atmosphere encouraging such freedom is particularly important when the child first begins to match tones and as he attempts the transition to upper-range tones.

One important goal of the singing program is to guide children toward the most pleasant and musical vocal sound. This goal should not be stressed too much with beginning singers, however, or with those who are attempting the transition to higher tones. The beginning singer will often produce some very loud and raucous sounds as he attempts to match tones in a limited range. These attempts are frequently quite successful and should not be discouraged. Later, a softer and more musical quality should be encouraged.

First attempts to place higher tones are difficult for many children. Some children try to force their voices upward and almost shout as they first attempt to sing higher. Others sing much more softly as they try to sing upper-range phrases. The transition to upper tones should eventually become as smooth as possible. Flexibility should be emphasized, however, as children practice phrases made up of higher tones.

One technique for helping children acquire a pleasant higher vocal sound is easily applied to many songs. A repeated upper-range phrase may be attempted first with a louder dynamic level, and then much more softly in an echo effect. "Hoosen Johnny" (page 273) has a higher section with a repeated phrase. The dynamic markings show that the phrase should be performed once loudly and again as an echo.

Audio-Visual Aids

The effective presentation of classroom singing activities is often enhanced by the introduction of audio or visual aids. These devices may be as simple as a chart showing a single musical element and as complex as the most recent electronic innovation. Teachers should use a variety of such aids to implement the preschool or primary-grade singing program.

Audio aids include the record player, tape recorder, and such recent inventions as the electronic chalkboard. A varied collection of outstanding recorded singing examples should also be included under this type of classroom music aid.

A *record player* should be standard equipment in every classroom. Classroom teachers with musical training may use recordings rather seldom and consider them merely as added singing examples or review material in the singing program. Teachers with little training will often rely upon the record player and excellent recordings as an indispensable part of singing activities.

All teachers, regardless of the amount of training they have had, should use recordings as adjuncts to the singing program for another important reason. The child will sing with recordings, radio and TV broadcasts, and in other situations outside of the classroom when he is introduced to this type of activity. Singing along with records will help the child achieve vocal independence by showing him one way to sing outside the classroom.

Tape recorders are seldom standard equipment in preschool and primary-grade classrooms, but they are available in many schools. The tape recorder will prove to be a valuable classroom aid to the singing program for several reasons. It may be used as a motivational device. The young child is delighted when he hears himself on tape and will respond eagerly as the teacher suggests recording a song. The use of the tape recorder in this manner early in the school year will prove to be an effective way to involve every child in singing.

Tape recording individual singing responses is another valuable way to make use of this audio aid. Evaluation is discussed in detail later in this chapter, but the importance of the tape recorder should be emphasized at this point. The teacher who is attempting to evaluate the singing progress of the individual child is a busy person. The tape recorder may be used to gather taped records of each child's singing for later evaluation.

Audio devices are effective only if they produce a musical and realistic sound. The cheap record player or tape recorder will often be a hindrance rather than an aid. Worn needles and recordings are equally ineffective. Teachers who want to present an effective singing program must be aware of aspects of the child's environment that may influence his tastes and musical models. He constantly hears music of poor quality performed on superb record players and supermarket sound systems. The child is *not* to blame if he prefers a well-recorded stereophonic performance of a "pop" song to a scratched recording of a beautiful folk song reproduced on a cheap record player with a worn needle.

Audio aids are appropriate and effective devices for any preschool and primary-grade classroom. *Visual aids* are generally planned to provide the child with an introduction to music reading and are therefore more appropriate for the primary-grade child. Those visual aids that introduce the child to music notation are extremely varied. Flannel and magnetic wall or easel boards are a flexible device for showing the child first examples of melodic and rhythmic notation. A large supply of notes of different rhythmic lengths should be available to make this visual aid useful as the teacher introduces prereading activities.

Concept charts and large song reproductions will also help the prereading and beginning reading program. The child will develop visual awareness of musical symbols as he sings while following these large reproductions of musical phrases.

Some teaching aids have both audio and visual qualities. Filmstrips with correlated records will help the young child acquire a readiness for music reading. The filmstrip provides visual examples, and the recording adds the sounds of music and narration.

Visual aids are traditionally used to help primary-grade children become aware of the meaning of music notation. They are often introduced as prereading activities to prepare children for reading. Actual reading is generally delayed until the intermediate grades. One approach to music reading, however, is planned for the primary grades. The charts that accompany Richards' book, *Threshold to Music*,[7] are carefully designed and structured to provide reading activities for young children. The approach is partially based on the work of the late Hungarian composer, Zoltán Kodály. Teachers who have developed a comprehensive basic music program and who have allotted sufficient time for music each day may wish to add these reading and dictation activities to the total program.

Many teachers will concentrate on children's basic musical needs and develop their capacities as fully as possible during the brief time allotted for music. As prereading visual aids are introduced occasionally after children have learned to sing a song or participated in some rhythmic activity, they will begin to see what they have performed. In this way they will acquire a fundamental understanding of the meaning of music notation.

The overhead projector and opaque projector are extremely helpful to the teacher who wants to continue reading experiences beyond the introductory or prereading level. The teacher will be able to continue to present musical symbols in a specific tonality or to present additional combinations of familiar notes by using one of these basic visual aids.

The teacher should never feel that prereading and reading activities will be effective *only* if each child is holding a music book. The child will often gain more understanding of the rudiments of notation if he follows a larger representation of a phrase or song while singing. Visual aids that present an example of larger and simplified notation are often more appropriate for the young primary-grade child than are small examples printed in song collections.

[7] Mary Helen Richards, *Threshold to Music* (Palo Alto, Calif.: Fearon Publishers, 1964).

Audio and visual aids add an important dimension to the classroom singing program. Teachers should be aware of the latest devices in this field and select those that are appropriate for specific classroom singing activities.

Vocal Independence

The child will not be able to use his singing ability fully unless he learns to sing without assistance from adults, accompaniments, or other children. He must develop confidence in his ability to sing alone if he is to sing at home and in other situations outside the music period.

After the child has learned a song, several steps will help him develop vocal independence:

> The teacher should stop singing with the class. The added support of the adult voice may become a vocal "crutch" if the teacher always sings.
>
> Accompaniment should, gradually be withdrawn. A harmonic accompaniment may be substituted for the melody of the song. Later, children should sing without any accompaniment.
>
> Portions of the music period should be planned to provide children with the opportunity to sing alone for others. Every child should have this opportunity at regular intervals. The child's solo performances will also help the teacher evaluate his singing progress.
>
> The teacher should discover whether the child is singing at home. The extent to which a child is transferring his song repertoire to other situations will show the extent to which he is becoming an independent singer. The teacher should also discover what songs the child is singing. This will provide information as to whether the songs the teacher selects are effective choices.

Young children have a tendency to separate school and home activities. A singing program that takes place only at certain scheduled times in the classroom is not an effective program. Music will become an important part of the child's life only if he uses music in situations away from the music period.

The child who has learned to sing tunefully and has confidence in his ability to sing without help will transfer this skill and attitude to other situations if the teacher uses one additional approach. The teacher must show in a positive way that this type of activity is appropriate and expected. The child should be asked what songs he has sung at home and which are his favorites. Children often adopt the attitudes of adults they admire and will sing outside the classroom if it is clear that the teacher considers this to be important.

PROGRAM OBJECTIVES

The process of vocal development and the materials, activities, and teaching techniques that will help children develop vocal ability have been described in detail above. The program must, nevertheless, be tailored to the needs of children in a specific classroom, and specific behavioral objectives must be developed.

The child in an early childhood classroom who participates in an effective program of singing activities should reach the objectives listed below. Every child should:

Sing accurately in a limited range of three to four adjacent diatonic tones.

Develop a wider lower range of five to eight diatonic tones.

Show that he has acquired a repertoire of songs of enduring quality.

Sing alone without assistance from the teacher, other children, or an accompaniment.

The child who has achieved sufficient physical maturation should reach still other objectives. He should:

Sing accurately and easily in a wider range from b to d".

Sing with a consistent and musical quality throughout this range, making a smooth transition between lower and upper range tones.

Demonstrate that he has added songs in a wider range to his singing repertoire.

The child will attain other related objectives as he participates in activities related to the vocal program. He will:

Play patterns on instruments and shape phrases with hand signals to show that he has acquired concepts of melodic direction.

Demonstrate his growing awareness of the meaning of melodic and rhythmic notation by his active and accurate use of line notation.

Many other objectives will occur to the experienced classroom teacher and music specialist. Every child should certainly become an enthusiastic singer. Children are enthusiastic about an activity in which they are successful, and the enthusiastic singer is therefore the child who has learned to sing well. Objectives concerning the child's motivation and interest in singing may be added for a specific classroom vocal program if the objectives described above are attained by every child.

PROGRAM EVALUATION

No singing program will be completely effective and meet the needs of each child unless evaluation is an important part of the program. This chapter contains many structured suggestions that will help the child develop singing ability. While the approaches are appropriate for both preschool and primary-grade children, they need thoughtful application to be completely suitable in a specific classroom.

Although all children pass through the singing development stages defined in this chapter, they make progress in quite different ways and at different rates of speed. The teacher who periodically checks individual singing ability will adjust singing repertoire to suit the child's level of singing development.

An informal singing game will provide a happy, relaxed setting as the teacher evaluates individual singing ability. The child thoroughly enjoys songs in which the entire group sings one part and individuals sing an answering part. "Who Built the Ark?" (page 261) is a folk song which may be introduced as an evaluation device. The child should be thoroughly familiar with the spirited song before the game is introduced. Either the musical question or the answer may be sung by one child:

"I See a Girl" (page 255) is another excellent choice for an evaluation singing game. The child who hesitates at other times will sing happily when this delightful question is asked.

Other songs may be used to check singing progress. The train-whistle imitation which serves as an introduction to "When the Train Comes Along" (page 281) is an excellent pattern for checking upper-range ability. The echoing phrase in "Hoosen Johnny" (page 273) is equally appropriate.

The teacher may listen to each child sing alone and discover later that it is almost entirely impossible to remember how well he performed. Several evaluation aids and techniques are necessary if the teacher is to obtain a valid record of each child's progress.

The tape recorder is an indispensable evaluation aid. The teacher may record each performance and listen later to evaluate the child's singing ability. The teacher who does not have access to this teaching aid may ask another teacher to help with the evaluation activity by taking notes as children sing.

The piano should be used for melodic accompaniment. The teacher will obtain an accurate record of a child's ability in a specific range if he sings a phrase with accompaniment.

Evaluation is often the weakest aspect of a potentially effective music program. Teachers must be fully aware of each child's singing progress if appropriate and sequential activities are to be planned and presented in the classroom. Effective planning and selection are possible only if the evaluation process is carefully applied.

SUMMARY

A carefully planned singing program is extremely important to the musical development of the young child. Singing should be emphasized in the early childhood classroom, since children develop vocal ability most easily during these formative years.

The program should be planned to meet the child's musical needs and to prepare him for further musical growth. While children develop singing ability in much the same way, the teacher must always be conscious of the individual child's progress as he develops ability within the ranges defined in this chapter and reaches the objectives set for the singing program. The vocal program should be further enriched by playing and prereading activities which will help the child learn to sing and also prepare him for later participation in music.

The child's future musical progress will be influenced greatly by successful early childhood singing experiences. He will want to continue to participate in singing activities if he has learned to sing well. His success in acquiring this important basic musical skill will also help him develop a positive attitude toward music and a continuing interest in other aspects of music.

QUESTIONS AND PROJECTS

1. Select a kindergarten or primary-grade basic series book. Use the vocal ranges and developmental stages described in this chapter to analyze the songs included in the book chosen. Arrange the songs in an approximate order of difficulty.
2. Analyze a book from a basic music series for word and melody repetition. List the songs that have these characteristics.
3. Prepare for a class discussion of the developmental characteristics of children in the early childhood age range by out-of-class reading assignments. Topics for investigation and discussion might include cognitive, physical, and emotional development.

4. Observe an early childhood classroom during a period set aside for music.
5. Explore the history of vocal range in songs published for young children through an examination of the basic music series published during the past twenty years.
6. What essential musical behaviors should be developed as a result of the early childhood vocal program?

REFERENCES

Basic Music Series

Birchard Music Series (Ernst et al.). Evanston, Ill.: Summy-Birchard Co., 1962.
Discovering Music Together (Leonhard et al.). Chicago: Follett Educational Corp., 1970.
Exploring Music (Boardman et al.). New York: Holt, Rinehart & Winston, 1966–69.
Growing with Music (Wilson et al.). Englewood Cliffs, N.J.: Prentice-Hall, 1966.
The Magic of Music (Watters et al.). Boston: Ginn and Co., 1965–67.
Making Music Your Own (Landeck et al.). Morristown, N.J.: Silver Burdett Co., 1968.
Music for Young Americans (Berg et al.). New York: American Book Co., 1966.
This Is Music (Sur et al.). Boston: Allyn and Bacon, 1967–68.

Supplementary Song Collections

Landeck, Beatrice. *Songs To Grow On.* New York: Edward B. Marks Music Corp., 1950.
Nye, Robert; Nye, Vernice; Aubin, Neva; and Kyme, George. *Singing with Children.* Belmont, Calif.: Wadsworth Publishing Co., 1962.
Pocket Folk Song Library. Delaware, Ohio: Informal Music, n.d.
Seeger, Ruth Crawford. *American Folk Songs for Children.* Garden City, N.Y.: Doubleday & Co., 1953.

Classroom Instruments

Autoharp (the 15-bar Educator Model is recommended for classroom use because of the addition of chord bars which are appropriate for accompanying songs for younger children).
Chromatic melody bells, chromatic resonator bells (sets extending from g to g″—25 bells—provide bells for any classroom music activity), diatonic step bells.

Suppliers

Children's Music Center, Inc., Los Angeles, Calif.
Harmolin, Inc., La Jolla, Calif.
Lyons Band Instrument Co., Chicago, Ill.
Peripole, Inc., Far Rockaway, N.Y.

Rhythm Band Inc., Fort Worth, Tex.
Wexler, Chicago, Ill.

Recommended Reading

McHugh, Catherine F. "The Uncertain Singer." In *Music Education in Action,*
edited by Archie N. Jones. Dubuque, Iowa: Wm. C. Brown Co., 1964.

Audio-Visual Aids

Useful visual aids are included in the following basic music series (see above).
For other audio-visual aids see the References at the end of Chapter 3.

Birchard Music Series (charts—large notation for songs; easels—accompaniments
for autoharps and other instruments).
Discovering Music Together (concept and notational charts for Book I).
Growing with Music, Book I, Chart Edition.
This Is Music (Wall Charts—reading aids, music for classroom instruments, pic-
tures of instruments).

3

VOCAL ACTIVITIES
FOR OLDER CHILDREN

Vocal development should be considered as a central focus in a music program planned for the older child. Children in intermediate-grade classrooms will have reached a readiness for a variety of singing activities after participating in the early childhood singing program described in Chapter 2.

The older child has a greater singing potential than the child in a preschool or a primary-grade classroom. His potential singing range is wider because he has reached a higher level of physical maturation and because of previous singing experience. His increased control of breathing and diction will allow him to sing longer musical phrases with ease.

Singing activities should be planned to challenge older children in the elementary school. They will continue to enjoy simple recreational songs and should add to their folk-song repertoire. They should also have the opportunity to sing more difficult vocal literature. Challenging singing activities will be appropriate for the older child's level of musical and vocal development. They will also help prepare him for a musical future. He will begin to develop an awareness of and an appreciation for outstanding vocal and choral performances.

Three general types of singing activities should be planned for children in the upper grade levels of the elementary school. Children should:

> Have frequent opportunities to sing more complicated and beautiful unison songs. The child becomes more sensitive to the beauty and complexity of melodies as he acquires a repertoire of such songs.

Participate in singing activities involving the performance of an added harmonic part. They will develop a strong harmonic feeling as they sing songs arranged in several parts. They will also become aware of and appreciate part-singing in performances by others.

Participate in singing activities planned to develop reading skills. They will become aware of the importance of music notation as they become independent in their uses of music through music-reading activities.

Singing programs planned for the older child vary greatly in terms of quality and frequency. The classroom teacher with little training or specialist assistance will present recreational singing activities at infrequent intervals. The classroom teacher who feels more confident when presenting music will introduce more varied and challenging activities. Music specialists and skilled classroom teachers should emphasize the activities described in this chapter to present a challenging and worthwhile singing program for older children.

The suggestions in this chapter are *not* based on the capacities of the classroom teacher with little training nor upon the minimum of assistance from special music teachers. These are, instead, the capacities every older child should develop through participation in a challenging and diversified singing program.

VOCAL DEVELOPMENT

The singing development of the younger child is described in Chapter 2. That description emphasizes the fact that the young child generally sings lower tones more easily than tones in a higher range. The older child also prefers to sing lower tones. He is, however, physically ready to expand his singing range. The singing problem between a' and d", which is heard so often as the young child attempts to sing higher tones, should be overcome in the upper grades of elementary school.

The teacher of the older child should plan singing activities to help him learn to sing well over a wide vocal range. The teacher may find, however, that the child is not ready for range-expansion activities. Some teachers of fifth- and sixth-grade children will discover a large number of poor singers at the beginning of the school year. The child with little previous singing experience should participate first in the types of singing activities described in Chapter 2.

Children who sing easily and accurately in a lower range of six to eight diatonic tones should gradually expand their range to an extreme lower tone of b-flat or a and an extreme high tone of f". Most of the songs older children sing after they have developed this range should be placed in a slightly narrower range from b to e". The teacher will help the child expand his range most effectively by introducing songs in a *transition range*.

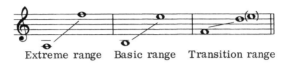

Extreme range   Basic range   Transition range

Transition Range

Most children have developed sufficient physical coordination to sing in a wide range by the approximate age of eight or nine. They often need careful vocal assistance if they are to develop the ability to sing with flexibility and consistent tone quality from the highest to the lowest tone. The teacher should introduce songs that will help the child learn to control tones in the transition range. He will learn to make an easy transition between lower and higher tones as he learns to sing songs similar to "Blow the Winds Southerly" (page 285). This quiet English round begins on c" and moves gradually down in sequential stepwise motion. "Ma Bella Bimba" (page 287) is another song that will help the child learn to sing easily in the transition range.

Transition-range songs should have the following characteristics:

The song should be in a range from f' to d" or e".
The melody should have phrases that begin high and move downward.
The song should feature descending scale-step motion if possible.

The teacher should introduce these songs by singing them softly and with a light vocal quality. The child will imitate this vocal example and learn to sing more easily in this portion of his range.

The older child should have many opportunities to sing songs in the transition range. He will gradually control this vocal problem area as he repeats these songs. His range will expand, and he will exhibit a consistent and pleasant quality after he has learned to sing several songs of this type.

Every child can sing and every older child can develop a wide and flexible vocal range. He will be eager to sing more complex songs in a wider range after he learns to sing transition tones without difficulty.

Quality in Song Literature

The older child will have reached a readiness level for other singing activities after he has developed the vocal coordination needed to sing in a wider range. He will be able to sing songs of excellent quality and will learn many things about music as he sings them. He will become more intensely aware of musical form, interpretation, and other aspects of music as he sings the songs described below.

The older child will discover that some songs are more interesting than others as he sings "The Ash Grove" (page 288) and compares it with other songs he has previously sung. This Welsh folk song will be easy to sing, but the form and complexity of phrases will become a part of the child's total musical experience and serve as a musical measuring stick for other melodies.

He should be led to discover musical form and contrast as he sings this song. Musical sequence is featured throughout. The A section moves downward to an interesting final cadence. The middle or B section is composed of ascending phrases which are repeated in a sequential manner. The B section ends in such a way that the child feels that more must follow. The repetition of the beginning A section provides an effective musical resolution to this outstanding melody.

"Simple Gifts" (page 291) is another melody that will provide the child with a highly musical singing experience. This Shaker song is melodically complex and is another example of music that has endured for many years because of its intrinsic musical quality.

These songs and others of equal musical value are described in detail in the Appendix. The musical characteristics that make them outstanding song examples are presented in terms of the older child's singing abilities and musical capacities.

SINGING IN PARTS

Some children are able to sing a harmonic part at an early age because of an unusually acute sense of hearing or an outstanding early program of singing activities. Part-singing is generally considered to be a major part of the singing program, however, in the upper grade levels of elementary school. Children begin to participate in part-singing activities at the approximate age of eight or nine.

The teacher who introduces part-singing activities in a well-planned and musical manner will help the child discover that this activity adds a new dimension to singing performances. The child who participates in the part-singing activities described in this chapter will find that:

Singing in parts is a pleasant and musically rewarding experience.

Harmonic structure becomes meaningful and vital as he develops harmonic sensitivity through singing.

Songs often acquire an added beauty when additional parts embellish the melody.

Part-singing will be a successful and pleasant experience for older children if the teacher considers three points in presenting any part-song activity. These points are as important when a sixth-grade class sings a complex harmonic arrangement as they are for the eight- or nine-year-old singing a harmonic part for the first time.

Groups must be balanced if a part-singing activity is to be successful. Teachers should not divide classes simply to have an equal number of children in each group. Instead, children with approximately the same range of vocal and musical ability should be included in each group.

Listening should be emphasized as a necessary element in any performance of a part song. Each child must listen as carefully as he sings. Musical cooperation is important in any part-singing activity. A simple chant is as necessary to the total effect as is the melody itself.

Every child should be thoroughly familiar with each part the class is singing together. Children who have learned to sing only the chant to "Sarasponda" (page 309) or the descant to "Goodnight" (page 297) may be unaware of the harmonic texture of the combined parts. Children should learn to sing each vocal line of a part song.

An Introduction to Part-Singing

Children should be introduced to part-singing by using previous musical learnings in new ways. They will achieve immediate success and enjoyment in singing parts if they find and sing *chord roots* as an introductory part-singing activity.

Children will have previously discovered simple chords on instruments in early childhood classrooms. They have accompanied melodies on bells, and they may have experimented with the chording possibilities of the autoharp or the piano. Singing chord roots as a harmonic addition to a familiar melody will present few problems since this activity will be based on the child's previous experiences with harmony.

The teacher should begin this new activity by introducing a simple melody that may be harmonized with a few chords. "Kum Ba Yah" (page 293) is an excellent choice. Children will discover, as they experiment with autoharp or piano chords, that two chords will provide a simple, yet effective accompaniment. The teacher will then explain that f is the root tone of the F Major I chord and that c is the root of the V_7 chord in this tonality.

These notes may be placed under the melody on the chalkboard, and children will take turns in groups singing them while others sing the melody. They will enjoy making musical decisions at this point concerning the words they want to sing with this simple added part.

They may decide to sing the entire text, or they may decide that a repetition of a single word phrase is just as effective. The child will be proud of his musical accomplishment as he sings the part *he* has created. The two examples shown here are typical of the harmonic form this song may take:

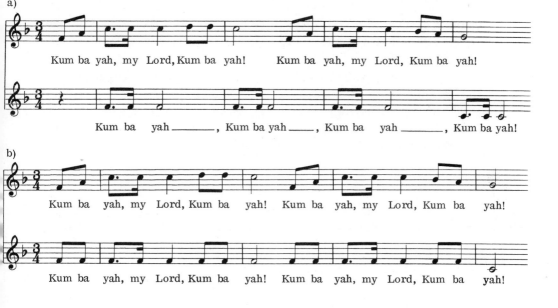

This introduction to part-singing will underline and intensify many other musical aspects as well. The child will solve musical problems such as chord selection, interpretation, and text suitability as he finds chord-root combinations and sings them.

Chants and Descants

The child learns to sing in parts most easily if the added harmonic line is simple and independent of the song melody. The chord-root harmonization just described shows one way to introduce part-singing. Chants and descants are the next type of harmonic part the teacher should introduce.

Chants are similar to chord-root harmonization since they consist of a simple phrase which is repeated and generally arranged below the melody. Chants always have more melodic interest than chord roots, however, since there is a short, repeated melodic phrase.

Descants are often as simple as chants, and occasionally the two terms are used for the same type of part. A descant is considered by many musicians, however, to be a simple, repeated phrase performed above the melody.

Since many chants are easier to sing than descants, they should be introduced as the next stage of part-singing development. Children should be thoroughly familiar with the song melody they will accompany with a chant. They should then learn to sing the chant itself while they listen to the melody.

Children's first attempts to sing chants in combination with song melodies will often be more successful if the teacher introduces an element of musical form. After reminding the class that some musical compositions begin with an introduction, the teacher will have one group begin to sing the chant as an introduction to the song. They will then easily maintain their part when other children begin to sing the melody.

"Masters in This Hall" (page 295) is a two-part arrangement with two chants. One accompanies the first half of this Christmas song, and the second adds harmonic interest to the second half:

Chants are often easier for children to sing if simple melody instruments are added to the performance. Bells will add a delightful and seasonal effect to performances of this holiday song.

Descants may be added to familiar melodies in a similar manner. The addition of a descant will be most effective for the child who is a beginning part-singer if the short melody is repeated. "Goodnight" (page 297) is an example. The simple four-tone descant is repeated in an identical way to accompany this lovely German lullaby.

One other musical feature adds to the effectiveness and easiness of this descant: the beginning tone is the same as the first tone of the melody. This eliminates any problem that might arise as the child attempts to find his beginning pitch.

The introduction of chants and descants will help the child develop harmonic independence as he sings. His experiences with this delightful and easy stage of part-singing are important to his singing progress.

Rounds and Canons

Children who sing chants and descants easily may be introduced to another type of part-singing. They should have frequent opportunities to sing rounds and simple canons. Chord roots, chants, and descants are generally short, incomplete musical ideas. Children sing an entire musical composition when they perform a round or canon. They therefore participate in a complete melodic and harmonic activity with each repetition.

The child should be introduced to the round as a part-singing activity by learning to sing "Blow the Winds Southerly" (page 285), "To the Dance" (page 299), or similar rounds. Rounds of this type begin high and the melody descends. Children who begin to sing after the first group has started will hear their entrance easily and maintain their part, since they will sing higher than the first group:

"Come Follow Me" (page 301) is a simple canon with similar harmonic characteristics. Although this canon is harder to sing in parts than the rounds mentioned above, the second and third entrances begin above the previous part.

Careful presentation by the teacher will give the child a feeling of satisfaction and success as he sings his first round. He should be highly motivated to continue this singing activity if the following teaching approaches are used:

The round should first be thoroughly learned as a unison song.

The teacher will then play or sing delayed entrances as children repeat the round as a unison song. This demonstration of the addition of different parts may be varied as the teacher sings a later entrance. A child may then find and play the second or third entrance on a melody instrument. This stage in learning to sing the round in parts might be used to give the child who has begun to study an instrument the chance to play while others sing.

The activity just described should then be reversed. The teacher will begin the round and the class will sing the second entrance.

The class is now ready to sing the round as a part song. Each child will have learned to listen carefully to another part while singing. The importance of listening should be emphasized when the class is divided into two sections of equal singing ability. If round singing becomes too loud and competitive, an echo repetition should take place.

As the child learns to sing rounds he may add further to his knowledge and understanding of musical form. Rounds are often very short and seem to end almost before they begin. They may be extended in a number of ways. One portion may serve as an introduction or coda. "I Love the Mountains" (page 303) may be transformed into a longer, more complicated choral arrangement as the child discovers phrases that may be used as introductions, codas, or added harmonic parts.

The melody of this round consists of simple phrases that gradually ascend in a sequential manner. Children will quickly learn to sing the basic melody:

They will then enjoy singing the round in two or three parts. The final phrase is a particularly effective musical ending, since the group that began to sing first can simply repeat it until the second or third group has reached the same place in the music. Many rounds seem to have no real ending when they are sung in parts. This one does. Children will discover that the ending phrase also makes an effective introduction. They may also decide that the melody will be enhanced as part of the class repeats this same phrase as a chant while others sing the melody:

The round melody may be further enhanced if the child experiments with chord tones and composes an appropriate descant.   The following is one of many possibilities:

These musical experiments with a simple round melody will result in a longer and musically effective arrangement. This is one of many ways in which "I Love the Mountains" can be performed:

Introduction (boom-ti-a-da)
Unison performance of the melody
Interlude (boom-ti-a-da)
Two-part performance (song melody and boom-ti-a-da chant)
Two-part performance (song melody and descant)
Three-part round repetition

There are other ways to arrange rounds. Chord roots may be added. Melody and rhythm instruments will add effective tone-color effects. The child will think of many ways to create new musical effects after he has been introduced to this exciting activity.

These experiments with melodic and harmonic elements will help the child's general musical growth as well. He will discover some of the ways in which composers and arrangers add complexity and color to a simple theme. He should become aware of style, form, and interpretation. A musical activity should never be presented to reveal just one aspect of music to a child. Instead, each activity may contain many varied musical experiences.

Harmonizing in Thirds and Sixths

The child who has participated in the singing of simple part songs has discovered how enjoyable these activities can be. He has also learned to maintain his own part as the group sings several harmonizing melodic lines. At this point the older child is ready for more challenging part-singing activities. Many part songs are harmonized in thirds or sixths. These intervals are often difficult for the child to hear and sing at first.

The adult who has not presented part-singing activities to this age group may assume that harmonizing parts at the interval of the third or sixth are extremely easy to sing. The experienced teacher, however, is aware of the fact that many older children hear these parts with great difficulty at first. There is a great difference between singing an easy, strongly melodic part and maintaining a dependent part that consistently moves a third or a sixth above or below the melodic line.

Songs that begin in unison and are then harmonized at the end of phrases or sections are an effective introduction. The arrangement should feature a third harmonization above the melody if possible. "There's a Meeting Here Tonight" (page 305) is typical. The thirds are added above the melody line at the end of each phrase. Since each harmonization is identical the child will learn to sing this song with ease.

Several other activities may be presented at this point to further strengthen the child's ability to sing in thirds. He will enjoy reviewing songs he has previously learned and then harmonizing them in thirds. The child will quickly discover that lower thirds are effective as he sings "Kum Ba Yah" (page 293).

Children will find lower thirds easy to sing as they add a harmonic part of this type to songs similar to "Tum Balalaika" (page 317). The thirds are easy to hear and sing because the song melody consists almost entirely of scale-step motion for eight measures.

Children should be introduced to sixth harmonizations after they have learned to sing thirds easily. They will easily understand the similarities and the differences by comparing these two harmonizing effects. "Sleigh Bells" ("Minka," page 307) may be used as an example. The melody may be harmonized with either thirds or sixths:

Thirds

Sixths

Several types of part songs have not been discussed here. Some feature echoing phrases, while others have two contrasting melodies which are sung together. Many part-song arrangements consist of a combination of types. The child should have many opportunities to sing each type of part song if he is to develop this important musical ability. A new type of part-singing activity should not be introduced until the teacher is certain that the class has had sufficient practice with familiar part songs.

READING VOCAL NOTATION

Vocal reading is a musical activity that is emphasized less than others as teachers plan a singing program for the older child. While most children learn to sing and many develop part-singing ability, very few learn to read music well.

Vocal reading receives less emphasis than other activities for a number of reasons. Many classroom teachers do not feel competent in this area. They may themselves read music well, but they do not understand the sequential stages the child must pass through as he develops vocal reading ability.

The classroom teacher who needs assistance in other music areas will find teaching aids available. The recordings that accompany the basic series books are an invaluable aid to the teacher of older children who needs assistance in presenting an effective singing program. Recordings are also available to help with the presentation of part-singing activities.

There are far fewer audio or visual aids planned to help the classroom teacher present an effective program of vocal reading activities. The teacher who does not feel competent in this area is either dependent upon the help of the music specialist or must ignore this facet of the child's musical growth.

Vocal reading should be considered a major part of the singing program for the older child whenever possible. Learning to sing songs by reading vocal notation is important for the following reasons:

> The child who has participated in a planned and sequential singing program will have developed a readiness for this more complex musical activity. He will have learned to recognize and understand visual aspects of notation while singing and will have developed a large variety of melodic and rhythmic concepts. He should, therefore, be shown how these previous learnings may be applied to reading and singing a vocal score.

> Learning to read will help the child acquire a larger repertoire of songs. Rote learning is a relatively slow procedure, while the child who reads will learn songs more quickly and will gradually become independent in his ability to learn to sing new songs.

The teacher who is planning a sequence of vocal reading activities should be aware of the differences between instrumental and vocal music reading. Since instrumentalists and singers read the same notation, a few comparisons will emphasize these differences.

The child who begins to learn to play an instrument in a class has a strong incentive to learn to read music. He must learn to read as he develops his playing technique and progresses with the group. The motivation to read vocal notation is not so strong. The child has been singing for years and may not understand at first why he should not continue to learn songs by listening and then singing.

Some teaching approaches that will place the young vocal reader in a situation comparable to that of the beginning instrumentalist are described below. The child should not have any rote-learning assistance as he begins to read. He should, instead, gradually acquire a vocabulary of visual symbols that are meaningful and that he can sing without hesitation.

Vocal music reading is not an activity that is suddenly introduced at a specific grade level. The older child who is learning to read vocal notation is simply using many previous musical experiences in a new manner.

Prereading Activities

The stages of music reading should always be presented as a problem-solving process. The child should begin with several prereading activities that are based on his previous musical experiences and will therefore lead to immediate success.

One of these activities involves the continued use of simple melody instruments. The teacher should provide selected bells or show children certain piano keys that will be used to find and play familiar melodies.

Some guidance from the teacher is appropriate when this activity is first introduced. Children may review a familiar song and shape the outline of the melody with hand or line notation. Children will then experiment with the selected bell or piano tones to discover the song melody. Songs similar to "Blow the Winds Southerly" (page 285) are ideal for this purpose. This song has a narrow range and consists almost entirely of scale-step motion.

Children will find the melody easily on the six bells or piano keys the teacher has selected for this first attempt. The song should then be placed on a chalk, flannel, or magnetic board in actual music notation. Large cards might also be used.

A collection might be made of the discovered notation of these familiar songs, and the teacher might later show the melodies as a guessing game. The child will learn to pay close attention to melodic notation as he participates in this musical game.

The teacher may then use these large examples of melodic notation to show how song phrases are constructed. The child will add a further dimension to his basic understanding of notation as he is helped to discover scale-step motion, chord outlines, and combinations of these two basic melody characteristics.

This melodic prereading approach is also appropriate for the younger child in some primary-grade classrooms. The child who has discovered hand and line notation and who has previously found simple melodies on tuned instruments will enjoy this additional prereading activity.

Other prereading activities are more appropriate for the older child. The child who discovers further principles of music notation in the following ways will discover that the early stages of music reading are musically rewarding *and* fun:

> The child should find and write the notation for familiar melodies. These should be songs with simple scale-step motion or repeated basic chord outlines. "Frère Jacques" ("Are You Sleeping?") is one of many appropriate choices.

> Children will learn a great deal about the rudiments of music notation as they create original melodies. A particular occasion or a suggestion from the teacher may be used to introduce this approach. The teacher might show the class the chord outlines that are characteristic of bugle calls. The child might then create a new bugle call of his own by playing tones on bells or the piano. While his first attempts may be crude, the child should compare his melodies with those other children have written. These creative experiments should then be written in music notation.

> At this point children will enjoy analyzing themes composers have written. They will discover melodic patterns and elements of musical form as their attention is directed to these themes.

Children will enjoy these introductory approaches to the reading of music. Musical symbols will become meaningful, and children will realize that they are necessary steps to understanding, performing, and creating music. Older children will be ready to read and sing vocal notation after they have participated in a number of these activities.

Reading Activities

The activities described above serve as an effective introduction to vocal reading. The child's attention will have been directed toward elements of melodic notation, and he will have learned a number of basic ways to manipulate and understand musical symbols. After this introduction to reading, he should participate in sequential activities that are planned carefully to help him actually learn to read and to sing vocal notation. The suggestions that follow are carefully organized in a musical and progressive sequence.

Many songs that are appropriate for the older child to read feature two types of melodic patterns. The melody of "Sarasponda" (page 309) has repeated chord-outline and scale-step patterns. Teachers should use the following techniques to help children learn to read and sing this song:

> The teacher should be quite certain that the class has never heard or performed the song before introducing the first reading activity.
>
> Chord outlines and scale-step patterns should be placed on the chalkboard. (Examples that show the melodic patterns in "Sarasponda" are given in the Appendix, page 308.) After showing the child these examples, the teacher will help him find the tones by playing them on a piano or other melody instrument. The difference between chord outline and scale-step motion will become immediately obvious to the child as he sings along.
>
> The child will then find these patterns in "Sarasponda." He will hear and sing the beginning pitch and then begin to sing the tonal combinations he has practiced.
>
> The teacher might suggest singing these pitches on a neutral syllable such as "la." Later the teacher will introduce a specific system for identifying these tones. Staff names, numbers, and syllables are all appropriate. Some teachers may introduce the Kodály-Richards hand signals as a vocal reading aid.

Teachers should always introduce a single approach to music reading. The teacher's training and general musical background will indicate the approach that should be introduced. A reading approach should never be introduced if the teacher does not feel completely at ease with it. A teacher who reads syllables, numbers, or staff names slowly and with difficulty will transmit a feeling of uneasiness and insecurity to children.

The Dutch song "Sarasponda" contains the characteristics that should be included in any song the teacher chooses for a beginning vocal reading activity. The following points should be considered in selecting songs for this purpose:

> The song should have repeated chord-outline and stepwise phrases.
>
> Rhythmic patterns should be extremely simple and match the basic meter as much as possible. Complicated rhythmic groupings will interfere with the child's first attempts to read vocal notation.
>
> The song should have musical appeal and value. The teacher should never select a song for music-reading practice solely because it contains repeated easy phrases. The song must also be appealing to the child.

Several important points must be considered as the teacher plans and organizes a sequence of reading activities:

Several songs should be presented as reading activities in the same key. If the first song introduced for this purpose is in the key of C Major, a number of other songs should be chosen and presented in C Major. The child who has not previously sung "Savez-vous?" (page 275) will easily identify and sing the C Major I-chord outline which is featured throughout this French folk song.

There must be continuity and repetition if reading activities are to be successful. This does not necessarily mean that an entire song must be learned through reading each day. It is advisable, however, to emphasize vocal reading at regular intervals. One portion of a song might be presented for reading practice and the remainder learned by rote. "The Deaf Woman's Courtship" (page 311) has repeated patterns which provide easy vocal reading practice. The child will *not* learn to read and reproduce vocal notation if this activity is presented only a few times, with weeks or months intervening between presentations.

Each reading activity featuring a new element should include familiar elements as well. Children who are introduced to the reading of the descending chord outline in "The Deaf Woman's Courtship" should compare this melodic outline to their previous reading of the ascending chord pattern in "Sarasponda."

The child will be ready for more challenging music-reading activities after he has successfully acquired a basic vocabulary of melodic intervals in notation. "I've Been to Haarlem" (page 312) has familiar notation patterns, since the ascending I-chord outline is repeated several times. This rollicking song also features a lower pattern which moves from the first scale step down to the lower fifth scale step.

The following teaching approaches will help the child learn to read and sing this longer and more difficult song:

A few preliminary explanations may be necessary if this is the first song the child has read in the key of E Major. The teacher may need to explain the key signature and show how familiar melodic patterns will appear in this new key. It will be appropriate to notate a song the child has previously read in the key of E Major.

The child should then scan the song, looking for familiar melodic notation patterns. He will discover the ascending I-chord outline in several variations. (The vocal notation examples for this song are given in the Appendix on page 311.)

The one new melodic notation element in this song should then be shown in large notation. The teacher will introduce the new phrase first by having children sing down from e' to b in a stepwise manner. Then the d-sharp' will be omitted, and they will sing the actual melodic phrase.

They will begin to sing the first half of the song, adding this new descending phrase to the tonal patterns that are familiar to them.

They will then analyze the refrain and discover that there are no reading problems. They will easily sing this second part from notation. The one new element is a slight rhythmic change involving the addition of half notes.

Songs that seem to be too difficult for the child to read are often appropriate for music-reading activities when they are carefully analyzed in terms of familiar and new elements of melodic outline. "Early One Morning" (page 314) is one of these. The first section is composed of two similar phrases which seem rather complex. When they are analyzed, however, patterns are discovered which make music reading a relatively simple procedure. The first phrase is composed of the following chord outlines:

I chord   II chord   V chord

The second phrase repeats two of these patterns in the same order. The refrain of this English song is equally simple for the child to read. One short phrase combining scale-step motion with a descending chord outline is repeated. The final phrase of this flowing melody combines an ascending chord outline with a descending major scale.

The child should also be introduced to the reading of songs in minor keys. "Tum Balalaika" (page 317) is an ideal choice for this purpose after the older child has had many other music reading experiences.

The teacher will introduce this song in D Minor by showing the key signature first on a chalkboard. Children with reading experience may identify this as the key of F Major. They will then become aware of the difference between F Major and D Minor as the teacher shows them both scales and compares them. Children will hear distinct differences as they sing each scale.

The child is ready to read and sing this melody after he has practiced reading scale patterns and chord outlines. He will realize that the beginning tone is the fifth scale step or the highest tone in the basic I chord. Finding the tone will be no problem when this is made clear. He should read and sing only the first four measures. The teacher will then ask him to compare the second phrase with the first. As the child compares the phrases, he will discover that the melodic pattern is the same but that the second phrase begins a step lower. The child will begin to realize the importance of comparing phrases as he discovers melodic sequence in this melody.

Measures nine through twelve will need additional preparation. The teacher will help the child sing this pattern most easily by placing the following pattern on the chalkboard:

The child will have previously recognized and sung chord outlines, but he may not have had the opportunity to sing them over such a wide range.

Measures thirteen and fourteen may be pointed out as another example of melodic sequence, since the pattern is very similar to the one preceding it. It is not an exact repetition, however, and the child may need assistance from the piano as he learns to sing this short pattern.

The reading procedure which has just been described may seem rather long and detailed. This detailed presentation is necessary, however, if the child is to learn to read. Later he will gain vocal reading speed because he is acquiring a vocabulary of familiar notational patterns.

The child will not learn to read vocal notation, of course, unless he understands rhythmic symbols as well. Suggestions for helping children learn to read rhythmic notation are included in Chapter 5.

Dictation

Dictation may be added to the music program as the child is introduced to the reading of music notation. The discovery of familiar melodies on melody instruments and the notation of original short songs are activities that have prepared the child for the procedure of writing music from dictation. The prereading activities described in this chapter and in Chapter 2 should also be considered as a preparation for dictation.

Dictation is an interesting and musical problem-solving activity. Children listen carefully to a melody and write what they hear, solving melodic and rhythmic notation problems as they proceed. Dictation is a simple procedure and an extremely effective way to train the musical ear. The activity makes the child aware of the importance of understanding musical symbols.

A detailed example will describe the dictation procedure. "Hush, My Babe" (page 318) may be used to introduce this activity. While dictation may be presented in several ways, the following procedure is effective:

Children will learn to sing this simple melody first as a rote song.

They will then practice chord and scale patterns that they will use to write this song. The following examples will prepare children to write the notation of "Hush, My Babe":

The entire song consists of arrangements of these melodic patterns. The child should hear and sing the melody again after he has practiced singing the chord and scale patterns.

The beginning tone of the melody should be firmly established. The teacher might play the first tone of the F Major scale and then the beginning tone of the song. Children will then be asked to identify the beginning tone.

The actual process of dictation will begin. The teacher will play the song phrase by phrase and repeat each as many times as necessary. Children will write the symbols for each tone without attempting to add the rhythmic element.

Rhythmic notation should be added after the class has transcribed all melody tones. Children will find this added stage an easy one if the following procedures are followed:

They will identify the meter first after they have decided whether the rhythmic groupings have a feeling of two or three. "Hush, My Babe" is a song arranged in a duple meter. A duple meter might be notated as 2/4, 4/4, or in several other ways. The length of the longest tone often indicates which meter is more appropriate. The longest tone in this song has the length of two metrical pulsations. The appropriate meter is therefore 2/4, or some other indication of two pulses per measure.

The song should then be divided into measures. The child will find these divisions easily as he taps the meter, counts, and places a bar line in front of the first note in each measure.

The lengths of individual notes within these measures will then be easy to hear and notate. The child might begin by finding first the notes that correspond exactly to the underlying meter. Thirteen measures in "Hush, My Babe" are identical to the basic meter of two quarter-note pulses per measure. He will discover that there are only two other note lengths to find and notate. The teacher might assist the child in his first dictation activity by showing the rhythmic groupings contained in the song. The following example will help the child see what he is hearing:

The older child will find dictation an absorbing way to learn to read music well. He will learn to "see with his ears and hear with his eyes" as he writes music in this way.

RELATED SINGING ACTIVITIES

Other singing activities should be introduced as the teacher plans a music program that is suited to the needs and capacities of every child. Children of different ages should discover the joy of singing together. Those children with an extreme interest in singing should be given additional opportunities to sing together in special choral groups.

Singing Together

Singing should be a joyous common denominator as children of different ages participate in an all-school activity. The kindergarten child and his older brothers or sisters will enjoy singing together the many songs that are suitable for all children. There are appropriate times throughout the school year for this joint musical experience. Holidays and other special occasions should be celebrated in song.

The young child hears older children sing the entire "Battle Hymn of the Republic." As he joins the refrain and sings "Glory, Glory, Hallelujah" he will feel an intense musical satisfaction in celebrating a patriotic occasion in this manner. The older child will benefit equally from this combined singing activity.

Cumulative song lists will be helpful as teachers plan singing activities that will involve all grade levels. These lists may be compiled in several ways. Some songs are popular with every grade level. Those requested often should be added to the cumulative list, and all children should learn to sing them.

Other songs have simple melodies and effective added harmonic parts. These should also be added to the cumulative list. Songs of this type are particularly suitable if they are appropriate for a holiday or other special occasion.

Special Choirs

Teachers often organize special school or school-system elementary choruses. This type of group should be formed to include all older children who want to sing. The choir or chorus should include those children who want to sing more often than time permits during the scheduled music program. The child should *not* be selected solely because of outstanding ability. Instead, each child who wants to join the group should be admitted.

The teacher who admits the child to a chorus solely because of the child's desire to sing must select singing repertoire with attention to a wide range of abilities and needs. One child may be a beginning singer and another may sing very well. There are many songs that will give each the opportunity to participate in a musically satisfying choral activity.

One group of songs in the Appendix has been included to cater to the variety of singing ability to be found in a school chorus. Many other songs included there are equally suitable for such groups.

"Die Musici" (page 321) is a simple German canon children will enjoy singing. The two parts are easy to sing together and yet very effective in a special performance.

"Ah, Robin" (page 323) is a very old English song. The child who does not sing well over a wide range will find a harmonic part suitable to his abilities. The competent singer will find another harmonic part challenging and enjoyable.

"Hosanna to the Living Lord" (page 325) is an outstanding example of a part song elementary choruses will enjoy singing. The early German chorale has distinct soprano and alto parts.

"He's Got the Whole World in His Hands" (page 326) will provide the teacher with an opportunity to introduce three-part singing in a simple and effective way. The two-part chant is easy for all older children to sing. The total musical effect is impressive, and yet the arrangement is not difficult.

THE TEACHER'S ROLE

The role of the teacher of the young child is carefully defined in Chapter 2. The specific teaching approaches described there are equally appropriate as the older child participates in singing activities. Teaching techniques that are appropriate for the presentation of part-singing or vocal reading activities must be carefully considered as the teacher adds these facets to the singing program. These are described in detail elsewhere in this chapter.

One general vocal teaching approach should be added to those described in Chapter 2. The teacher should help the older child learn to establish pitch before he begins to sing. The beginning tone of any song may be found in relation to the scale or I-chord outline of that key.

An example will indicate the general approach the teacher should use in helping children establish the pitch of the beginning tone of any song. "Tum Balalaika" (page 317) is in the key of D Minor. The child should be familiar with the key signature, the D Minor scale, and the I-chord outline in D Minor before he finds the starting tone of this song. The teacher will play the tone d', which is the first tone in the D Minor scale and the root tone of the I chord in this key. The child will then sing up to a', the fifth scale step and the third note in the I chord.

The child discovers several things about music as he finds his own beginning pitch. He becomes thoroughly familiar with key signatures, scales, and chord outlines. The harmonic setting of a melody becomes meaningful as he finds his pitch in this harmonic context. He acquires musical learnings that will help him to become increasingly independent in the performance of music.

Audio-visual aids are also described in Chapter 2. Equipment is equally important in the singing program for the older child. The teacher will use visual aids to a greater extent as the child participates more and more in melodic reading activities.

One type of teaching aid that will increase the effectiveness of the reading program and save time as the teacher presents visual examples is a magnetic or flannel board with a music staff and a variety of music symbols. This will enable the teacher to present visual patterns quickly and accurately. Visual aids of this type are much more efficient to use than the chalkboard. Few classrooms have sufficient chalkboard space to permit the teacher to have a permanent music staff painted on one section. The magnetic or flannel board with a staff and moveable symbols is an efficient classroom aid.

A new reading pattern should be reproduced, in large notation if possible. Magnetic and flannel boards are ideal for this purpose. Song charts may also be purchased. They are less flexible and adaptable to a specific classroom situation, however, since the notation cannot be adjusted in any way.

Teachers and children may work together to create their own reading charts. The child will understand the need for these visual aids as he finds he must "tune up" each time he solves a new notation prob-

lem. A collection of charts displaying scale-step patterns, chord outlines in different inversions, and melodic patterns will prove invaluable
to the teacher who presents an effective vocal reading program.

A list of teaching aids appropriate for the activities described is
included at the end of the chapter.

PROGRAM OBJECTIVES

An effective singing program for older children should be based on
specific behavioral objectives. These objectives must be chosen with
careful regard to the child's specific needs and capacities. They should
also be selected in direct relation to the overall purposes of the music
education program.

Specific objectives for the singing program are grouped in three
general categories. One group of objectives is related to the child's
vocal development; a second presents attainable goals in the area of
learning to sing in parts; the third category of objectives is concerned
with helping children learn to read vocal music.

Vocal Development

The older child has the capacity to develop a wide vocal range and
a flexible and expressive tone quality. Teachers may set high goals
for children in this age range. The following objectives should be
attained by the time the child has completed the sixth grade. The
child will:

Sing accurately in a wide vocal range with consistent and expressive
tone quality.

Show by his song preferences that he enjoys singing a large repertoire
of songs of lasting musical quality.

Show by his comments that he has developed critical standards regarding vocal performances. He will not be satisfied with performances that are not of excellent quality.

Display repeatedly the satisfaction that accompanies a successful vocal
performance.

Show by his participation in singing activities that he has developed
a positive attitude toward music as a result of many satisfying experiences in the classroom.

The above objectives should be reached by all older children in the
elementary school. They can develop the ability to perform in and
appreciate vocal performances of excellent quality. Their capacities
should be fully developed during these formative years.

Singing in Parts

Objectives regarding the development of part-singing proficiency are equally important. The older child has the ability to learn to sing an independent part, and he should have many opportunities to develop this capacity.

Part-singing is important to the child's musical growth for several reasons. He learns to participate in a more complex musical texture as he sings part songs. His ear becomes acutely tuned to the harmonic element in music as he performs. He develops an appreciation for choral music which will lead to a later interest in choral performances.

Objectives related to the development of part-singing ability should be quite specific and carefully stuctured. Part-singing may become a frustrating experience to children if too-difficult materials are presented without sufficient preparation. Part-singing activities may, on the other hand, become boring if they are not challenging and sequential. The following objectives should be achieved by the child as he learns to sing part songs. The child will:

Maintain his part in performances involving chord roots, chants, and descants.

Demonstrate his ability to sing his part in the performance of rounds and canons.

Sing accurately in part-song performances featuring harmonizations of thirds and sixths.

Demonstrate by his eagerness to participate that part-singing has become a pleasurable and musically satisfying activity.

The teacher who implements the structured suggestions in this chapter will discover that part-singing is a popular activity with older children. Part-singing often becomes the core of the music program.

Vocal Reading

Vocal reading should be considered an important and necessary part of a comprehensive music program for older children. Vocal reading experiences will help children acquire a song repertoire more efficiently than rote teaching methods. They will, in addition, be prepared for later secondary-school choral activities. Teachers should help children reach a number of vocal reading objectives in the intermediate grades. The child will:

Complete notational problem-solving activities involving instrumental exploration and the identification of melodic outlines.

Notate familiar melodies and create original melodies which he is able to write in music notation.

Read simple songs consisting of chord outlines and scale-step motion.

Acquire a vocabulary of melodic intervals and demonstrate that he can transfer this vocabulary to new reading situations.

Notate music from dictation and show that he understands the importance of music notation.

Demonstrate that he considers music reading to be a challenging, worthwhile, and enjoyable musical activity.

Some teachers and administrators consider music reading to be the responsibility of music consultants. Classroom teachers with some knowledge of music, however, may be of great help to the reading program. The beginning aspects of the reading program may be developed quite successfully by the classroom teacher. Pupils with instrumental experience are important resources to call upon.

PROGRAM EVALUATION

Evaluation as an important aspect of the educational process has been defined and discussed in previous chapters. Evaluation is as important to the intermediate-grade vocal program as it is to any other facet of education. Program planning and progress are not complete unless the teacher has included the important step of evaluating the progress each pupil has made.

Vocal Development

All older children who have participated in an effective singing program should have developed tonal accuracy and learned to sing easily within the ranges defined earlier in this chapter. The teacher should periodically check each child's ability, however, in order to select the types of songs that will be most appropriate for sequential singing activities.

Vocal problems most often occur in the range from f' up to d". Each child should be able to sing comfortably throughout this range if he has participated in the singing activities described earlier in this chapter. The number of songs chosen to help children sing in this range, however, will depend on an individual evaluation of the child's ability.

The evaluation procedures described in Chapter 2 are also appropriate for measuring the singing ability of the older child. He should sing alone several times during the school year, and his performance should be tape recorded whenever possible.

Some music specialists and classroom teachers cooperate in checking the child's singing ability. The specialist may conduct the testing in a relaxed atmosphere by having each child sing all or part of a familiar song. The classroom teacher assists by taking notes regarding each child's performance.

Question-answer songs and those with solo-chorus combinations are ideal for this purpose. They provide the relaxed atmosphere and the vocal phrases that will help the teacher evaluate the child's ability to sing.

Songs with high descants and low chants are helpful as the teacher evaluates the child's ability to sing in a wider range. "Masters in This Hall" (page 295) has an accompanying chant that will clearly show the child's ability to sing extreme lower tones. There are many descants that will give the teacher an opportunity to check his ability to sing higher phrases.

Singing in Parts

Evaluation should play an important part in determining the pace of the part-singing program. A new part-singing activity should be introduced only after the majority of the class has successfully achieved the preceding level of accomplishment.

Teachers should introduce a new part-singing activity, therefore, after a careful evaluation of individual progress. This is easily accomplished within the setting of an informal classroom music program. Small groups may be chosen to sing familiar part-songs. The teacher will be able to evaluate the child's ability to maintain a part when a few children are singing.

Evaluation of part-singing independence is particularly important as children reach the level at which part-songs become more harmonic than melodic. Songs with interdependent parts represent the final and most difficult stage of part-singing development in the intermediate grades. The teacher should evaluate individual ability carefully before presenting songs of this type.

Vocal Reading

A successful music reading program will require careful evaluation of the child's progress in this activity. The child's understanding of music symbols and his ability to sing from notation must be checked at periodic intervals.

Some parts of the vocal reading program are easy to evaluate. The child will show clearly his early understanding of music symbols as he finds familiar melodies and identifies phrases of songs by looking at the notation. The child's ability to write melodies and rhythmic patterns through dictation also provides the teacher with a means of evaluating growth in this activity.

The following examples show appropriate ways to evaluate the child's ability to read vocal notation:

The child listens to a performance of a musical phrase. He compares the performance with two examples of music notation, e.g.:

The child who has learned to read vocal notation will realize that the second example is an accurate representation of the performance while the first example contains three errors.

The child studies an example of musical notation. He has been told that there are mistakes which he should circle as he listens to an accurate performance of the example:

This short test might be extended. The child may write a correct version of the phrase as he continues to listen to the example.

Short tests of this type provide useful information concerning a child's understanding of vocal notation symbols. They do not, however, measure his ability to sing the symbols he recognizes. Teachers will be able to evaluate the total success of the vocal reading program as children perform unfamiliar melodic examples by reading and singing. The child who can sight-sing has reached a high level of reading competence.

SUMMARY

A singing program planned for the older child should include varied and challenging activities. Singing should be scheduled daily and involve far more than simple, recreational songs.

Several types of singing activities should be included to develop the child's musical potential. Older children should learn to sing easily in a wide vocal range. They should develop the ability to maintain a harmonic part as other children sing additional harmonic lines. They should also become familiar with a large vocabulary of music symbols and learn to read music notation.

Singing should always be planned in relation to the goals of the total music program. The songs the child learns to sing should contribute to his general musical development and prepare him for future musical growth.

QUESTIONS AND PROJECTS

1. Analyze an intermediate-grade basic series book (see References, below) to discover and list those songs that are appropriate for the development of vocal range expansion, part-singing ability, and vocal reading skills. Use the criteria defined in this chapter for your analysis.
2. Organize a class discussion dealing with the topic of vocal music reading. Students should be prepared to discuss the relative effectiveness of syllables, staff names, and number notation as reading aids.
3. Survey SA and SSA choral arrangements to find additional vocal-choral selections that are appropriate for children in the intermediate grades. Attempt to find examples of medieval, Renaissance, baroque, and contemporary compositions.
4. Prepare to report on one of many possible ways of using a singing activity as an impetus for a comprehensive music learning experience. How can a child's awareness or knowledge of choral, orchestral, chamber music, or operatic literature be heightened through singing?
5. How can a music specialist develop sequence between the early childhood vocal program and a singing program for older children?
6. What musical competencies are essential as a basis for successful participation in part-singing activities?
7. Develop a specific procedure for evaluating the results of one aspect of the vocal program for older children.

REFERENCES

Basic Music Series

Eight basic music series are listed at the end of Chapter 2.

Supplementary Song Collections

Dallin, Leon, and Dallin, Lynn. *Heritage Songster.* Dubuque, Iowa: Wm. C. Brown Co., 1966.

Ehret, Walter, and Evans, George K. *International Book of Christmas Carols.* Englewood Cliffs, N.J.: Prentice-Hall, 1963.

Hood, Marguerite. *Art Songs for Treble Voices.* New York: Mills Music, 1965.

Landeck, Beatrice. *More Songs To Grow On.* New York: Edward B. Marks Music Corp., 1954.

Luboff, Norman, and Stracke, Win. *Songs of Man: The International Book of Folk Songs.* Englewood Cliffs, N.J.: Prentice-Hall, 1965.

Nye, Robert; Nye, Vernice; Aubin, Neva; and Kyme, George. *Singing with Children.* Belmont, Calif.: Wadsworth Publishing Co., 1962.

Pocket Folk Song Library. Delaware, Ohio: Informal Music, n.d.

Tobitt, Janet E. *The Ditty Bag.* New York: Plymouth Music Co., 1960.

Audio-Visual Aids

(See also the visual aids available with the *Birchard Music Series* and *This Is Music,* listed at the end of Chapter 2.)

Developing Skills in Music (filmstrips and records), Society for Visual Education, Chicago.

Howard Music Staff Chalkboard (green chalkboard with four music staves on one side and blank chalkboard on reverse), Lyons Band Instrument Co., Chicago.

Judy Music Flannel Board Kit (flannel board with treble and bass staves and music symbols), Lyons Band Instrument Co., Chicago.

Magne-Music Board (magnetic music symbols), Lyons Band Instrument Co., Chicago.

Mills Music Board (erasable music-staff board with non-wax crayons), Mills Music, New York.

The Music Board (electronic chalkboard with music staff and adjustable pitches), Educational Tools, Orchard Park, N.Y.

Music, The Expressive Language and *Introduction to Music Reading* (films that prepare the older child for music reading), Sutherland Educational Films, Los Angeles, or Sam Fox Publishing Co., New York.

Place-A-Note (magnetic staff and moveable notes), G. Schirmer, New York.

Sight of Music (transparencies for overhead projector, including statics and overlays), Educational Audio Visual, Pleasantville, N.Y.

Staffs, notes, and other visual aids, Musicard, Hollywood, Calif.

4

THE EARLY CHILDHOOD RHYTHMIC PROGRAM

The young child is always eager to participate in rhythmic activities. "Let's move!" is a frequent request after children in early childhood classrooms have been introduced to rhythm through movement. Practically any rhythmic activity will satisfy the child, since he thoroughly enjoys physical responses. The teacher should be aware, however, that some activities are much more appropriate than others in helping the child develop rhythmic responsiveness.

It is often difficult to separate rhythmic activities that help the child's musical development from others that simply involve physical movement. Singing games, circle dances, and other simple folk dances are often presented as the only rhythmic activities in the classroom. These games and dances are actually more closely related to physical education and dance than they are to the child's musical development. A rhythmic program planned for the young child should emphasize those activities that will develop his capacities to the fullest and prepare him for further experiences with music. The program outlined in this chapter stresses this approach to the rhythm program.

The young child has an intense desire to move and should gradually learn to channel this energy into expressive movement. Activities planned to help him develop expressive responsiveness will also prepare him for later listening and rhythmic development. He should also begin to acquire a basic understanding of rhythmic symbols as he responds actively to rhythmic patterns and has the opportunity to see visual representations of these same patterns. Rhythmic activities should involve far more than activity for activity's sake. The program should be carefully planned to develop the rhythmic potential every child possesses.

THE EXPRESSIVE MOVEMENT PROGRAM

The central focus of the rhythmic program should be expressive movement in which the young child uses his entire body This does not mean, however, that the teacher should expect beautiful and well-coordinated responses as the child first responds to the music he hears. The process of rhythmic movement development may be compared to the way the child learns to speak. He experiments with sounds, gradually develops a vocabulary of words, and finally combines them in a meaningful way. Expressive movement is developed in a similar manner. The child gradually acquires a movement vocabulary and then combines these movements in a more complex and expressive way.

The rhythmic program should be planned to help the child progress through three general stages of rhythmic movement development. During the *introductory stage* he will develop the ability to make appropriate movement responses to simple rhythmic patterns he hears. He will also learn to express basic musical concepts with his body. The child will begin to combine his basic movement and conceptual vocabulary in a more expressive way as he reaches a *second stage* of development. He will listen and respond to simple compositions with a repeated rhythmic pattern. The child will begin to move more expressively after he has passed through the first two stages of expressive movement development. As he reaches the *third stage* he will be able to respond to longer, more complicated musical forms. Tempo changes and form contrasts will present few problems as he listens and moves.

The child should never be expected to pass through these stages of expressive movement development at a certain time or in exactly the same way as another child. The preschool child may move expressively and show that he has reached a third stage of development consistent with his level of physical maturation. He may, at the same time, not have reached a coordination level for some basic patterns such as skipping.

The primary-grade child, on the other hand, may be extremely clumsy and able to respond at first only to the most basic introductory activities. This will frequently happen if he has not had previous experience with well-planned expressive movement activities.

Introductory Stage

This is the critical stage of movement development. The child who learns to listen attentively and who gradually develops the rhythmic responses described here will continue to think of expressive movement as an exciting musical activity. The child who is not introduced to movement in this manner will often be frustrated by more complex music as he is asked to respond with his body.

The child should develop two types of rhythmic response during the introductory stage of expressive movement. He should learn to identify and move to rhythmic groupings that suggest basic foot patterns. He should also develop a vocabulary of basic musical concepts which he expresses through physical movement.

Basic foot patterns are generally grouped as even and uneven pulses. The even patterns (walking or marching, running, and moving slowly) are often easier for the young child to hear and reproduce. Uneven patterns (galloping and skipping) may be more difficult. The child will experience success through movement more quickly and easily if even patterns are introduced first:

(The rhythmic notation included to show these patterns is only one of several ways to indicate each rhythmic grouping.)

The child will find many other foot patterns as he listens and moves. The ones listed here and on page 74 are the most basic, however, and are necessary to further development. Additional patterns will be described in connection with the later stages of expressive movement.

The child should gradually learn to express musical concepts through movement during the introductory stage. The musical elements he will identify in this way consist of other aspects of music in addition to rhythm. As he shows highness and lowness with his body, he is expressing melodic outline. As he tiptoes to express his feeling of a soft musical pattern, he is indicating a concept of dynamic contrasts.

The child must show that he is acquiring a vocabulary of many such concepts if he is to develop expressive movement ability. As he expresses the following concepts through movement he will show that he is acquiring an understanding of musical elements which he will also transfer to other musical activities:

High—Low	Short—Long
Fast—Slow	Even—Uneven
Loud—Soft	

The above list seems quite simple, and some teachers may assume that the child already has an awareness of these contrasts. All concepts are learned, however, and the child must learn to identify them, label them, and express them through movement. The older child who seems to lack musical ability as he is asked to sing, move, or listen is simply indicating that he has not acquired this basic understanding of musical elements.

The child's first introduction to rhythmic pulses suggesting basic foot patterns should be carefully planned. The following procedure will make this introductory activity a pleasant and successful one for every child:

> The teacher should introduce a single pattern by clapping or by playing a drum or other simple rhythm instrument. The rhythmic cue will be much easier for the child to hear than a presentation that also includes melodic and harmonic elements.

> The child will identify a pattern that suggests a specific movement response. He may then volunteer to show the others what he has heard by moving around the room. Every child will enjoy showing *his* movement idea if there is time for this solo activity.

> The class will then stand and move about the room together. Children may move freely in any direction if the room is large and there are no desks or other obstructions. In many rooms, however, some direction for moving must be established. This is particularly necessary in smaller classrooms, with younger children, and during faster movement activities.

> This activity may be varied in several ways as the teacher repeats the same pattern on subsequent days. Half of the group may help the teacher by clapping or by playing a simple rhythm instrument. They will then exchange places with the group that has been moving. The teacher may suggest after a few days that the child find ways to move his arms, hands, and body as he repeats this introductory foot pattern.

A rhythmic cue suggesting a walking or marching response is often the most successful introduction to expressive movement. Other even patterns (running and slow moving) may be introduced and contrasted with this pattern.

These simple but necessary activities should be repeated a number of times. As the child hears a familiar rhythmic cue time after time he will gain confidence in his ability to move rhythmically and his movements will become more and more expressive.

The child should begin to acquire musical concepts through body movement in a similar manner. The following example shows one effective approach:

> The teacher may introduce the elements of *high* and *low* by playing extremely high and low tones on the piano. The child should be asked where each of these tones is. He might show highness by raising his arms and lowness by moving as low as possible while seated.

> The activity may be varied to provide greater contrast as the teacher asks the child how he can move even higher as he hears extremely high tones. The child will respond by standing. He may stand on his toes and raise his arms. Extreme lowness may be expressed by lying on the floor.

> Other activities should be introduced to help the child feel and identify these paired concepts. He will enjoy finding high and low tones on resonator bells, on the piano, and on other melody instruments. As he experiments with these instruments, he will become more acutely aware of differences in pitch level.

> The teacher may then help the child become conscious of these conceptual differences while moving around the room. A walk may become a high tiptoe as a simple, even pattern is played at a moderate tempo high on the piano keyboard. A pattern the child has previously identified as a march will suggest a different response as it is performed at a very low pitch level. The child begins to combine concepts and basic foot patterns as he participates in this satisfying movement activity.

Children should add other foot patterns and concepts to their movement vocabulary after they have shown that they are listening carefully and moving in different and appropriate ways to several rhythmic pulses. They should also become conscious of uneven rhythmic groupings during the introductory stage of expressive movement development. Patterns that suggest galloping or skipping should be introduced and repeated. The young child will often distinguish between these two rhythmic cues simply because of a difference in dynamic level. He will tend to gallop if he hears an uneven pulse that is louder and lower. Skipping often takes place as the child hears a higher or softer uneven pattern. The following patterns are therefore merely suggestions. The child *may* reverse these under certain musical conditions.

Galloping

Skipping

The teacher should not expect every child to respond to these patterns in exactly the same manner. The preschool child may walk faster or run as he first hears a fast, uneven pattern. Some children will hop on one foot or jump. While a skipping or galloping response *will* convey the uneven pattern in a more appropriate way, the teacher should always be flexible and conscious of individual differences in maturation and experience as the child first responds to a new rhythmic pattern.

Additional elements should also be introduced. The child will feel that ascending-descending contrasts are a delightful game as he responds to these sounds through body movement. Teachers may introduce these elements in the following way:

> Children should be seated and waiting for a rhythmic activity to begin. The teacher will explain that musical sounds will begin in one location and then move down or up. An ascending pattern might then be played. The following is an example of the form this musical cue may take:

> The child who has learned to listen carefully will discover that the music moved upward (ascended). The teacher may then ask him to show through movement what he has just heard.

> A descending pattern should be presented in the same way. This contrasting musical element will become a real musical problem to solve if the child hears the following pattern while he is seated:

> He will identify the pattern as one that moves downward (descends). He will then realize that he must begin to move on a higher level if he is to reproduce the sound he hears through movement.

The teacher may then add these new elements to expressive movement activities. The ascending pattern becomes a musical way to stand and prepare to move. The descending pattern provides the child with an equally musical way to return to his place after participating in expressive movement.

These ascending and descending patterns may become a musical game which will help the child learn to listen more carefully. The teacher may play only a few chords of the ascending pattern and then play down to the beginning position:

The child must listen very carefully if he is to make an appropriate response. He will thoroughly enjoy this musical guessing game. He will also become intensely aware of ascending and descending motion.

Teachers will notice great differences in physical coordination as children in early childhood classrooms make their first expressive responses. Some will move gracefully from the very beginning, while others will be less well coordinated. These extreme differences will be much less noticeable after children develop a movement vocabulary. The shy or awkward child may be one of the first to discover ways to move his hands or arms as he marches around the room. He may quickly discover what a new rhythmic pattern *means* and volunteer to show his idea to the class.

This description of rhythmic patterns may lead teachers to the false assumption that children should be rhythmically *accurate* as they move. Precise accuracy while moving should not be a major goal of the early childhood program of expressive movement activities. The child should simply develop a basic rhythmic vocabulary consistent with his developmental level which will introduce him to expressive movement.

The child's excitement and interest in this introductory stage of expressive movement will be a strong motivating force as he continues to move. The second stage will provide more complex activities which build on this rhythmic and musical foundation.

Second Stage

The second stage of expressive movement development is related to the introductory stage, but there are some important distinctions. The child has developed the ability to move well and to listen equally well. He is now ready to respond to music of different periods and styles. Several points should be considered as the teacher selects recordings or piano compositions appropriate for this stage of movement development:

The composition should have a consistent tempo and repeated rhythmic patterns. Compositions with these characteristics will enable the child to solve one rhythmic problem at a time.

Compositions should be selected to provide a variety of musical periods and styles. The child should have the opportunity to respond expressively to music ranging from the baroque period to the twentieth century.

Any composition chosen for the second stage of development should have a definite rhythmic pulse. Some recordings are not appropriate for this reason.

Musical quality should be considered as music is selected. Compositions composed specifically for rhythmic activities are often of inferior musical quality. "Soldier's March" by Schumann (BRL–R–2; MSB 78303),[1] a well-known composer of the romantic period, is one example of a second-stage composition. The rhythmic pattern is always repeated in exactly the same way. The rhythmic pulses are clear and easy for the child to hear.

As the child listens to a performance of the "Soldier's March" for the first time, he will hear a repeated, even pattern with strong accents.

He may march as he responds to these patterns. The child may begin to move his arms or head in a stiff manner. He may also lift his knees as he responds expressively to this composition.

The teacher should not expect every child to respond by marching. A short, uneven pattern introduces each rhythmic phrase. The child may respond with a skip or a hop. He may continue this pattern since it is repeated often:

This movement is an appropriate response and should be encouraged. The teacher should never expect only one type of response from a group. The child who is marching stiffly is moving in an expressive manner. The child who is adding a skip or a hop to his performance may be showing that he is listening with even greater care as he moves.

"March, Little Soldier" from *Memories of Childhood* by Pinto (BOL #68; BRL–L–1) is another excellent choice for an introductory

---

[1] These codes identify recordings in the basic record series listed at the end of the chapter.

second-stage expressive movement activity. Some teachers may find that their children make the transition from the introductory stage to the second stage if even faster selections are presented. Most children will respond immediately, however, to the accents of these marches.

The child should have an opportunity to respond through expressive movement to several recordings or piano performances which will sug--gest each of the even and uneven patterns he has felt through movement during the introductory stage. He should also identify familiar musical elements as he listens and moves to a variety of performances of excellent quality. Appropriate recordings are listed at the end of the chapter.

Third Stage

The child who has moved expressively while listening to many performances on the second-stage level is ready for more complex activities involving expressive movement. Compositions representative of the third stage of development have longer and more varied musical forms. Two-part, three-part, and rondo forms may be presented as the child learns to use his expressive movement vocabulary in a challenging and exciting way.

"Ballet of the Unhatched Chicks" from *Pictures at an Exhibition* by Moussorgsky (AIM–I) is an example of a third-stage composition in ABA form. The teacher may introduce the third stage of development by presenting this colorful selection in the following manner:

> The recording should be presented first as a quiet listening activity. The child will be told he will hear familiar musical sounds before he listens to this unfamiliar selection.
> He will identify a light, high, rather fast sound in the first and third sections. These will remind him of previous expressive movement responses involving light running and a concept of highness. He will recognize a slower, heavier sound in the B section.
> The teacher will play the composition again after children have discussed these familiar musical sounds. As they listen a second time, they will be asked to find a new element in the recording.
> The child will recognize the new form combination as he listens to the recording a second time. He will hear the faster high A section followed by the slower B section. The return of the first section will be obvious.
> At this point the child is ready to demonstrate this three-part form through expressive movement.

Many compositions may be introduced in this way to provide children with an opportunity to hear and feel more complex music through movement. Outstanding examples of recordings appropriate for the third stage of development are listed at the end of this chapter.

This delightful activity should be presented often in the early childhood music program. Children will always respond eagerly to the opportunity to express musical form and contrast through movement.

OTHER RHYTHMIC ACTIVITIES

Expressive movement should be an important rhythmic activity in preschool and primary-grade classrooms. Other rhythmic activities should also be introduced and repeated if the child is to develop his rhythmic capacities to the fullest.

The young child should be introduced to rhythmic symbols and become aware of the way they show visually what he hears and feels through movement. Simple rhythm instruments should be added to the program to intensify the child's perception of the rhythmic element in music. Every preschool and primary-grade child will enjoy and benefit from participation in expressive movement and the playing of simple instruments. The introduction of rhythmic notation should be delayed, however, until the primary-grade child has had many previous experiences with rhythm through movement.

Rhythmic Notation

The primary-grade child should be introduced to notation in an informal manner. The teacher may show him how a familiar rhythmic pattern looks by displaying it in line notation. The child who has made a galloping or skipping response to an uneven rhythmic pattern will quickly understand why the following simplified notation example represents the sound he has heard:

— — — — — — — —

A number of these visual patterns may be introduced after the child has listened to and moved to a variety of even and uneven rhythmic patterns. The following examples will show the child how familiar rhythmic patterns appear in line notation:

Walking or marching   — — — — — — — —

Running or fast walking -- -- -- -- --

Slow moving   ——— ——— ———

This simple visual introduction to notation may be followed by the presentation of specific rhythmic symbols. In many primary grade music programs, however, there is not sufficient time allotted to music to permit this stage in the recognition and understanding of rhythmic symbols.

Teachers who do introduce rhythmic notation will also introduce a change of emphasis in the child's physical response. In expressive movement activities the child is not expected to be precise in a metrical way, although many children do match metrical pulses with accented foot patterns as they move. The child must be able to match metrical pulses as he identifies and reproduces rhythmic notation patterns. The primary-grade child is ready for this more precise response.

Rhythmic symbols may be introduced and become meaningful to the child if music is a daily activity in the classroom. The child should first understand how different patterns are related through symbols and changes in tempo. Even tempos may be displayed first in relation to the quarter note:

The child should never be told that a quarter note always represents a "walking" pulse or that an eighth note or sixteenth note is a "running" note. He should learn from the beginning that there are no fixed tempo values to rhythmic symbols. He should begin to understand, instead, that different symbols represent different subdivisions within a measure grouping.

The teacher may show the flexible use of rhythmic symbols by establishing a different grouping of symbols another day. The eighth note may be established as a symbol of moderate tempo. Faster and slower patterns will be written in relation to this new basic rhythmic unit:

The child will begin to understand the relative time value of rhythmic symbols as he compares these two groupings of symbols. He will be ready to recognize some of these relationships by identifying rhythmic notation in familiar songs.

The child should become aware of meter and meter signatures after this introduction to rhythmic symbols. After a brief explanation of the 2/4 meter signature the teacher may divide the class. Half will clap the basic meter while the other half claps faster or slower rhythmic patterns. New patterns may be introduced in this way. The child will become aware of the visual difference between even and uneven patterns as he claps a dotted grouping while others maintain a steady metrical pulse:

The child should begin to use this new knowledge of the rhythmic element in music after he has developed a vocabulary of rhythmic symbol relationships. He will be ready to read rhythmic notation in unfamiliar songs. He will be able to identify familiar patterns as he listens to unfamiliar recordings or piano performances.

Teachers who have the time and the training necessary for introducing notation in the primary-grade classroom will be interested in comparing different techniques that have been developed for making the child aware of musical symbols. Several methods are described in Chapter 5 (pages 105–11).

Rhythm Instruments

The rhythmic notation suggestions presented above are more appropriate for the primary-grade child. The introduction and repeated use of rhythm instruments is appropriate for any preschool or primary-grade child.

The teacher should always have a *musical* reason for adding instruments to a musical activity. They should never be introduced simply to allow the child to make a "joyful noise" or to involve him in some hit-or-miss physical activity.

Rhythm instruments may be used quite effectively as the child begins to experiment with basic foot patterns during the introductory stage of expressive movement. The child may play the pattern as others move. He often shows an increased sensitivity as a result of playing a pattern before moving.

The child will often become more aware of musical elements as he helps the teacher reproduce them on a simple instrument. Accelerando-ritardando and other paired rhythmic elements may be performed in this way.

Instruments should not be added to second- and third-stage expressive movement activities. The recordings the child will hear and respond to through movement will provide sufficient rhythmic pulse. The addition of instruments may distract him, and he will not listen well as he moves.

The teacher should also add instruments to the rhythmic program when the child is introduced to rhythmic symbols. The basic rhythmic symbol identification activities described above will often become more meaningful to the child as he plays patterns on a rhythm instrument. Performances on simple rhythm instruments are particularly effective when a new visual symbol is presented. Rhythm instruments may also be added to the music program in other ways. Suggestions are included in Chapter 2 (pages 25–27) and in Chapter 8 (pages 169–70).

While other activities may be added to the rhythmic program for early childhood, the ones described here are important to the child's rhythmic development and each makes a direct contribution to his musical growth. These activities will increase the child's perception and understanding of the rhythmic element in music. They should therefore, be emphasized as teachers plan an effective and varied music program for young children.

THE TEACHER'S ROLE

Most children are eager to participate in rhythmic activities. The excitement of expressive movement and other rhythmic activities, however, may interfere with the effectiveness of the program. The suggestions that follow are described primarily to help teachers transform each rhythmic activity into a musical activity as well.

Motivation

Many children will respond immediately to any new activity in the classroom. A few other children, particularly at the beginning of the school year, may hesitate or attempt to withdraw from an unfamiliar situation. There are always a few children who feel unsure of themselves when a physical activity is introduced.

The first few weeks of school may set a pattern for participation or withdrawal that may continue for a much longer time period. Teachers should help hesitant children discover the satisfaction that is always present in rhythmic activities. A few simple introductory approaches will involve every child in the excitement of rhythm.

1. One activity suggested during the introductory stage of expressive movement development (pages 73–75) will involve the hesitant child in rhythmic activities. Since he is asked to find high and low sounds with his body as he listens to these musical cues, he may do so while seated. He will feel quite "safe" and still respond to the music. He will gain confidence in his physical ability as these cues are repeated. When another child demonstrates an even higher response by standing high and reaching higher with his arms, the shyest and most hesitant child will usually join him.

2. The teacher may introduce rhythmic activities by singing a few "action" songs at the beginning of the school year. The song should be learned first during a singing activity. Then the teacher will substitute words that suggest physical activity. The first action suggestions should involve the use of hands or other parts of the body as the child is seated. As he claps, nods, or sways he will feel at ease and participate in a relaxed manner. The activity will be enjoyable and exciting. The teacher may then substitute other words when every child is making a physical response. Word substitutions such as "stamp," "jump," or "leap" will bring the child to his feet. He will thoroughly enjoy this physical release and stimulation. He will also be ready to participate in additional rhythmic activities.

"If You're Happy" (Example 4-1) is an example of the type of song the teacher may use to introduce children to rhythmic activities. "Action" songs should not, however, be considered as an adequate rhythmic program to such an extent that other more musical rhythmic activities are excluded. Songs that suggest actions are merely an introduction to rhythm. If they are emphasized too much in the music program, young children will simply learn to match actions to words rather than to the varied and exciting pulses of music itself.

These two simple approaches will effectively draw each child into the rhythmic activity. The child who seems to withdraw from a new physical activity at first will quickly forget his feeling of hesitation as he participates in these activities.

Learning To Listen

A rhythmic activity that is well planned in other respects may fail because the teacher is not conscious of one important detail. The child will learn to respond rhythmically and expressively to the music he hears only if his attention is centered upon the sound of the music itself. The teacher who introduces a simple uneven pattern by saying,

Example 4-1

IF YOU'RE HAPPY [2]

Action verses:

    2. Clap your hands!

    3. Stamp your foot!

    4. Jump with me!

[2] From *Discovering Music Together—Early Childhood* by Robert B. Smith and Charles Leonhard. Copyright © 1968 by Follett Educational Corporation. Reprinted by permission of the publisher.

"This is galloping music," is telling the child to listen for verbal directions rather than the rhythmic patterns he should learn to identify. If this teaching approach is consistently used, the child may become completely dependent upon his teacher's directions, and he may not learn to listen to rhythmic pulses and expressive changes in music.

This teaching mistake takes place most frequently at the beginning of the school year. Children may not be listening carefully to a specific rhythmic pattern at first as they begin to move. They seem to wander aimlessly around the room as the teacher plays a rhythmic cue which should result in a marching response. At this point the teacher often labels the music by telling the child he is hearing a "marching" pattern. This remark is intended to be helpful, but verbal directions are always a hindrance when the child first begins to move.

Learning to listen carefully may take a relatively long period of time. The child will eventually show by his responses that he is hearing different patterns. The teacher will help him most at this point by repeating simple patterns day after day and by not telling the child to move in a specific way.

Some teachers attempt to help the child find expressive ways to move by suggesting that he move in an imitative or dramatic way. As the child hears a slow pattern at a low pitch level he may be told that this pattern sounds like "elephants" moving. Other patterns are often described as movements other animals make. This is a false and unmusical approach. Music is *not* a descriptive art form. The child is restricted by this approach, and he does not learn to listen attentively as he attempts to move. He simply becomes dependent upon the teacher's directions instead of listening attentively to the music when a new composition or pattern is introduced. The child should, instead, be guided to listen attentively to a new pattern and to become gradually more expressive in his body responses as he hears an example time after time.

Some teachers defend an imitative or dramatic approach to movement because the child who is self-conscious forgets his feelings of hesitation or withdrawal when he is asked to move like a rabbit or a giant. This approach is not necessary, however, if children have participated in the activities included in the introductory stage of expressive movement. Children should become self-confident in musical and expressive ways rather than as animals or as fictional characters.

Four teaching examples provide an appropriate setting for any expressive movement activity:

> Children should always identify a new pattern through movement or by describing what they have heard. The teacher may supply a term if the child is unable to supply a verbal label for what he has

heard, but the pattern should never be described in any specific way for the child before he has moved or talked about the new pattern.

Teachers should not introduce a large number of new patterns or compositions, and they should repeat familiar selections many times. These frequent repetitions will provide children with the opportunity to become more and more expressive as they explore the varied ways they can manipulate their feet, arms, and bodies. A child may simply walk at first as he responds to a second-stage selection with an accented even pattern. On a second day he may begin to discover the accents with his feet as he listens, by lifting his knees and stamping with one foot. He may, as he listens and moves on subsequent days, find expressive ways to move his arms as he listens to the same composition or pattern.

Children should begin a new movement activity by listening attentively in a seated position. They will identify familiar sounds and hear new patterns much more easily than they will if they immediately try to respond through movement. The teacher may use this seated prelude to movement to ask several children to show the class what they have heard. As children develop the habit of listening attentively before moving, they also have the opportunity to observe a number of movement possibilities.

As the child develops a more varied repertoire of foot patterns and concepts, he may combine them in an unusually expressive way as he moves. The teacher should watch carefully as the group moves. Occasionally a child may be selected as outstanding in his expressive response. When this approach is introduced, the teacher should attempt to select at least one other child as well. If the group watches just one child as an example, they may well conclude that his response is *the* way to move. If more than one child moves as an expressive example, the child who is observing sees variety and flexibility in expressive movement responses.

The teacher should never begin a movement activity by deciding which movements will be appropriate to express musical sounds. Children often hear many expressive possibilities in music that the adult ear does *not* hear. Activities will become truly expressive both to the child and to the teacher if the approaches described here are followed.

Facilities and Equipment

Several practical considerations must precede the effective presentation of a program of rhythmic activities. The child must have space in which to move. Several types of musical equipment must be available, and maintenance of the equipment must be provided.

The teacher should have at least one drum of excellent quality. A tuneable drum is ideal, since adjustments in tension are easily made. This type of drum may be used in introductory movement activities and for many other rhythmic purposes in the classroom.

Rhythm instruments should be available for the child as well. A small drum should be provided for approximately one-third to one-half of the class. Rhythm sticks might also be supplied in similar quantities. The selection of additional instruments will depend upon specific classroom situations and the child's level of coordination.

A library of fine recordings is an absolute necessity if the child is to participate in expressive movement activities beyond the introductory stage of development. Teachers who play the piano well may be able to perform appropriate selections, but few will play well enough to provide the child with performances equal to the recordings listed at the end of the chapter.

An excellent record player should be provided for rhythmic and other music activities. The teacher who attempts to present musical examples on a player of poor quality is seriously hampered by inferior sound reproduction.

Funds must be available for the maintenance and replacement of equipment. Record-player needles must be checked regularly and replaced when worn. Records with worn surfaces should also be replaced. Pianos and rhythm instruments must be kept in excellent repair.

Available space is often a problem as the teacher plans rhythmic activities, since small classrooms with fixed desks are not adequate for an expressive movement activity. Many schools have special music rooms, but few of these have sufficient space for movement activities. The school community room or gym is a better choice. Large areas of this type may cause problems in terms of discipline at first. The available space, however, is conducive to free and expressive movement, and these space benefits far outweigh any possible disadvantage.

The teacher should plan cooperatively with children the ways to make a room more suitable for movement activities. Classroom equipment may need to be moved to provide more space. The gym or community room may have more space than is needed. Children should also be involved in planning how they will behave as they move from the classroom to a larger room for this activity. They will often volunteer many helpful suggestions.

PROGRAM OBJECTIVES

Expressive movement is an exciting activity for the young child since this aspect of his rhythmic growth is suited to his need for physical release. Expressive responses will also prepare him for future experiences with this fascinating aspect of music. The first category of objectives for the rhythmic program is directly related to the stages the young child must pass through to develop expressive responses to music.

The child should also begin to develop an awareness of rhythmic symbols. The objectives directly related to this facet of his rhythmic development are more suitable for children in primary-grade classrooms.

Expressive Movement

The child who has participated in an effective program of expressive movement activities should:

Develop a repertoire of basic foot patterns and musical concepts.

Combine this repertoire in an expressive manner as he hears and responds to compositions during the second stage of rhythmic movement.

Respond to more complex selections in a variety of musical forms.

Demonstrate that expressive movement has become a satisfying and musical experience which he wants to continue.

Rhythmic Notation

The primary-grade child who has participated in a daily, effective rhythmic program should:

Develop an understanding of simple rhythmic symbols and identify those line-notation patterns that correspond to familiar foot patterns.

Read rhythmic notation. He will show that he has developed this music-reading skill as he identifies rhythmic notation patterns in unfamiliar songs and participates in other musical activities involving the recognition of rhythmic symbols.

PROGRAM EVALUATION

The process of evaluation must be applied periodically as the teacher plans an effective and sequential program of rhythmic activities. The child's developing physical coordination and his rhythmic vocabulary or repertoire level must be checked carefully before a new activity is introduced.

Evaluation of rhythmic development may seem at first to be a much easier procedure than an evaluation of singing development. The child is moving or otherwise actively participating, and his responses may be observed as he responds with the group. An evaluation during a group rhythmic activity can be extremely misleading, however, since the child may be merely imitating the responses of another child. He may be looking instead of listening.

The teacher will discover the child's ability to listen and respond only by introducing solo movement or other rhythmic activities. The child will enjoy these gamelike activities very much as he is asked to guess what the rhythmic pattern is and then to show the pattern. As the teacher presents this evaluation game, the child's ability to respond and his readiness for new activities or stages of development will be accurately measured.

The child's ability to identify basic patterns and elements at the introductory stage of development may be checked in the following manner:

> Several patterns and elements should be listed before the activity begins. The teacher should also plan to play these patterns on only one instrument if possible. The child's ability may not be measured accurately if high-low elements are played on bells and a rhythmic pattern is played on the piano. He may be simply responding to different instruments rather than to rhythmic elements. The piano (or another melody instrument) is, therefore, more appropriate, since both rhythmic and melodic patterns (high-low, ascending-descending) may be played.
>
> The evaluation activity should extend for several days, and a few children should respond each day. The activity takes too much time to be completed during one music period.
>
> The patterns should be presented in a different order as each child responds alone. The teacher may plan several different orders of presentation before the activity is introduced. If the patterns are presented in the same order for each child, children who observe the sequence several times may memorize the order of patterns.

The teacher may plan similar evaluation activities as the expressive movement program progresses. Familiar and unfamiliar recordings and piano selections may be presented to evaluate further progress.

The young child who listens to an unfamiliar composition featuring a variety of patterns and contrasting elements and then responds in an appropriate and expressive manner has reached a high level of rhythmic and expressive ability.

Teachers who emphasize the reading of rhythmic notation in the primary grades should evaluate progress periodically before they introduce a new activity. Children will enjoy playing the following evaluation games:

The patterns with which the class is familiar may be written on large charts. The teacher will present the charts in random order and give each child a turn to identify one or more patterns. The child will clap the pattern he recognizes on the chart.

The charts may be used in another type of game. The teacher will display all patterns together. After the teacher claps one pattern, or plays it on a rhythm instrument, a child comes to the charts and points to the pattern which has been played.

Dictation tests may be presented periodically to check progress. The teacher plays familiar patterns, and the class writes them in line or staff notation.

These notation-reading evaluation activities are as appropriate for children who can identify only a few simple patterns as they are for those who are becoming competent in the reading of staff notation. The success of a reading program depends to a great extent upon the periodic evaluation of each child's progress.

SUMMARY

Rhythm must be a carefully defined element in the young child's music education. Activities must be selected to lead to those experiences that will develop the child's rhythmic capacities.

The rhythm program described in this chapter carefully considers the child's rhythmic capacities and needs. Expressive movement is presented in a detailed and sequential manner. This aspect of rhythmic growth should be emphasized in every early childhood classroom. Activities with instruments are also appropriate for both the preschool and the primary-grade child. Rhythmic reading may be introduced in primary-grade classrooms.

The child is highly motivated to participate in the excitement of any rhythmic activity. Teachers must select these activities with great care, however, to provide continuing musical growth rather than mere recreation.

QUESTIONS AND PROJECTS

1. Examine one of the basic record series listed below in terms of recorded selections that are appropriate for early childhood movement activities. What supplementary recordings would be needed in a school system to provide selections representative of all periods and styles?
2. Examine several record albums from the various series that emphasize music for fundamental movement activities. What are their positive attributes? Do they have negative characteristics? Listen to each selection as you make this critical analysis.
3. Select two or more elementary music methods textbooks and compare their

approaches to helping children develop rhythmic responsiveness. Outline the sequence of rhythmic development described in each text.

4. Discuss the contribution of the rhythmic program to the development of the young child's creative potential.

5. How does each of the following types of rhythmic activity affect the child's rhythmic development?

Singing games   Expressive movement
Action songs   Folk dances

REFERENCES

Classroom Instruments

Tuneable head drum (primarily for the teacher—children will play it at times).
Small tomtoms (several should be provided).
Sticks, tambourines, tone blocks, and other appropriate instruments that the child can play easily.

Suppliers

Children's Music Center, Inc., Los Angeles, Calif.
Lyons Band Instrument Co., Chicago, Ill.
Peripole, Inc., Far Rockaway, N.Y.
Rhythm Band Inc., Fort Worth, Tex.
Wexler, Chicago, Ill.

Audio-Visual Aids

Basic Record Series

Adventures in Music. New York: RCA Victor Educational Sales.

AIM–I, Grade 1
AIM–II, Grade 2
AIM–III–1, Grade 3, Vol. 1
AIM–III–2, Grade 3, Vol. 2

Basic Record Library for Elementary Schools. New York: RCA Victor Educational Sales.

BRL–L–1, The Listening Program, Vol. I
BRL–L–3, The Listening Program, Vol. III
BRL–R–1, The Rhythm Program, Vol. I
BRL–R–2, The Rhythm Program, Vol. II
BRL–R–3, The Rhythm Program, Vol. III

Bowmar Orchestral Library. Los Angeles: Bowmar Records.

BOL #53, Pictures and Patterns
BOL #54, Marches
BOL #55, Dances, Part I
BOL #62, Masters of Music
BOL #63, Concert Matinee

BOL #64, Miniatures in Music
BOL #68, Classroom Concert

Musical Sound Books. Scarsdale, N.Y.: Musical Sound Books.

MSB 78000 series, For Young Listeners
MSB 78300 series, Tiny Masterpieces

Second-Stage Recordings

Slow tempo

Corelli-Pinelli: "Sarabande," *Suite for String Orchestra* (BOL #63)
Handel: "A Ground" (BOL #53)
Kabalevsky: "Pantomime," *The Comedians* (AIM–I)
Mahler: "Second Movement," *Symphony No. 1* (BOL #62)
Moussorgsky: "Bydlo," *Pictures at an Exhibition* (AIM–II)
Schumann: "Northern Song" (BRL–R–3)
Tchaikovsky: "Dolly's Funeral" (BRL–R–3)

Moderate tempo (walk, march)

Couperin: "Little Windmills" (BOL #64)
Handel: "Bourrée," *Fireworks Music* (BOL #62)
Pierne: "Entrance of the Little Fauns" (BOL #54)
Pinto: "March, Little Soldier," *Memories of Childhood* (BOL #68; BRL–L–1)
Prokofiev: "March," *Love for Three Oranges* (BOL #54)
Rossini-Britten: "March," *Soirées Musicales* (AIM–I)
Schumann: "Soldier's March" (BRL–R–2; MSB 78303)
Tchaikovsky: "March of the Tin Soldiers" (BRL–R–3)
Walton: "Country Dance," *Façade Suite* (BOL #55)

Fast tempo (run)

Beethoven: "Scherzo," *"Eroica" Symphony* (BRL–L–1)
Bizet: "Impromptu" (BRL–L–1)
———. "The Ball" (AIM–I), "The Top" (BOL #53), *Children's Games*
Copland: "Hoe-Down," *Rodeo* (BOL #55)
Gluck: "Ballet" (BRL–R–1)
Kabalevsky: "Intermezzo," *The Comedians* (BOL #53)
Khatchaturian: "Galop," *Masquerade Suite* (BOL #55)
Mendelssohn: "Tarantelle" (BRL–R–2)
Prokofiev: "Departure," *Winter Holiday* (AIM–II)
Rossini-Respighi: "Tarantella," *The Fantastic Toyshop* (AIM–III–2)
Schubert: "The Bee" (BOL #64; BRL–L–3)

High

Corelli-Pinelli: "Badinerie," *Suite for String Orchestra* (BOL #63)
Liadov: "Music Box" (BOL #64; MSB 78016)
Rossini-Respighi: "Pizzicato," *The Fantastic Toyshop* (BOL #53)

Uneven

Corelli-Pinelli: "Gigue," *Suite for String Orchestra* (BOL #63; MSB 78304)
Gluck: "Sicilienne" (BRL–R–1)
Handel: "Siciliana" (BRL–R–3)
Schumann: "Jaglied" (BRL–R–1)

Musical contrasts

Bizet: "The Ball," *Children's Games* (AIM–I)—high-low, loud-soft
————. "The Changing of the Guard," *Carmen Suite No. 2* (AIM–III–2)—crescendo-decrescendo
Grieg: "In the Hall of the Mountain King," *Peer Gynt Suite No. 1* (AIM–III–2)—low-high, soft-loud, accellerando
Kabalevsky: "Pantomime," *The Comedians* (AIM–I)—crescendo, low-high
Moussorgsky: "Bydlo," *Pictures at an Exhibition* (AIM–II)—crescendo-decrescendo
Prokofiev: "Departure," *Winter Holiday* (AIM–II)—crescendo-decrescendo
Rossini-Britten: "March," *Soirées Musicales* (AIM–I)—loud-soft, low-high
Shostakovitch: "Pizzicato Polka," *Ballet Suite No. 1* (AIM–I)—accellerando

Third-Stage Recordings

Bizet: "Trumpet and Drum," *Jeux d'Enfants* (BOL #53; MSB 78008)
Copland: "Circus Music," *The Red Pony* (AIM–III–1)
Gluck: "Air Gai," *Iphigénie in Aulis* (AIM–I)
Grieg: "In the Hall of the Mountain King," *Peer Gynt Suite No. 1* (AIM–III–2)
Grieg: "Wedding Day at Troldhaugen" (BOL #62)
Ibert: "Parade," *Divertissement* (AIM–I)
Kabalevsky: "Gavotte" (BOL #55)
————. "March and Comedians' Gallop," *The Comedians* (AIM–III–1)
Lully: "Marche," *Ballet Suite* (AIM–III–2)
McDonald: "First Movement" (AIM–II–2), "Third Movement" (AIM–II), *Children's Symphony*
Moussorgsky: "Ballet of the Unhatched Chicks," *Pictures at an Exhibition* (AIM–I)
Mozart: "Minuet," *Symphony No. 40* (BOL #62)
Pinto: "Run, Run," *Memories of Childhood* (BOL #68; BRL–L–1)
Schumann-Glazounov: "German Waltz—Paganini," *Carnaval* (BOL #53)
Shostakovich: "Petite Ballerina" (AIM–II), "Pizzicato Polka" (AIM–I), *Ballet Suite No. 1*
Thomson: "Walking Song," *Acadian Songs and Dances* (AIM–I)

Other Aids

Doll, Edna, and Nelson, Mary Jarman. *Rhythms Today!* Morristown, N.J.: Silver Burdett Co., 1966. (Two correlated recordings are also available.)
Saffran, Rosanna. *First Book of Creative Rhythms.* New York: Holt, Rinehart & Winston, 1963. (Many valuable materials and references.)

5

RHYTHMIC ACTIVITIES
FOR OLDER CHILDREN

Rhythmic activities are as important for the older child as they are for children in early childhood classrooms. The older child is able to participate in rhythmic activities which are too complex for the younger child because he has reached a higher level of physical coordination. He has also developed a sensitivity to rhythmic pulsation and the expressive qualities of music through his participation in previous rhythmic activities.

Children should continue to participate in movement activities and the element of musical form should be stressed as expressive movement is continued. The older child will discover form through movement and understand this important musical element as he listens to unfamiliar compositions. The older child should also become aware of different musical styles and periods. He will feel and understand stylistic differences easily as he continues to participate in expressive movement.

The child should learn to read and reproduce rhythmic notation. He should develop a large vocabulary of rhythmic notation patterns, and he should be able to recognize and perform them as he sings and plays.

The older child should reach two major goals as he continues to participate in rhythmic activities:

> He should become aware of musical form, style, and periods of composition as he participates in expressive movement.

He should learn to read rhythmic notation well and use this reading ability in singing and instrumental activities.

Other rhythmic activities are appropriate in a daily music program. The child will often find rhythmic patterns more easily as he plays rhythm instruments. Patterned dances may be introduced to make him aware of a specific musical style or period.

The basic areas of the rhythmic program, however, should be continued expressive movement and a thorough understanding of rhythmic notation. These two activities will develop the child's rhythmic capacities and prepare him for further musical growth.

EXPRESSIVE MOVEMENT

The child who listens to music and then responds with expressive movement is participating in an activity that involves far more than the element of rhythm. He is developing concepts of form, style, period, and melodic direction as he responds to a number of compositions. He is also, of course, continuing his developing conceptualization of rhythmic elements in music. Expressive movement is therefore an activity that may lead to many related musical experiences. The child is constantly growing in his appreciation and understanding of music as he responds to a large repertoire of music.

Introducing Movement

The older child who has participated in an effective early childhood program of expressive movement will want to continue to make expressive responses to music. He will have developed a large repertoire of ways to move, and he will feel confident of his ability as he listens and moves.

The child without previous movement experience will often feel much less confident and may need to begin at a more basic level if he is to want to participate in a movement activity. The teacher should not expect expressive or relaxed responses from a child if his previous participation in the primary grades was limited to adding actions to a song or to playing a few rhythm instruments.

A few simple techniques will help the child overcome any feeling of hesitation and lead him to the point where he wants to move. The teacher should begin with movement activities that will help the child develop the basic movement patterns and concepts necessary for expressive movement. Some of the activities described in Chapter 4 are appropriate for the older beginner.

Older children will want to move expressively after they have listened to two marches with a similar rhythmic pulse but completely different musical moods. "Marche Joyeuse" by Chabrier (AIM–IV–1) [1] and the "March" from *Love for Three Oranges* by Prokofiev (BOL #54) are excellent introductory examples. Each is a march with a consistent rhythmic pulse. The child will hear two entirely different musical effects, however, as he listens and moves.

> Each selection should be presented first as a listening activity. The teacher may introduce the recordings by saying that each suggests a way to move.
>
> After listening to both marches the child should be asked how they are similar and at the same time quite different. He will have heard striking differences in rhythm and tone color while comparing the two selections.
>
> The teacher might then introduce seated movement by asking the child to show rhythmic pulses with his arms or body as he sits and listens to each recording a second time.
>
> While these seated responses may be expressive, the child will realize that they are not adequate to express some of the sounds he has heard. The teacher may then suggest that he think of ways to move about the room as he listens again.
>
> These selections should be repeated later several times. As the child grows in his ability to respond expressively he will discover that highness-lowness, loudness-softness, and other musical elements he will hear may be expressed through movement.
>
> *Related activities:* The child will be interested in hearing and responding to other marches. The teacher may use this opportunity to introduce him to other styles of music. The child may begin to identify instruments as he listens and moves. The colorful cymbal crashes in the Prokofiev march will capture his attention.

Children who are introduced to expressive movement in this way may be learning much more than a simple rhythmic response. They are also discovering that composers of one period composed marches that are typical of that period and quite different from another. They may find that a title is often of little help in identifying a musical mood or effect. Some marches are slow and majestic while others are faster and exhilarating. The musical effects in a march may convey much more than the title implies.

Other types of activities may be presented to introduce older children to expressive movement. Two of these activities are more closely related to helping the child feel at ease in a movement activity than they are to expressive movement itself.

Rhythmic canons may be introduced. As the child participates in

[1] See the References at the end of this chapter for identification of the recordings mentioned.

a rhythmic canon activity he maintains his own rhythmic presentation of the canon patterns as other children enter at different times. The teacher might suggest "Come Follow Me" (see the Appendix, page 301) as an appropriate choice. The three sections of this canon have contrasting rhythmic patterns. The class may be divided into three groups. Each group will learn to clap just one pattern at first. Then these patterns will be combined with one group beginning and continuing to repeat the first pattern. The second group will begin after the first group has performed the complete pattern one time. Later the third group will enter:

The child should thoroughly enjoy this activity and be motivated to try the rhythmic canon in another way. The teacher may then suggest that each group find its pattern by foot tapping rather than by clapping. The class should proceed from this stage to producing the pattern while moving about the room. In this way, the child is involved in movement in an enjoyable manner.

Other rounds and canons that have phrases with contrasting rhythmic patterns may be performed in this manner. The child will often perform his designated rhythmic pattern more quickly and easily if he begins by chanting the words in rhythm and clapping at the same time.

Rhythmic rounds and canons may be continued as a more challenging activity. Children may perform the canon rhythmically as they would if they were singing it. One group will begin and clap or step the entire sequence of rhythmic patterns. They will maintain their part as other groups begin later and clap or step the same patterns in a delayed sequence.

These simple introductions to movement are necessary if the older child is to participate successfully in more complex movement activities. He will develop a basic confidence in his ability to move and he will want to join further activities of this type. Movement activities are relaxing and enjoyable for the child who has found success in his first attempts.

Experiencing Form Through Movement

The older child is ready to acquire knowledge about music. He should become aware of the many elements that are combined to form a complex musical selection. The form of music should fascinate him, and the most delightful way to learn about musical form is to experience it through movement.

Some musical forms that are used in contemporary composition were developed hundreds of years ago. The child should become familiar with the most frequently heard forms of musical organization through expressive movement. He should then learn to identify these forms as he listens to unfamiliar selections.

The *ABA or ternary form* has been used frequently by composers of many styles and periods. The form will be easy to identify through movement. Compositions with strong rhythmic or mood contrasts should be chosen as the child first identifies the ABA form through movement. The "Minuet" from Mozart's *Symphony No. 40* (BOL #62) is an example. The A section has a strong, thrusting accent and a melodic outline with a jagged, leaping quality. The B section (Trio) provides a contrast since the theme, dynamic level, accompaniment, and texture are combined in a lyrical manner. The A section returns and completes this simple example of ABA form:

Section A theme

Section B (Trio) theme

The child should listen to the "Minuet" after the teacher tells him that he will hear two contrasting sections.

The two main themes should then be played and displayed in large
notation.

The child should listen to the "Minuet" again and identify the number
of times each theme appears. He should also become conscious of
the fact that there are three main sections to the selection.

The child might show the rhythmic contrasts in the two sections while
remaining seated. The A sections may suggest strong arm thrusts
and the B section horizontal movements with the arms or upper
body. This activity will help the child who is learning for the
first time that a complete section of a composition may consist of
more than one theme. Seated movement will also help those without previous expressive movement experience.

Every child who has participated regularly in movement activities at
the preschool and primary-grade levels will be ready to move
rhythmically around the room as he listens again to the "Minuet."
Children who are just beginning to participate in this type of activity may move more freely if the class is divided into smaller
groups. Boys might respond at first to the strongly rhythmic A
sections, while girls move as they hear the B section begin. The
groups should be reversed later if this approach is followed.

The child should hear this symphonic movement later and continue to
add expressive responses. He may show the melodic direction of
melodies through arm and body motions. He may hear and respond to different rhythmic patterns.

Related Activities: The child should hear and identify this same musical
form in other selections which are chosen as examples of different
musical styles and periods. The "Norwegian Dance" by Grieg
(BOL #63) is a composition in ABA form written by a composer
of the romantic period. The class may learn an eighteenth-century
minuet and compare this more highly stylized dance to the Mozart
"Minuet." Musical terms will become more interesting to the child
as he reads and gathers information concerning the minuet, the
symphony orchestra, and the classical period.

Rondo form will be easy for the older child to identify after he has
become thoroughly familiar with ABA form. The first three sections
of a typical rondo form will remind the child of ABA form. He will discover, however, that additional sections often include a third theme
and that the A section returns time after time.

The "Waltz" from *The Sleeping Beauty* by Tchaikovsky (AIM–IV–
1; BOL #67) is a typical example of rondo form. The composer has
added a dramatic introduction and coda to the basic form. The selection clearly shows the dominant characteristic of this musical form.
The A section is performed four times:

The teacher may prepare the child to listen by asking him to compare this selection with the compositions in ABA form he has previously heard. The child might also be told before listening that the composition begins with an introduction. After he has heard the waltz he will realize that the form is longer and more complex than a selection with a three-part (ABA) form.

The three main themes should be placed on the chalk board. The child may listen to them at this point. He will be able to sing the first theme easily.

The child should then discover the form while listening, and the order of themes should be placed on the board.

(Introduction) A - B - A - C - A - B - A (Coda)

The class should then discuss and select movement patterns that will express each contrasting section. Different groups may then move expressively to different sections of this selection in rondo form.

Related Activities: The child will enjoy listening to the waltz another time to hear the brilliant instrumental combinations the composer has selected. The class might discuss the manner in which different combinations of instruments add to the contrast between sections. The story of the Tchaikovsky ballets provides fascinating reading for the child. He should also find definitions for the terms "introduction" and "coda." The child should listen to other compositions in rondo form. One example, "The Cowboys" by Thomson (BOL #65), is more appropriate for a quiet listening activity. The child will enjoy discovering how a contemporary American composer uses this same form and selects folk songs for his themes. As the child listens to the "Scherzo" from Beethoven's *Symphony No. 7* (BOL #62), he will hear accented pulsations which suggest an expressive response.

Children who have learned to identify ABA and rondo forms through their movement responses should have the opportunity to react expressively to other rhythmic selections based on these musical forms. They should also be introduced to other musical forms through movement.

Variation form is one of the oldest and, at the same time, one of the newest of musical forms. Serious composers still write variations of themes, and many jazz and popular selections are based on variants of a theme. Composers change the original theme in many ways as they write variations. They may vary the melodic, rhythmic, or harmonic element; they may combine changes in these elements in a single variation.

One section of the *Appalachian Suite* by Aaron Copland was written in variation form. This composer selected the Shaker melody, "Simple Gifts," as his theme and wrote five variations. Four of these are included in the recording, *Music U.S.A.* (BOL #65). Copland's variations are easy to identify, and the theme is always present. He changes tempi and rhythmic pulses beneath the melody. Varied tone-color effects contribute to the unique quality of each variation. The clarinet plays the theme after a short, slow introduction composed of parts of the melody. Variation I begins with the oboe, and then strings enter as this fast, high variation continues. Variation II is much slower and is majestic in mood and tempo. The third variation is fast and brilliant; a trumpet fanfare is featured. The short Variation IV is slower and woodwinds are prominent.

> The child should learn to sing "Simple Gifts" first. This song is included in the Appendix, page 291.
>
> After a very simple explanation of variation form, the child should listen to the "Simple Gifts" variation part of the *Appalachian Suite* by Copland. He might listen to decide which variations sound most like the song he has sung.
>
> Appropriate movements will be easy to choose after the child listens to the variations several times. The class may decide to move rhythmically in two groups since the composition may be divided into slow and fast sections.
>
> The class may then be introduced to more subtle elements in the variations. Instruments imitate each other in the introduction and in Variations I and II. These imitations will remind the child of rounds he has sung. Groups might decide to move in an imitative, contrapuntal fashion.
>
> *Related Activities:* The child should identify variation form as he listens to other recordings. The second movement of the *Surprise Symphony* by Haydn (BOL #62) is an example from the classical period. The child will want to hear other compositions by the

American composer Aaron Copland. "Hoe-Down," from the *Rodeo* ballet suite (AIM-IV-2; BOL #55), provides a complete contrast to the variations the child has heard and shows the versatility of this famous contemporary composer.

Three compositions mentioned earlier in this chapter have short contrapuntal effects. The overlapping thematic effects in the A section of the "Minuet" from *Symphony No. 40* by Mozart will remind the child of rounds he has sung. The echo effect in the third theme of the "Waltz" from *The Sleeping Beauty* is easy for the child to hear and respond to. The echoes are short and barely overlap the melody. The contrapuntal lines in the introduction and first two variations of the "Simple Gifts" section of the *Appalachian Suite* by Copland are longer and more complex.

Children will become aware of one aspect of contrapuntal music as they listen to "Jesu, Joy of Man's Desiring" by Bach (AIM-V-1; MSB 78316). The following activities will introduce them to this baroque-period composition:

> The class should learn to sing the chorale, "Jesu, Joy of Man's Desiring," which is included in the Appendix, page 334.
>
> They should then be told that they will hear this familiar melody in an instrumental arrangement as they prepare to listen to the recording. They will identify the chorale melody without difficulty as they listen to the recording. They will also become aware of the fact that another melodic line is repeated with some variations several times. The teacher may explain some characteristics of the *chorale-prelude* form at this point: (1) This musical form developed as organists introduced new melodies to the congregation. Later these "chorales," as they were named, were sung. (2) The organist often added contrapuntal lines to embellish these melodies.
>
> The chorale melody may be compared to the contrapuntal melody, and children will understand one aspect of contrapuntal form more clearly as they see the following examples:

> The teacher may sugggest at this point that these two melodic lines may be expressed through movement in quite different ways. The

class will then listen to the chorale-prelude again to select expressive movement patterns that are appropriate for the chorale and the contrapuntal accompaniment. The following ideas may be suggested: (1) The children may decide that the chorale melody should be expressed by a dragging or a slow processional type of movement. (2) They will select quite different movements to express the feeling of the chorale-prelude melody. The repeated groupings of three eighth notes may suggest a swaying or circling motion. (3) Children may suggest that two groups move expressively to the chorale-prelude. One group will express the mood of the chorale as the second group responds expressively to the contrapuntal accompaniment.

The child who has learned to identify contrapuntal forms in several selections will respond to the horizontal texture of a fugue. The "Little Fugue in G Minor" by Bach (AIM–VI–1) is a clear example of fugue form. Many of the activities described previously are appropriate as children respond to this selection. The child may respond to the entrances of the fugue subject more easily in a seated position since the tempo of this recording is rather fast. He may indicate the entrances by appropriate arm movements.

Some children will indicate an intense interest in expressive movement. They should have the opportunity to respond to more complex forms. Selections composed in sonata-allegro form will provide these children with challenging expressive movement opportunities.

Sonata-allegro form may be explained to the child as a more elaborate and complex variant of the familiar ABA form. The first section (*exposition*) contains two or more theme groups which are often quite different and provide obvious contrast. The middle section (*development*) often features fragments of themes which were presented in the exposition section. The third section (*recapitulation*) is very similar to the exposition and is often extended by the addition of a *coda*. Some composers begin a sonata-allegro movement with an *introduction*.

The first movement of the *Symphony No. 5* by Schubert (AIM–V–1) is an example of this form which is appropriate for expressive movement activities. The theme groupings are easy to identify and to respond to through movement, and the entire movement is rhythmically interesting to the child.

The expressive movement activities described above will add an exciting element to the music program for older children. They will have frequent opportunities to respond to music with large, expressive movements, and their knowledge of music will be expanded as they find form and style through movement. Expressive movement activities also help children to learn to listen more attentively and acquaint them with a wide range of musical literature.

READING RHYTHMIC NOTATION

Older children should continue with rhythmic notation activities which were introduced in the primary grades, and they will have a rich and varied background upon which to build. They have felt basic patterns through movement, and they have identified and produced rhythmic pulses by clapping or by playing simple instruments. They will also, in many cases, have learned to recognize visual symbols for the patterns they have heard and reproduced.

Rhythmic reading, like any other facet of musical growth, is a continuous process. The ability to read rhythmic patterns depends upon previous rhythmic experiences. The older child who has not participated in the prereading and basic reading activities described in Chapter 4 should be introduced to rhythmic notation by first making physical responses to the rhythmic pulse of music.

The process of rhythmic reading is just one aspect of the total process of reading music. Rhythmic notation is easier to understand and reproduce, however, than combinations of rhythmic patterns and vocal intervals involved in the total reading process. The child is often able to learn to read rhythmic notation before he has reached a level of readiness for the reading of melodic patterns.

Older children will learn to read and reproduce rhythmic symbols easily by participating in carefully structured activities. The reading process should proceed gradually from simple to more complex patterns. They should have many opportunities to recognize and produce notation groupings at each level of their development.

Prereading Activities

The older child should be introduced to rhythmic notation by participating in activities that are more basic than the actual reading of symbols. Prereading activities will prepare him for reading activities in the following ways:

His attention will become focused on printed notation.

He will learn to understand such basic terms as "meter" and the names for the symbols he will later use in reading.

He will transfer his previous rhythmic experiences to the beginning stages of reading rhythmic notation.

He will find success in these beginning activities and understand the relationship between seeing and feeling rhythmic pulses.

The child should begin by distinguishing between duple and triple meter. He has previously heard and felt these differences through movement and will now become aware of them as they appear in simple notation. Songs chosen for this introductory reading activity should feature metrical patterns. "Vesper Hymn" (page 329) is an example. Quarter notes appear almost exclusively in the rhythmic notation of this majestic hymn in 4/4 meter.

The following activities will help the child become aware of duple meter as he listens to the "Vesper Hymn":

> The teacher should define the term "meter" and explain that musical selections have a basic pulse which is repeated throughout the composition.
>
> The teacher should present the hymn melody in a simple, accented performance as the child listens. A piano presentation is preferable since the child will more easily hear the metrical repetitions without the distraction of the text. Melody bells may be substituted for this presentation.
>
> The child should respond to the meter during a second performance by lightly clapping or tapping the meter groupings he hears. He will discover that the hymn has a metrical structure of two rather than three steady pulses.
>
> The notation should be presented as the child listens a third time. The child will see and identify the notation which represents the metrical groupings he has discovered.
>
> At this point the child should be ready to understand several musical terms. He will easily understand the meaning of the meter signature, 4/4, since he has felt and seen the groupings indicated by this signature. The significance of "measures" and "bar lines" will also become meaningful.
>
> The child should then learn to sing this melody. He will learn it easily because he has heard it several times and because he already understands the repeated rhythmic pattern.
>
> *Related Activities:* This hymn is simple to sing and yet dignified and majestic. The child will enjoy singing it, and he will understand why a soft dynamic level is appropriate as he sings the stanza. The "Jubilate" refrain may be added to other songs as an effective introduction. It is particularly appropriate as an introduction to Christmas songs such as the "Echo Carol." The "Jubilate" phrases may be performed as a simple round. The class may be divided into two groups of equal singing ability. The second group should begin after the first group has sung either one or two measures.

The child should learn to identify triple meter in a similar manner. "Sweet Betsy from Pike" (Appendix, page 331) is an example of a song that consists almost entirely of metrical groupings of three quarter notes in each measure. The child should participate in activities similar to those just described as he listens to this American folk song.

Children should also understand the difference between the terms "meter" and "rhythm" before they participate in activities involving the actual reading of rhythmic notation. The teacher may add to the child's developing awareness of rhythmic notation by playing a recording of the "Triumphal March" from *Aida* by Verdi (Bol #62; MSB 78048).

> Children should listen to the theme, performed first by the trumpet and then by a symphony orchestra.
>
> They will clap the rhythmic patterns of the theme softly as they listen a second time.
>
> The teacher may suggest at this point that the class listen again as the theme is performed. They will hear steady, even pulsations accompany the performance of the theme.
>
> As they clap these, the teacher may explain that they are almost identical to the meter underlying the rhythmic changes in this selection. Children will hear and clap a few uneven patterns as they clap the meter. The accompaniment has few of these changes, however, and consists almost entirely of an even meter.
>
> The class may be divided into two groups to prepare for another activity involving a rhythmic response to this recording. One group will clap the rhythmic patterns of the theme or melody, while the other group claps the steady meter of this march.
>
> *Related Activities:* This recorded selection may also be repeated as an introductory movement activity. The child who reproduces the rhythmic patterns of the theme or the metrical repetitions of the accompaniment is acquiring further experience with the contrast between meter and rhythm. He is also participating in an activity that involves moving about the room. This stirring triumphal march may also be repeated as a listening activity. The child will identify instruments and elements of musical form as he continues to listen.

The child will begin to read rhythmic notation with more sensitivity and understanding after he has participated in a few simple prereading activities of this type. He will have developed a basic vocabulary of rhythmic terms and an understanding of metrical structure.

Rhythmic Reading Activities

The teacher should always consider the importance of motivation as rhythmic reading activities are planned and introduced. The child must see the musical value of each activity and succeed in solving each rhythmic reading problem.

There is one important difference between prereading and reading activities. The child discovers meter in prereading activities by listening. Reading activities must be presented in a different manner. The child must discover the meaning of each new symbol or pattern through actual reading before he reproduces the pattern he sees.

The child should begin to read and reproduce rhythmic symbols by becoming aware of even subdivisions. "An American Vow" (page 332) has repeated rhythmic patterns which will help him discover and practice basic rhythmic subdivisions within a duple meter.

> The child should see this song first in large rhythmic and melodic notation. The teacher may begin the reading activity by asking him to identify the familiar rhythmic elements in this song. The child will recognize the meter and the relationship of the quarter note and half note to the meter. He should then be asked to point out the unfamiliar rhythmic elements. The repeated groupings of two eighth notes may be new. He will also find patterns of four eighth notes.

> These new rhythmic patterns should be placed on the board. The basic meter should be presented below each pattern to show the child the relationship between meter and rhythmic patterns:

> The class should be divided. Half will clap the meter as the other half finds the new patterns and claps them against the steady meter. The new rhythmic pattern will become obvious as this visual presentation is reproduced in rhythmic sound. The child should then clap the rhythmic pattern of the entire song. The text may also be chanted in rhythm.

> The child should learn to sing this attractive patriotic melody. He will discover that he learns the song much more quickly because he has already become acquainted with the rhythm.

Similar activities should be introduced to provide the child with additional reading practice. The teacher might add one new element each time by selecting a song with a similar rhythmic pattern but a different meter. The duple meters 2/2, 2/4, 4/8, and ¢ (alla breve) should gradually be added to the child's rhythmic reading vocabulary.

Subdivisions within a triple meter should be practiced in a similar manner, "Jesu, Joy of Man's Desiring" (page 334) is an example that will introduce the child to this new aspect of rhythmic reading.

> The child should see the notation for this chorale and discover familiar and unfamiliar rhythmic elements. He will identify the 3/4 meter and realize that he has previously read all of the rhythmic symbols. The relationship of the repeated half note to the triple meter is the new rhythmic element.

> The class will discover, while half claps the meter and the other half claps the new rhythmic pattern, that this relationship is easy to read.

> The child should learn to sing this lovely chorale. He may then study the text and plan interpretive effects that will reflect the meaning of the words.

> *Related Activities:* The child should hear a recording of an organist performing the chorale-prelude based on this melody. He will enjoy listening to the song in this different setting, and he will also become aware of the registration possibilities of the pipe organ. These experiences with one aspect of music of the baroque period may stimulate the child's desire to learn more about this period of composition. The child may read about Bach's life, about the *chorale-prelude* as a musical form, and about the pipe organ as a musical instrument.

He should also discover that many songs have a meter that combines duple and triple pulses. Songs with a compound meter are often included in the basic music series, and the child should learn to recognize and reproduce these more complex patterns.

The child will recognize the difference between simple and compound meters easily as he sees the notation for "Blow the Wind" (page 336). The rhythmic patterns consist almost entirely of two groupings of three eighth notes in each measure.

> The child should be asked to look for familiar elements in this song. He will quickly discover that none of the rhythmic symbols is familiar in this new context.

> The teacher will explain this new type of meter. There are two main pulses in each measure, and three basic subdivisions to each pulse. The child should begin to understand that a 6/8 meter is really a combination of duple and triple meters. The main accents or pulses have a duple feeling, while each half of a measure is similar to the triple meters he has experienced.

He should clap the meter and the rhythm. He will discover that they are almost identical.

Every child will enjoy singing the first part of this wistful English song. The class may decide that the B section is more appropriate for girls to sing because of the text.

The child will enjoy finding and singing other songs of the sea after he has sung this song. He will discover that most songs about sailing are much more lively. The chantey or river-boat song bears little resemblance to this sad melody.

One other easy rhythmic reading pattern should be introduced before the child begins to read more complicated notation. He has identified two subdivisions to one metrical pulse. Many songs also have four subdivisions to a single pulse. "Tirra-lirra-lirra" is an example (page 339).

As the child looks at the notation of this song, he will identify several familiar rhythmic elements. The meter signature and the relationship of the eighth notes and quarter notes to the signature will be quite clear.

He will find one new rhythmic combination. Four sixteenth notes appear four times. The child will be able to understand the relationship of these symbols to the meter and to the other note lengths as he compares the three types of notes:

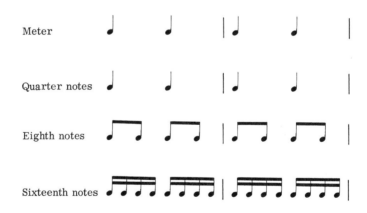

He should clap each of these groupings while other children clap the meter. The activity may become a game as the class is divided into three sections and each section claps a different note-value combination.

The rhythmic patterns of the song will be easy to read and clap after this introduction. The child should establish the meter well, however, before he claps or chants the rhythm of this song.

He may have enough experience by this time to perform both the meter and the rhythmic patterns at the same time. He might maintain the meter by tapping his foot while he claps the rhythmic patterns.

At this point more challenging rhythmic reading activities may be introduced. Songs should be selected with repeated uneven rhythms or syncopated patterns.

The dotted quarter note followed by an eighth note is one of the most common uneven rhythmic patterns. "A Murmuring Brook" (page 340) has five examples of this pattern.

> Many of the rhythmic elements in this song will be familiar. The child will recognize the meter signature and most of the rhythmic combinations. He will discover one new pattern. While he will feel this new pattern easily as he claps it against the meter, one step should be added to the learning process to help him see and feel this pattern:

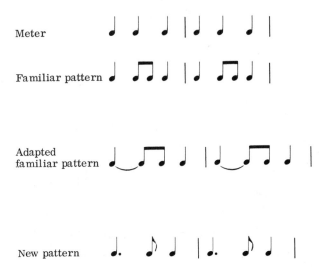

> The child will understand the significance of a dot added to a note as he sees and feels the extension of the quarter note.
> The child should learn to sing this art song by Schubert. He will discover as he sings that many songs with a triple meter have a strong accent on the first pulse of each measure. A waltz-like swing is often appropriate as the child sings songs in this meter.
> The composed art song is a fascinating subject for further study. The lives of the composers of Lieder or German art songs will provide interesting reading for the child.

Other songs with repeated uneven rhythmic patterns should be introduced. Children should learn to recognize and to reproduce accurately the dotted eighth—sixteenth note pattern as they sing.

Syncopated patterns should also be added to the child's rhythmic reading vocabulary. These patterns are often found in spirituals and American folk dances. "Eliza Jane" (page 343) has a simple, repeated syncopated pattern.

> Every other rhythmic pattern in this song will be familiar to the child. He will find, however, that one repeated pattern has familiar symbols arranged in an unfamiliar way. The teacher will facilitate his understanding of this new pattern by placing the following examples on the board:

> The child may begin by clapping the familiar pattern as he taps the duple meter. Half the class may then clap the familiar pattern as the other half claps the tied eighth notes by clapping the first one and pressing the hands slightly on the second. The new pattern should be clearly understood after this activity.
>
> This new pattern may be added to the song as a rhythmic accompaniment after the child has learned to sing "Eliza Jane."

Other songs with a repeated syncopated pattern should be introduced for rhythmic reading activities. Songs of the Caribbean such as "Tinga Layo" are excellent choices.

The activities described in this section will help children become aware of the importance of reading rhythmic notation. They should be highly motivated to continue to read music symbols because of these successful experiences.

RELATED ACTIVITIES

Other rhythmic activities may be introduced to help the older child become more aware of this important musical element. The teacher may introduce additional rhythmic reading activities by adapting the highly structured European systems described below for classroom use. Other rhythmic movement activities may be added to the classroom music program, and instruments may be used in a more complex manner than in preschool and primary-grade rooms.

Two approaches to rhythmic reading have been brought to this country from Europe. The first of these, *French Time Names,* is an English adaptation by Reverend John Curwen of a system invented by Aimé Paris. The system has an appropriate sound for each rhythmic symbol, and they may be instantly combined by the pupil who has developed a vocabulary of these symbolic sounds. The following example shows the way these symbols are combined to help the child read rhythmic notation:

taa–aa   taa   taa – tai   ta – fa – te – fe

This system is widely used by instrumentalists. Very few elementary music educators in this country, however, use French Time Names as a beginning aid to rhythmic reading. A reference describing this system in more detail is given at the end of this chapter.

A second European system is gaining in popularity in this country. Mary Helen Richards has adapted some of the music teaching approaches of the Hungarian composer, Zoltán Kodály, in a system designed for the young American child. *Threshold to Music* [2] is a step-by-step approach to music reading which the classroom teacher can easily understand and may therefore introduce with little assistance. The Experience Charts that accompany this method are visual aids for the teacher who chooses this method for classroom use.

Teachers may introduce rhythmic activities based on the educational approaches of Carl Orff as they continue the older child's music education. The Orff principles of "elemental music" and the rich and flexible use of original instruments are particularly helpful to the older child who has not previously participated in rhythmic activities. He may be introduced to the fascination of rhythm quite easily as the Orff principles of rhythmic and instrumental participation are added to the music program.

Echo clapping and rhythmic canons are two activities included in the Orff method. These activities are also introduced quite often by teachers with a different musical orientation. An example of a rhythmic canon appears on page 96. The music specialist who is thoroughly conversant with the Orff principles of music education may add many other activities to the basic rhythmic program.

Dance is another activity included in the music program for the older child. Patterned dances most frequently selected are American square dances and circle dances. Dances of different cultures and historical periods are other examples of the patterned dance category.

The term *patterned dance* indicates that the child's movement responses will conform to a set pattern. He will move in a prescribed manner, often to verbal directions or to a memorized sequence of dance steps.

Teachers should introduce dances of this type only after careful consideration. The goals of the rhythmic program and the amount of time allotted to music will help the teacher make a decision about this type of movement activity. The patterned dance *does* involve movement, but this activity will *not* help the child reach the basic objectives of the rhythmic program. He must listen to directions or recall memorized patterns. The musical accompaniment seldom provides an expressive cue for movement.

The child may develop a deeper understanding of another culture or period of history by learning an appropriate dance. Patterned dances are therefore an appropriate way to add music and movement to a social studies unit. Dances of this type should also be considered as recreational and physical education activities. The child is involved in physical movement and may also develop increased physical coordination through participation in patterned dances.

The specialist in physical education has received training in the presentation of patterned dances, since movement activities of this type are closely related to his general field of physical development. The music specialist, on the other hand, is concerned with the child's expressive movement responses to selected musical examples. The classroom teacher must be aware of different goals in physical activities and maintain a balance between movement responses that are related to physical education objectives and those that will help the child's musical growth.

James Mursell underlined the differences in purpose between music education and physical education when he made this statement:

> To be sure there is a correlation here between physical education and music education, just as music makes contacts with all sorts of subjects in the school curriculum. The distinction should always be drawn in terms of aim and purpose. When we employ large physical movement to build grace and skill of body, we are in one field. When we employ large physical movement to help the pupil sense and feel the rhythmic structure of music, we are in another.[3]

[3] James L. Mursell and Mabelle Glenn, *The Psychology of School Music Teaching* (New York: Silver Burdett and Co., 1931), pp. 190–91.

Decisions concerning additional rhythmic activities are generally dependent upon a specific classroom situation. The time allotted to music, the goals or objectives of the program, and the training of the teacher are all important considerations. The older child should participate in the basic activities described here, however, before other rhythmic areas are emphasized.

PROGRAM OBJECTIVES

Rhythmic objectives for the older child may be listed in two separate categories. The first category involves much more than rhythmic development. These objectives are related to the child's growing ability to identify form and style through expressive movement. A second category of objectives should be attained as the older child develops the ability to read and perform rhythmic notation. Other objectives will be achieved as these specific goals are fulfilled. The child will develop positive attitudes toward the rhythmic area and be highly motivated to continue to participate in rhythmic activities as he develops the musical skills listed below.

Expressive Movement

The child who participates in the expressive movement activities described in this chapter should attain several specific objectives. He should:

Develop a vocabulary of basic movement patterns and learn to express musical concepts through body movements if he is participating in expressive movement for the first time.

Identify basic musical forms by responding actively to many selections of different styles and historical periods.

Identify familiar forms as he responds to unfamiliar compositions.

Increase his knowledge about composers, musical terms, and related subjects suggested by his active response to music.

Show by his enthusiasm for expressive movement *and* attentive listening that he is constantly growing in his interest in music.

Reading

Other specific objectives should be achieved by the child as he develops the ability to read rhythmic notation. He should:

Identify a wide variety of rhythmic patterns and demonstrate this identification by his rhythmic and singing responses.

Show by his participation that he understands that rhythmic reading is a worthwhile musical activity.

PROGRAM EVALUATION

The child's rhythmic development should be evaluated as carefully as any other aspect of his musical growth. The teacher will determine the success, direction, and pace of the program as this important element is emphasized.

Expressive Movement

Informal evaluation techniques are appropriate if the child participated in expressive movement activities as a younger child. The older child will indicate, as the teacher observes his responses, that he is listening and responding to music itself and not merely imitating other children.

The child's verbal identification of elements of form will indicate that he is acquiring understanding and knowledge about this aspect of music. The teacher will evaluate each child's ability periodically to be certain that he is able to identify familiar forms.

Reading

The teacher will measure rhythmic reading development in a more detailed manner. The child's reading skill may be evaluated in several ways.

A game atmosphere may be established as individual children clap patterns that are shown quickly on cards. Cards containing a variety of familiar rhythmic patterns may be prepared by the class. This type of project also involves the child in the analysis of music to find familiar patterns.

A similar evaluation technique may be used in a more complex way. Cards containing melodic-rhythmic combinations are prepared. The child has learned to read rhythmic notation well if he finds and repeats the rhythmic element on the card by clapping or by playing a simple rhythm instrument.

The child's ability to identify and reproduce rhythmic notation may be measured by the completion of a written test. A printed example containing the melodic outline of a phrase is prepared and distributed to the class. The child studies this printed example as he listens to a performance containing the missing rhythmic elements. He then adds the appropriate rhythmic notation to the incomplete example of notation.

The teacher may use this basic test in several ways. A relatively simple version asks the child to add rhythmic notation to a familiar melody. The test is much more discriminating if he is to add rhythmic symbols to a phrase he has never heard.

The child should ideally be able to read the rhythmic notation of an entire song containing a variety of rhythmic patterns. Teachers will be able to evaluate this skill only by checking individual attempts.

Evaluation procedures of this kind will help the teacher plan and present an effective program suited to the child's level of rhythmic development. Activities that require previous musical understanding for success will be frustrating if the child has not reached an adequate level of readiness. The teacher who evaluates rhythmic progress carefully will never present a new activity before children are ready to complete it successfully nor continue to present activities on an easier level when the class is ready for more challenging activities.

SUMMARY

Rhythmic development is an important part of the older child's music education. His increased physical maturation and his previous experiences with rhythm enable him to participate successfully in rhythmic activities that are too complicated for younger children.

Teachers should set two major goals for the program of rhythmic activities. The first of these involves expressive movement. Older children should continue to move expressively as they listen to music. They will become more aware of form in music as they participate. They will also learn to recognize differences in musical styles and in periods of music composition.

The second goal of the rhythmic program concerns reading rhythmic notation. The older child should demonstrate, after his participation in an effective reading program, that he can read and reproduce rhythmic symbols as he sings and plays.

Other goals may be added to the rhythmic program when these two main areas of concentration are well established. The objectives and activities described in this chapter should be emphasized, however, since they will effectively satisfy the child's rhythmic needs and prepare him for further musical development.

QUESTIONS AND PROJECTS

1. Assume that a group of children has never had the experience of reading a syncopated rhythmic pattern. Prepare a lesson plan progressing from a review of familiar patterns to the identification, reading, and performance of a selected syncopated pattern. Expand your lesson plan into a more comprehensive musical activity (you may wish to include a listening project involving an example of contemporary music).

2. Prepare for a class discussion of the ways in which audio-visual devices will contribute to the effectiveness of the rhythmic reading program.
3. Analyze one or more intermediate-grade basic series books to list the rhythmic patterns that should be added to the rhythmic reading program planned for older children.
4. Examine the recent issues of a selected research journal (the *Journal of Research in Music Education* is recommended) to find reports that might have some bearing on a rhythmic program for older children. Abstract an appropriate article and show its relevance to the rhythmic reading program.
5. Assume that you will teach in a classroom in which older boys have not participated previously in expressive movement activities. Develop a lesson plan, including specific materials, that will aid you in involving these boys in movement activities.
6. What rhythmic concepts should the older child develop as the result of participation in rhythmic activities?

REFERENCES

Recommended Readings

Humphreys, Louise, and Ross, Jerrold. *Interpreting Music Through Movement.* Englewood Cliffs, N.J.: Prentice-Hall, 1964.

Orff, Carl, and Keetman, Gunild. *Music for Children.* Adaptation by Doreen Hall and Arnold Walter. New York: Associated Music Publishers, 1960.

Reichenthal, Eugene. "French Time Names." In *Music Education in Action,* edited by Archie N. Jones, chap. 6. Dubuque, Iowa: Wm. C. Brown Co., 1964.

Richards, Mary Helen. *Threshold to Music.* Palo Alto, Calif.: Fearon Publishers, 1964.

Audio-Visual Aids

The audio-visual aids listed at the end of Chapter 3 are appropriate for the rhythmic reading activities described in this chapter.

Basic Record Series

Adventures in Music. New York: RCA Victor Educational Sales.

AIM–IV–1, Grade 4, Vol. 1
AIM–IV–2, Grade 4, Vol. 2
AIM–V–1, Grade 5, Vol. 1
AIM–V–2, Grade 5, Vol. 2
AIM–VI–1, Grade 6, Vol. 1
AIM–VI–2, Grade 6, Vol. 2

Bowmar Orchestral Library. Los Angeles: Bowmar Records.

BOL #53, Pictures and Patterns
BOL #54, Marches
BOL #55, Dances, Part I
BOL #56, Dances, Part II
BOL #60, Under Many Flags
BOL #62, Masters of Music
BOL #63, Concert Matinee

BOL #65, Music U.S.A.
BOL #67, Fantasy in Music
BOL #68, Classroom Concert

Musical Sound Books. Scarsdale, N.Y.: Musical Sound Books.

MSB 78000 series, For Young Listeners
MSB 78100 series, Music to Remember

Introducing Expressive Movement Activities

Alford: "Colonel Bogey March" (BOL #54)
Bizet: "Farandole," *L'Arlésienne Suite No. 2* (AIM–VI–1)
————. "Trumpet and Drum," *Jeux d'Enfants* (BOL #53; MSB 78008)
Chabrier: "Marche Joyeuse" (AIM–IV–1)
Coates: "Knightsbridge March," *London Suite* (AIM–V–2; BOL #60)
Gould: "American Salute" (AIM–V–1; BOL #65)
Gould: "American Salute" (AIM–V–1); BOL #65)
Khatchaturian: "Galop," *Masquerade Suite* (BOL #55)
————. "Russian Dance," *Gayne Suite No. 2* (BOL #56)
Kodály: "Entrance of the Emperor and his Court," *Háry János Suite* (AIM–IV–2)
Prokofiev: "March," *Love for Three Oranges* (BOL #54)
Smetana: "Dance of the Comedians," *The Bartered Bride* (AIM–VI–2; BOL #56; MSB 78109)
Tchaikovsky: "Trepak," *Nutcracker Suite* (BOL #58)
Verdi: "Triumphal March," *Aida* (BOL #62; MSB 78048)

Three-Part Forms

Bizet: "Trumpet and Drum," *Jeux d'Enfants* (BOL #53)
Copland: "Hoe-Down," *Rodeo* (AIM–V–2; BOL #55)
Grieg: "Norwegian Dance in A (No. 2)" (BOL #63)
————. "Wedding Day at Troldhaugen" (BOL #62)
Khatchaturian: "Mazurka," *Masquerade Suite* (BOL #55)
Lecuona: "Andalucia," *Suite Andalucia* (AIM–IV–1)
Mozart: "Minuet," *Symphony No. 40* (BOL #62)
Pinto: "Run, Run," *Memories of Childhood* (BOL #68)
Schubert: "Marche Militaire" (BOL #54)

Rondo Forms

Beethoven: "Scherzo," *Symphony No. 7* (BOL #62)
Falla: "Spanish Dance No. 1," *La Vida Breve* (AIM–VI–1)
Gottschalk-Kay: "Grand Walkaround," *Cakewalk Ballet Suite* (AIM–V–1)
Sibelius: "Alla Marcia," *Karelia Suite* (AIM–V–1)
Smetana: "Dance of the Comedians," *The Bartered Bride* (AIM–VI–2; BOL #56; MSB 78109)
Tchaikovsky: "Waltz," *The Sleeping Beauty* (AIM–IV–1; BOL #67; MSB 78108)

Variation Forms

Anderson: "The Girl I Left Behind Me," *Irish Suite* (AIM–V–2)
Copland: "Shaker Tune" (BOL #65); "Simple Gifts" (MSB 78152) *Appalachian Spring*

Gould: "American Salute" (AIM–V–1; BOL #65)
Haydn: "Theme and Variations," *"Surprise" Symphony* (BOL #62)

Polyphonic Forms

Bach: "Jesu, Joy of Man's Desiring," *Cantata No. 147* (AIM–V–1)
————. "Little Fugue in G Minor" (AIM–VI–1)
Bizet: "Farandole," *L'Arlésienne Suite No. 2* (AIM–VI–1)

6

THE EARLY CHILDHOOD LISTENING PROGRAM

Young children are fascinated by colorful sounds. They show this interest as they listen attentively to sound after sound during the school day. They constantly experiment with the sound possibilities of equipment in the classroom, at home, and as they play out-of-doors. It is therefore a simple matter for teachers to introduce listening activities as an important part of the music program. The young child is ready and eager to participate in any activity featuring sounds.

The listening activities described in this chapter and implied in other parts of the text are based on three general aspects of listening. These listening activities will help young children become more sensitive to the expressive qualities in music; they will develop their ability to interpret music through singing, moving, and playing; they will contribute to their ability to analyze and to understand the many elements that are combined in a single musical composition.

The child must develop sensitivity in listening if he is to respond to beauty and expressive quality in the music he hears and performs. This heightened sensitivity will be evident as he sings more expressively, responds with increasingly expressive movements, and finds ways to use musical elements in a flexible and creative manner.

The young child must learn to interpret what he hears in a discriminating manner if he is to develop other musical capacities. He will learn to sing tunefully as he identifies melodic elements and expresses concepts of melodic direction. He must listen equally well to express other concepts through movement responses.

Analytic listening is complementary to other types of listening; it is also a distinct musical skill. The child will show the development of this listening skill as he distinguishes between tone colors, identifies themes, and becomes aware of form and structure, period and style.

One major goal at any level of the child's music education is to help him reach the point where he listens carefully in any musical activity. He must listen actively as he sings, plays, or moves. He must listen in an equally attentive manner as he indicates that he is becoming receptive to many types and styles of music.

THE CHILD'S WORLD OF MUSICAL SOUNDS

The teacher should plan activities that will transform the child's world of sound into a world of musical sounds. This is an achievable goal as the child is introduced to the different but equally fascinating ways in which composers of different periods have combined musical timbres, themes, harmonic effects, and rhythmic patterns.

Some teachers hesitate to present musical examples of excellent quality as an integral part of the music program. They observe the many different levels and types of musical tastes adults exhibit as they select music and apparently conclude that the child enters the early childhood classroom with fixed musical tastes and preferences. While many children enter the classroom with an interest in colorful sounds, few young children have listened to so many musical examples of one type of music that they have developed a preference for it. Children and adults who do show a preference for musical listening on one level are indicating a certain type of background of experience. The older child or adult who prefers music of enduring quality to music of dubious worth is simply showing a rich background of listening experiences that has included many types of music.

The child should be exposed to many types of music as listening is included in his general music education. There are times when listening is a relaxing musical activity and other times when music is a necessary acompaniment to some form of recreation. There are also situations in which the pleasure and beauty of music are revealed most fully through quiet, attentive listening to a composition created by a well-known composer.

The child will become aware of some of these types of music through informal exposure. He will certainly hear many examples of relaxing and recreational music on radio and television. He will hear similar music as he participates in other activities during the school day.

Children should therefore be introduced to music of enduring quality as listening becomes a part of the daily music program. There is a large heritage of music literature that has been passed on from generation to generation. The young child should become acquainted with examples of this heritage that are appropriate for his level of experience and suited to his musical capacities.

The child who never has an opportunity to hear music other than obvious selections with superimposed stories will not develop his capacity to respond to excellence in music. He will simply decide that listening activities at school are a form of recreation and that the quality of the music is similar to the music he hears on television, in supermarkets, and as a constant musical background to his daily life.

The child who is introduced to the exciting world of music literature through carefully planned activities that will develop his capacities and capture his attention will enter a far more musical environment. He will begin to develop listening habits and a receptive attitude toward many types of music as he responds to exciting tone colors and recognizes familiar musical elements in new settings.

THE LISTENING PROGRAM

Listening is a critical factor, often determining the success or failure of any early-childhood music program. The young child must learn to listen attentively if he is to develop his other musical capacities. He should also begin to realize that listening to musical selections is an exciting activity in itself.

Listening: The Basic Skill

The importance of listening has been stressed in other chapters. The child must learn to listen carefully if he is to learn to sing, move, or play. Teaching suggestions that will help the child constantly listen before and while he is actively engaged in musical performance have been stressed in Chapters 2 and 4. These suggestions are reinforced and amplified here.

The young child is eager to participate in any musical activity. He therefore tends to sing, move, or play without listening attentively as a prelude to action. He must, however, learn to listen before he actively participates if he is to develop his musical capacities. Helping children in early childhood classrooms develop attentive listening habits is therefore of crucial importance. Children who have learned to listen before singing an unfamiliar song will hear phrases clearly and then attempt to sing them. Children who immediately join in the performance of a new song will not hear a melodic example from the teacher, piano, or recording.

The teacher must create an environment that will help the child realize the importance of attentive listening before he attempts to participate. One effective approach involves the presentation of any new song or recording first as a listening activity. It is often appropriate to introduce a new song at the end of the daily music program. The teacher will perform the song with complete attention to interpretation, expressiveness, and tone quality. The child will hear the song as a vocal model. He will learn to sing it much more easily when, on a subsequent day, it is presented as a song he is to learn to sing.

The teacher must also make the child conscious of the importance of listening before he participates in a movement activity. Helping the child establish the habit of listening before moving is a relatively simple procedure. The teacher should introduce a new selection or review a familiar composition while children are seated quietly at their desks or near the piano or the record player.

Groups occasionally become too excited as they respond to a fast, loud selection. The class may be divided into smaller groups in such a situation, and the teacher will stress the importance of attentive listening. Extremely excitable or immature children may need further assistance in developing attentive listening habits. Teachers who emphasize soft, slow rhythmic patterns will help these children learn to listen attentively while they move.

Listening: An Added Musical Dimension

Listening activities offer the teacher the opportunity to present the child with an added dimension of music. The young child is limited musically to some extent by his capacities and maturation level. He will learn to sing with accuracy, but he has not yet developed the vocal quality and expressive potential of older children. His expressive movement ability is also limited to some extent by his level of physical coordination. These performance limitations extend to other areas of music as well. The younger child has definite limitations as he participates in instrumental, rhythmic, and creative activities.

The young child is not limited or hampered by his level of maturation as he participates in listening activities. While he may not be able to perform the music of Bach, he is able to listen to compositions of this well-known baroque composer and to become aware of many characteristics of music of this period. Through attentive listening, he may respond to many other compositions that are beyond his capacities as a young performer.

The young child's musical horizons are extended by this type of activity. He will develop listening abilities far beyond his ability to make active responses. He will develop sensitivity through listening as he responds to changing expressive moods and subtle tone color combinations. He will develop interpretive and analytic listening ability as he compares selections of different periods, identifies instruments and themes, and discriminates between performances of varying quality.

The teacher may help the young child develop listening skills in several ways. Children should learn to identify the characteristic tone colors of several instruments and then recognize them in performances with other instruments. They should also learn to identify melodies and themes. Primary-grade children should, in addition, become aware of form in music as they participate in an effective program of listening activities.

The child will learn about musical form in two different but complementary ways. Some of the activities described in Chapter 4 will help him become aware of this element of music through his expressive movement responses. He should also become more aware of the formal element as he participates in quieter attentive listening activities.

The child should also be introduced to a new educational area in a way which will provide him with immediate success and with a strong motivation for further participation. His first experiences with listening should therefore involve the identification of instrumental tone colors. Children will immediately discover that *identifying instruments* is an interesting activity. They are captivated by colorful sounds and will become absorbed in listening as the teacher introduces instruments.

The teacher may begin by introducing those instruments the young child is able to play. The child will be interested in listening to examples of percussion tone colors after he has experimented with the tonal possibilities of simple drums and other percussion instruments.

He should have the opportunity to hear several drums. While adults or older children may show the timbres of different drums in a classroom demonstration, the young child will learn to recognize their characteristic sounds equally well as he listens to a recording planned for this purpose. Meet the Instruments [1] is one of many recordings issued to help the child learn to identify instruments.

The child should listen attentively as he compares the different timbres of the snare drum, the tympani, and other percussion instruments. He should learn to identify these percussion instruments by name as he listens to these simple performances several times. He should then have the opportunity to recognize the instrument in a recording that features a number of instruments playing together.

Selections suitable for the identification of a familiar instrument should feature the instrument in an easily identifiable, repeated per-

[1] Bowmar Records, Los Angeles, Calif.

formance. "Pantomime," from *The Comedians* by Kabalevsky (AIM–I), is a typical example. The snare drum is easy to identify in this contemporary Russian composition. The following activities will help the child recognize the timbre of the snare drum in this more complex setting:

> The class should have the opportunity to review the sounds of different percussion instruments before they listen to "Pantomime."
>
> The teacher will mention the fact that they will hear one of these familiar instruments as they listen to this unfamiliar recording. The child should be able to identify the snare drum easily as he listens. He may recognize other instruments as well.
>
> He will hear other musical effects as he continues to listen. The music begins at a low pitch and at a soft dynamic level. The child will acquire concepts of dynamic elements as he listens to the entire composition. A consistent, gradual crescendo is a basic characteristic of this selection.
>
> *Related Activities:* Children who have participated in expressive movement activities may want to move as they continue to listen to this slow composition. They will often respond with sliding foot patterns and arm and body movements. The teacher should not suggest appropriate ways to respond. The child will find his own ways to move expressively to "Pantomime." Children will enjoy identifying the snare drum in other recordings. "March–Trumpet and Drum" from *Jeux d'Enfants* by Bizet (BOL #53) includes easily identifiable performances by this percussion instrument. Other selections featuring the sound of the snare drum are listed at the end of this chapter.

Other percussion instruments should be introduced in a similar manner. Children will enjoy experimenting with the sound possibilities of some. The teacher may introduce others through the use of a recorded solo performance accompanied by a picture of the instrument.

The child will find great pleasure in his successful attempts to identify instruments in this way. The method is effective for two major reasons. Percussion instruments are easy to identify since each instrument has a distinctive, unique tone-color. The teaching approach is equally effective because the child hears a familiar element in each listening situation. He experiences something familiar at first because he experiments with some of these instruments before he hears them on a recording. Later he again encounters a familiar situation as he recognizes an instrument he has previously identified in a different recording.

The child will be eager to identify the sounds of other instruments after he has become acquainted with several instruments in the percussion section. The teacher should introduce woodwinds next since the instruments in this section also have distinctive tone-colors. The child should have no trouble distinguishing the sounds of double reeds from those of single reeds. The woodwind instruments heard most frequently are the flute, oboe, and clarinet. The child should have the opportunity to hear each play alone. After he has identified each instrument in a solo recording performance he should have further opportunities to identify each by listening to a recording with varied tone colors and many instruments.

Selections featuring a woodwind solo should provide the child with an opportunity to hear the instrument as easily and as often as possible. "Badinerie," from *Suite No. 2 in B Minor* by Bach (AIM–III–1), is an example. The following activities will help the child identify the flute in this baroque dance:

> The child should be introduced to this listening activity as the teacher tells him he will hear a familiar woodwind instrument play a solo accompanied by other instruments. The teacher may review woodwind tone-colors and show pictures of several familiar instruments before playing the recording.
>
> The child will easily recognize the timbre of the flute since the instrument is featured throughout this selection.
>
> The child will also hear string instruments accompany the flute solo. The teacher may mention the fact that the string section provides the accompaniment, describe the different ways in which these instruments produce a musical tone, and show pictures of several stringed instruments.
>
> *Related Activities:* The "Badinerie" is rhythmically exciting. At times the child may want to move expressively as he continues to listen. The primary grade child who has been introduced to music symbols will enjoy watching the notation of the theme as the flute plays. He may shape the rise and fall of the melody with hand and arm motions to make this activity more meaningful. The child will have become aware of basic formal elements in music through participation in singing and rhythmic activities. The teacher may direct his attention toward the two sections in this dance after he has listened to it several times. He will hear each section twice. The flute is quite "acrobatic" in this performance. The child should also have the opportunity to hear this woodwind instrument perform a slower, more melodic solo. "En Bateau" by Debussy (BOL #53) is an appropriate choice.

The clarinet and oboe should be presented in a similar manner. Each will be easy for children to identify if the procedure just outlined is repeated for each instrument. The compositions listed at the end of the chapter have been carefully chosen to provide these listening opportunities.

After the child has learned to identify other woodwind instruments in this manner he should become acquainted with the brass section. A similar procedure should be followed. These additional listening activities should always contain a familiar element.

Children who have learned to identify percussion, woodwind, and brass instruments will enjoy listening to the sounds of the string section. Appropriate selections are described in Chapter 7.

The child will then be ready for many other listening activities featuring instrument identification. He will enjoy identifying instruments of different types as they are featured in the same musical selection. The teacher may review the selections the child has heard at this point before selecting a recording that features solos by several instruments. Children who have participated in the specific listening activities described above have heard a contemporary Russian composition (Kabalevsky: "Pantomime") and a selection representative of the baroque period (Bach: "Badinerie"). The "Berceuse" by Gabriel Fauré (AIM–II) will introduce the child to another period of musical composition. This selection is typical of the nineteenth-century romantic period. The orchestration, while it is quite simple, has the rich and colorful textures often heard in romantic selections.

The child will enjoy the following activities as he listens to this quiet orchestral lullaby:

> The recording may be introduced as a musical guessing game as the teacher tells the child he will hear familiar instruments in a new musical setting. Children who have learned to identify instruments will recognize the flute, the French horn, the clarinet, and the oboe. The first two are particularly easy to hear because they play the entire theme as a solo. The clarinet and oboe are slightly more difficult to identify because they are featured in shorter solos. The clarinet begins one theme, and the oboe completes it.
>
> The teacher may continue this listening activity in order to emphasize the expressive qualities and the mood of this selection. Children should be told that the title, "Berceuse," is a French word meaning *lullaby*. As they listen to the recording again they will hear several musical devices that heighten the expressive mood suggested by the title: (1) Strings play an accompaniment that suggests rocking or swaying. (2) The melody is similar to a lullaby a mother might sing to her baby. (3) The dynamic level is consistently soft, and there are no strong accents or faster rhythmic patterns.

The child will continue to develop attentive listening skills and habits as he identifies familiar songs and melodies in instrumental and choral arrangements. His first listening experiences of this type should involve the identification of melodies he has sung or heard many times.

The Third Movement of the *Children's Symphony* by McDonald (AIM–II) is an orchestral composition featuring themes that every young child will recognize with delight. The following activities will introduce the child to the identification of melodies as he listens:

> The teacher may prepare the class for this listening activity in a simple manner. They will understand that they will hear two songs they have heard or sung before. The children will recognize "The Farmer in the Dell" and "Jingle Bells" as they listen. They may also identify familiar instruments. The trumpet is featured in this recording.
>
> The class should listen to the recording a second time to hear these familiar songs as they are transformed into instrumental themes. They will hear each song in a complete presentation and may count the number of times each appears. They will also hear melodic fragments that will remind them of one of these melodies, and they should identify the song the fragment represents.
>
> *Related Activities:* The teacher may reinforce the child's awareness of ABA form as he continues to listen to this delightful recording. The child will become aware of this basic musical form as he hears "The Farmer in the Dell" begin and end the composition while "Jingle Bells" is prominent in the middle (B) section. The child will then enjoy moving expressively after he has listened to the recording several times. He will easily feel the form of the composition as he makes expressive responses. The A sections have repeated rhythmic patterns which suggest a skip or light gallop, while the B section has a repeated, fast, even pattern with strong accents.

The teacher should present several listening activities that feature familiar songs as themes. This aspect of listening-skill development should be expanded in several ways. The child should also identify familiar songs in choral arrangements. The record albums that accompany the basic music series will provide appropriate examples.

Children should learn to identify many other melodies as they listen to instrumental and choral arrangements. They should learn to identify the theme first by listening as the teacher or a child plays the theme.

The listening activities suggested here have two common elements. In each case the child identifies instrumental tone colors or a theme. He is prepared to listen attentively because he knows there will be something interesting to hear. A second element common to each of these activities is that the child always recognizes something familiar in a new musical setting.

The child will enjoy listening activities that are presented in this manner, and develop the habit of attentive listening as he discovers old friends in new and colorful instrumental or choral arrangements.

THE TEACHER'S ROLE

Learning to listen attentively is a skill and habit the child *must* develop if he is to participate in any musical activity. The child who does not develop attentive listening habits will be unable to develop singing and rhythmic skills. He will be hampered to the same extent as he participates in listening as a separate musical activity. The teacher will play an important role in helping the child learn to listen attentively as he participates in any musical activity.

The teacher's role in helping the young child learn to listen as he engages in other musical activities is described in Chapters 2 and 4. Some additional suggestions for leading the child to discover the pleasures that are involved in listening to music are appropriate at this point.

The teacher must always be certain that a *familiar element* is present in any listening situation. The teaching suggestions in this chapter consistently emphasize this important part of the learning process. The child who has explored the tonal possibilities of a percussion instrument before identifying the instrument in a recording is listening for a familiar element. As he hears a familiar song or melody in an unfamiliar arrangement, he also recognizes the familiar as he listens to the new.

The *teacher's attitude* toward music is another factor that contributes to the success of the listening program. The teacher who shows that listening to music is an exciting experience is providing an example for the child to observe and imitate. Listening activities will be interesting and enjoyable for every child when the teacher creates an appropriate atmosphere for this activity and displays a positive attitude.

The environment for listening must be *flexible*. Children in early childhood classrooms often become excited as they listen, and they may make expressive movement responses. There is no arbitrary distinction between quiet, attentive listening and expressive movement. A listening experience may become a movement experience as well. The teacher should always be conscious of this and expand a planned activity in this manner when the child's responses indicate that he wants to move.

The teacher should carefully avoid including any *extramusical elements* in the listening program for the young child. Superimposed stories actually interfere with the child's listening development, although they are often added to the listening situation to attract the child's attention and prepare him for listening. It should be repeated here that music is *not* a descriptive art form, and even selections with titles that suggest a possible story should be presented to the child first without the title. Stories and other descriptive suggestions are false learning cues and will interfere with the child's ability to identify musical elements in a selection.

Careful *preparation* is another important factor contributing to the success of the listening program. The selections listed at the end of this chapter have been chosen very carefully to provide outstanding examples. The teacher should listen to them first, however, before presenting them to the child as a listening activity. Instruments that can be heard very clearly when a record is played on one machine may be almost impossible to identify when it is played on another.

Teachers need to develop knowledge and skills in order to present an effective listening program for the young child. The teacher who is unable to identify instruments will often project a feeling of inadequacy when attempting to present a listening activity. Additional knowledge may be gained by listening carefully to one of the instrumental identification recordings listed at the end of this chapter.

The *equipment* available in the classroom is another major factor that will help determine the success or failure of a listening program. The teacher who is presenting carefully selected listening activities is also presenting the child with examples of musical excellence. Equipment in poor condition will interfere seriously with the effectiveness of these activities.

The child hears music wherever he goes. The music heard in supermarkets, restaurants, and shopping centers is often trite, but the quality of sound production is generally excellent. The young child is fascinated by tone color and may prefer the music he hears in these other locations if the selections he hears during the music program are played on cheap phonographs with worn needles and scratched records.

Many factors contribute to the success of the listening program. The teacher's background, attitude, and flexibility are extremely important. Careful preparation must be accompanied by consistent attention to learning and motivation. The quality of classroom equipment is an equally important element in the implementation of a successful listening program.

PROGRAM OBJECTIVES

A music program planned to aid young children in developing their listening capacities has two major goals. The child must acquire those listening skills and habits that will assist in the development of his other musical capacities. He should, in addition, acquire skills directly related to listening as an independent musical activity.

Two categories of specific behavioral objectives are considered here. The first describes the behaviors a child should exhibit as he demonstrates that he has learned to listen attentively during other musical activities. The second category describes in a sequential manner the musical behavior of a child who has developed the ability to listen to music in a discriminating and receptive manner.

Listening: The Basic Skill

The success of all other aspects of the music program depends upon the extent to which the child attains the objectives in the first category. Each child will:

Listen attentively before he attempts to sing a new song and continue to listen while he sings with others.

Listen in a discriminating manner before he participates in an expressive movement activity, and show by his movements that he continues to listen carefully while he responds to musical cues.

Develop varied concepts about the elements of music as a result of the acquisition of attentive listening habits. He will demonstrate this concept formation while he sings, moves expressively, and describes what he hears.

The objectives in this first category should be successfully attained by every child who has participated in the singing and rhythmic programs described in Chapters 2 and 4. Children will not develop these specific listening skills, however, unless attentive listening is consistently stressed in these areas of the music program.

Listening: An Added Musical Dimension

As children attain the objectives in this second category, they will develop listening skills, habits, and a receptive attitude toward the varied and absorbing activity of listening to music of many types and styles. Each child should be able to:

Identify the basic percussion, woodwind, and brass instruments.

Recognize the above instruments in orchestral and band performances.

Identify familiar melodies and themes in choral and orchestral arrangements.

Show by his enthusiasm that listening to many types of music has become an exciting experience which he wants to repeat.

In addition, the primary-grade child should be able to:

Identify simple musical forms by recognizing contrasting sections in two- and three-part forms.

Each of these objectives will be achieved through the successful presentation of the listening activities described in this chapter. The child will develop his listening capacities in a manner consistent with his musical potential. He will develop a sensitivity to musical sounds that will also contribute to the success of the listening program for older children.

PROGRAM EVALUATION

Evaluation devices should be carefully and periodically applied to determine the young child's progress in developing listening skills. Portions of the listening program that are directly related to singing and rhythmic activities may be evaluated by the procedures described in Chapters 2 and 4. Additional evaluation approaches should be introduced to determine the extent to which the child has reached the other listening objectives listed in this chapter.

The teacher may evaluate the child's ability to identify instruments or themes informally as children discuss the sounds they have heard. Careful individual evaluation will be difficult, however, since a few children often dominate the discussion while others do not respond. The following suggestions provide more precise measurements of the child's level of listening skill development:

The teacher may introduce the first procedure after children have learned to identify instruments of various types. Unfamiliar recordings featuring a solo by a familiar instrument may be selected from the lists at the end of this chapter. Several of these may be used as an individual guessing game. The recorded selections will be played in a random order, and children will take turns identifying the instrument featured on one of the recordings. A similar procedure may be followed in discovering the extent to which a child is able to identify familiar themes in compositions he has heard before.

The primary-grade child will be able to complete a simple written test which will measure his ability to identify instruments. The teacher will select an unfamiliar composition with prominent solos by several familiar instruments. A test sheet may be prepared and duplicated, or the items may be placed on the chalkboard. The following simple test will measure the child's ability to identify the instruments featured in one recording:

Listening Test

Thompson: "Walking Song" (AIM–I)

Trumpet ( )   Flute ( )   Clarinet ( )

The teacher will tell the class that the names of the instruments are not necessarily in the order in which they appear. The child will indicate the proper order by placing a number in each bracket. Recordings featuring performances by several solo instruments are listed at the end of the chapter. The teacher may find others that are appropriate by listening carefully to recordings available for classroom use.

Tests of the above type represent a few of the many evaluation techniques that will occur to an imaginative teacher. The teacher must evaluate each child's ability in some specific manner if the pace and direction of the listening program are to be appropriate to his level of development.

SUMMARY

Attentive listening is the most basic musical skill. Children who have not learned to listen well are not able to participate successfully in other parts of the music program. Listening to music is also an important activity that provides an added dimension to the child's experiences with music. The young child should be introduced to varied listening activities as he enters school, and he should continue to participate in such activities which are planned and presented as a regular and important part of the total music program.

The child will learn to enjoy listening to many types of music as he develops listening skills, habits, and a receptive attitude toward any situation involving attentive listening. He should learn to identify tone colors, themes, musical forms, and stylistic tendencies as he participates in a varied and challenging program of listening activities.

Listening experiences are extremely important in the music education of the young child as a means of helping him develop performance skills and as a way to develop his capacity to enjoy many types of music. Experiences with listening are equally important as one way to prepare the young child for further musical growth. Many musical activities that should be appropriate for the older child are dependent upon the extent to which he has developed the habit of attentive listening.

133

QUESTIONS AND PROJECTS

1. Analyze a basic record series to list those instruments young children identify most easily (use the guidelines in this chapter for selection purposes). You may find that some instruments are not featured or that some styles or periods have few examples. Analyze additional supplementary recordings to balance your list.
2. What are the advantages and disadvantages of programmatic music in the early childhood listening program?
3. Prepare for a class discussion of the following topic: "What are the relative merits of a highly structured and a loosely structured approach to the presentation of listening activities?"

REFERENCES

Recommended Readings

Britten, Benjamin, and Holst, Imogen. *The Wonderful World of Music.* Rev. ed. Garden City, N.Y.: Doubleday & Co., 1968.
Buchanan, Fannie, and Luckenbill, Charles L. *How Man Made Music.* Chicago: Follett Publishing Co., 1959.
Copland, Aaron. *What To Listen for in Music.* Rev. ed. New York: McGraw-Hill Book Co., 1957.

Audio-Visual Aids

Instrument Identification

Instrument display boards, J. W. Pepper & Son, Philadelphia.
Instruments of the Orchestra. New York: RCA Victor Educational Sales (22 display boards, recording).
Meet the Instruments. Los Angeles: Bowmar Records (25 posters, study prints, film strips, recording).

Basic Record Series

Adventures in Music. New York: RCA Victor Educational Sales.

AIM–I, Grade 1
AIM–II, Grade 2
AIM–III–1, Grade 3, Vol. 1
AIM–III–2, Grade 3, Vol. 2

Bowmar Orchestral Library. Los Angeles: Bowmar Records.

BOL #53, Pictures and Patterns
BOL #54, Marches
BOL #55, Dances, Part I
BOL #58, Stories in Ballet and Opera
BOL #62, Masters of Music
BOL #63, Concert Matinee
BOL #64, Miniatures in Music
BOL #65, Music U.S.A.
BOL #68, Classroom Concert

Musical Sound Books. Scarsdale, N.Y.: Musical Sound Books.

MSB 78000 series, For Young Listeners
MSB 78100 series, Music to Remember
MSB 78300 series, Tiny Masterpieces

Percussion Instruments

Cymbals

Bizet: "The Changing of the Guard," *Carmen Suite* (AIM–III–2; MSB 78136)
Elgar: "Pomp and Circumstance No. 1," final section (BOL #54; MSB 78120)
Handel: "A Ground" (BOL #53)
Ibert: "Parade," *Divertissement* (AIM–I)
Khatchaturian: "Galop," *Masquerade Suite* (BOL #55)
Meyerbeer: "Waltz," *Les Patineurs* (AIM–II)
Prokofiev: "Departure," *Winter Holiday* (AIM–II)
———. "March," *Love for Three Oranges* (BOL #54)
Sousa: "Stars and Stripes Forever" (BOL #54; MSB 78120)

Snare Drum

Bizet: "Trumpet and Drum," *Children's Games* (BOL #53)
Kabalevsky: "March and Comedians' Galop" (AIM–III–1), "Pantomime"
(AIM–I), *The Comedians*
McDonald: "Allegro," *Children's Symphony* (AIM–III–2)
Prokofiev: "March," *Love for Three Oranges* (BOL #54)
Sousa: "Stars and Stripes Forever" (BOL #54; MSB 78120)

Tambourine

Guarnieri: "Danca Brasileira" (BOL #55)
Hanson: "Children's Dance," *Merry Mount Suite* (AIM–III–1)
Massenet: "Aragonaise," *Le Cid* (AIM–I)
Moussorgsky: "Ballet of the Unhatched Chicks," *Pictures at an Exhibition*
(AIM–I)
Rossini-Respighi: "Tarantella," *The Fantastic Toyshop* (AIM–III–2)

Triangle

Brahms: "Hungarian Dance No. 5" (BOL #55)
Copland: "Circus Music," *The Red Pony Suite* (AIM–III–1)

Tympani

Kabalevsky: "Intermezzo," *The Comedians* (BOL #53)

Woodwind Instruments

Clarinet

Bartok: *Three Compositions* (BOL #68)
Bizet: "Cradle Song," *Children's Games* (AIM–I)
Gounod: "Funeral March of the Marionettes" (BOL #64; MSB 78021)
Khatchaturian: "Galop," *Masquerade Suite* (BOL #55)
Schumann-Glazounov: "Chopin," *Carnaval* (BOL #53)

Tchaikovsky: *Album for the Young* (BOL #68)
→ Thomson: "Walking Song," *Acadian Songs and Dances* (AIM–I)
Walton: "Country Dance," *Façade Suite* (BOL #55)

Flute

→ Bach: "Badinerie," *Suite No. 2 in B Minor* (AIM–III–1)
Bartok: *Three Compositions* (BOL #68)
Bizet: "The Changing of the Guard," *Carmen Suite No. 2* (AIM–III–2)
→ ———. "Cradle Song," *Children's Games* (AIM–I)
———. "Impromptu—The Top," *Jeux d'Enfants* (BOL #53)
Debussy: "En Bateau" (BOL #53)
→ Delibes: "Waltz of the Doll," *Coppélia* (AIM–I)
Gluck: "Dance of the Happy Spirits" (MSB 78315)
Grieg: "Elfin Dance" (MSB 78315)
Haydn: "Allegro" (MSB 78315)
Liadov: "Music Box" (BOL #64)
Mozart: "Menuetto" (MSB 78315)
Mozart: "Tamino's Air," *The Magic Flute* (MSB 78315)
Pierne: "Entrance of the Little Fauns" (BOL #54; MSB 78015)
→ Shostakovich: "Petite Ballerina," *Ballet Suite No. 1* (AIM–II)
Tchaikovsky: *Album for the Young* (BOL #68)
→ Thomson: "Walking Song," *Acadian Songs and Dances* (AIM–I)
Walton: "Country Dance," *Façade Suite* (BOL #55)

Oboe

Bartok: *Three Compositions* (BOL #68)
Grieg: "Norwegian Dance in A (No. 2)" (BOL #63)
Tchaikovsky: *Album for the Young* (BOL #68)
———. "Puss-in-boots and the White Cat," *The Sleeping Beauty* (AIM–III–1)

Piccolo

Bizet: "The Changing of the Guard," *Carmen Suite No. 2* (AIM–III–2)
→ Shostakovich: Petite Ballerina," *Ballet Suite No. 1* (AIM–II)
Sousa: "Stars and Stripes Forever" (BOL #54)

Brass Instruments

Trumpet

Bizet: "The Changing of the Guard," *Carmen Suite No. 2* (AIM–III–2)
———. "Trumpet and Drum," *Jeux d'Enfants* (BOL #53)
→ Copland: "Circus Music," *The Red Pony* (AIM–III–1)
Ibert: "Parade," *Divertissement* (AIM–I)
→ Kabalevsky: "March and Comedians' Gallop," *The Comedians* (AIM–III–1)
→ McDonald: "Third Movement," *Children's Symphony* (AIM–II)
Pierne: "Entrance of the Little Fauns" (BOL #54; MSB 78015)
Prokofiev: "March" (BOL #54)
→ Rossini: "Finale," *William Tell Overture* (AIM–III–1)
→ Rossini-Respighi: "Can-Can," *The Fantastic Toyshop* (AIM–II)
→ Thomson: "Walking Song," *Acadian Songs and Dances* (AIM–I)
Verdi: "Triumphal March," *Aida* (BOL #62; MSB 78048)

Familiar Melodies

Cailliet: "Pop! Goes the Weasel" (BOL #65; MSB 78114)
Gould: "American Salute" (BOL #65)—"When Johnny Comes Marching Home"
McDonald: "First Movement," *Children's Symphony* (AIM–III–2)—"London Bridge"; "Baa, Baa, Black Sheep"
McDonald: "Third Movement," *Children's Symphony* (AIM–I)—"Farmer in the Dell"; "Jingle Bells"
"Yankee Doodle" (MSB 78306)

Two- and Three-Part Forms

Bach: "Badinerie," *Suite No. 2 in B Minor* (AIM–III–1)
Bizet: "Trumpet and Drum," *Jeux d'Enfants* (BOL #53; MSB 78008)
Brahms: "Hungarian Dance No. 5" (BOL #55; MSB 78110)
Copland: "Circus Music," *The Red Pony* (AIM–III–1)
Corelli-Pinelli: *Suite for Strings* (BOL #63; MSB 78101)—"Sarabande"; "Gigue"; "Badinerie"
Debussy: "Golliwogg's Cakewalk," *The Children's Corner Suite* (MSB 78037)
Gluck: "Air Gai," *Iphigénie in Aulis* (AIM–I)
Grieg: "Norwegian Dance in A (No. 2)" (BOL #63)
Handel: "Bourrée" and "Minuet II" (AIM–III–2; MSB 78002), "Minuet I" (MSB 78002), *Royal Fireworks Music*
Kabalevsky: "Gavotte" (BOL #55)
Khachaturian: "Mazurka," *Masquerade Suite* (BOL #55)
Lully: "Marche," *Ballet Suite* (AM–III–2)
McDonald: "Third Movement," *Children's Symphony* (AIM–II)
Moussorgsky: "Ballet of the Unhatched Chicks," *Pictures at an Exhibition* (AIM–I)
Mozart: "Minuet" (BOL #53)
Offenbach: "Barcarolle," *The Tales of Hoffmann* (AIM–III–1)
Pinto: "Run, Run," *Memories of Childhood* (BOL #68)
Prokofiev: "March" (BOL #54)
Schumann-Glazounov: "German Waltz—Paganini," *Carnaval* (BOL #53)
Shostakovich: "Petite Ballerina" (AIM–II), "Pizzicato Polka" (AIM–I), *Ballet Suite No. 1*
Tchaikovsky: "Dance of the Toy Flutes" (BOL #58; MSB 78034), "March" (BOL #58; MSB 78033), *Nutcracker Suite*
Vaughan Williams: "March Past of the Kitchen Utensils," *The Wasps* (AIM–III–1)
Villa-Lobos: "Let Us Run Across the Hill" (BOL #68)

Several Instruments (evaluation)

Fauré: "Berceuse," *Dolly* (AIM–II)—flute, oboe
Handel: "Minuet" (MSB 78318)—clarinet, oboe
Kabalevsky: "Gavotte" (BOL #55)— oboe, clarinet
Kodály: "Viennese Musical Clock," *Háry János Suite* (AIM–II)—snare drum, triangle, trumpet, flute, cymbals
Thomson: "Walking Song," *Acadian Songs and Dances* (AIM–I)—clarinet, trumpet, flute
Walton: "Country Dance," *Façade Suite* (BOL #55)—flute, clarinet, oboe

7

LISTENING ACTIVITIES FOR OLDER CHILDREN

Older children are eager to participate in additional listening activities. They have learned to listen attentively through participation in the listening program described in Chapter 6 and they have developed a positive attitude toward this aspect of music as the result of many satisfying experiences. The child's ability to listen to music attentively has been further developed by means of the activities described in Chapters 2 and 4. Each child has learned to identify musical elements through singing experiences and through responses involving expressive movement.

A variety of additional sequential listening activities should be provided for older children. They should learn to identify a larger number of instruments, and they should recognize them in more complex instrumental textures. Older children should be introduced to choral and chamber-music literature as well as to additional orchestral and band selections. They should become increasingly familiar with a variety of musical forms representing several periods of musical composition.

THE LISTENING PROGRAM

Teachers should consider three aspects of listening when they plan a program for older children. They should organize activities to help children (1) identify a wider range of instrumental tone colors, (2) recognize a variety of musical forms and styles of composition, and (3) become aware of additional performance media.

These three aspects of listening are often closely related. The child may become conscious of a musical form or style as he participates in an instrumental identification activity. The example he hears may be a form of chamber music, thereby providing him with the opportunity to become acquainted with another performance medium. These related experiences may, in addition, become closely identified with the program of activities involving expressive movement responses. The child may wish to move expressively as he listens.

Introducing Listening Activities

The activities suggested later in this chapter and in Chapter 5 are based on the assumption that the older child will have had many previous opportunities to develop listening skills and to make expressive responses. Children who have not had previous experiences should participate first in some introductory listening activities.

Any new aspect of education should include a familiar element. The child who has had limited experiences in listening to music will become interested in this activity as he recognizes familiar melodies in new settings. "American Salute" by Morton Gould (AIM–V–1)[1] will provide the child with a rousing introduction to listening as he hears "When Johnny Comes Marching Home" in this brilliant arrangement.

The class should learn to sing "When Johnny Comes Marching Home," if possible, before the listening activities begin. This popular song is included in several of the basic series books.

The teacher may introduce this listening activity by simply remarking to the class that they will hear a familiar song in a new setting. Children will immediately identify the melody, and they will become engrossed in listening to the brilliant orchestration.

The teacher should then briefly explain *variation* form and suggest that the children listen again to discover the ways in which the composer has created variations of this melody. The form might be placed on the chalkboard as the class identifies each variation.

Children should have repeated opportunities to listen to this selection. They will identify other characteristics of this musical form as they continue to listen. "American Salute" begins with an introduction, the variations are separated by short interludes, and a coda provides an effective finale.

[1] Sources of recordings are listed at the end of the chapter.

Related Activities: Children will enjoy listening to the varied ways other composers have arranged musical settings for familiar melodies. (Appropriate recordings are listed at the end of the chapter.) Additional selections composed in a similar form should be presented. These listening activities should include compositions representative of different historical periods and several styles of composition.

Teachers may decide that children need even more opportunities to participate in introductory listening activities. Those described in Chapter 6 will make children aware of tone-color differences and prepare them for the materials in this chapter.

Instrument Identification

Listening activities planned for older children should be based on their previous experiences with the identification of the timbres of several instruments. They should be able to identify basic percussion, woodwind, and brass instruments in solo performances and as these instruments are heard in performances with a variety of other instruments. Children who have not had the opportunity to become acquainted with the tone colors of the most commonly heard instruments should participate in the activities described in Chapter 6.

Children in intermediate-grade classrooms should also become acquainted with the distinctive timbres of lower instruments in the woodwind and brass sections of the orchestra or the band. The bassoon, English horn, French horn, and tuba are appropriate examples.

The older child should learn to identify the tone colors of string instruments. Although string instruments are difficult for the younger child to recognize, the older child will identify their timbres with greater ease. The violin, viola, cello, and string bass (bass viol) should be introduced in the same way that other instruments were presented in Chapter 6. The instrument should first be heard in a solo performance and then identified in a performance with other instruments.

Many other instruments will provide fascinating listening experiences for older children. The harp and the celeste add colorful effects to many orchestrations. The harpsichord and pipe organ are important instruments the child should also learn to identify.

Children should acquire additional knowledge about instruments. They should become aware of the different ways in which they produce sounds. They may perform simple acoustical experiments and read about the acoustical differences that contribute to distinctly different tone colors. Children who play instruments are an important musical resource in the classroom. They may demonstrate the way they play their instruments and explain the way sounds are produced.

Musical Form and Style

There are some similarities between the following discussion and one part of Chapter 5. Both suggest ways to help the child learn to identify form and to become sensitive to different musical styles. Chapter 5 describes ways to help the child recognize form through expressive movement responses. The activities described here complement those in Chapter 5, offering another approach to the recognition of musical form and style.

The two approaches to listening discussed in these chapters are both important to the child's musical development. He may first become conscious of formal and stylistic elements by making expressive movement responses as a young child. These activities should continue and become more complicated, leading the older child to the point where he can analyze and identify these elements while responding to unfamiliar compositions.

The child will also develop sensitivity to form and style as he is actively engaged in quiet listening. The young child will discover the excitement of different tone colors and learn to identify instruments. The older child will apply these previous learnings to more complex listening activities involving formal and stylistic recognition.

Binary (AB) forms provide a simple transition between form in familiar songs and form recognition while listening to unfamiliar selections. Two-part forms are often short, and the contrasts between A and B sections are similar to the melodic contrasts the child has identified in songs.

Binary forms are characteristic of one style of composition typical of the baroque period. Many of the dances arranged in suites feature this two-part structure. The "Sarabande" from the Corelli-Pinelli *Suite for String Orchestra* (AIM–VI–2; BOL #63; MSB 78101) is an example. The child should be able to identify two-part form easily as he participates in the following listening activities:

> The child should be aware of the formal element in music before listening to this selection. The teacher might begin by reviewing familiar songs that have two contrasting sections. Many songs the child has sung contain this type of contrast. "Masters in This Hall" (page 295) and "Vesper Hymn" (page 329), are simple examples of two-part form.

> He should listen to the "Sarabande" before he sees the themes, and he should attempt to identify the two sections. He will discover as he listens that this slow baroque dance is more complex than songs composed in binary form.

The child should then follow the themes as he listens again. The A section begins with this melody:

The melody is performed twice and ends in an incomplete manner, which seems to demand a contrasting section:

The B section is longer and begins with a contrasting melody:

The child will enjoy humming or singing these simple themes. He will identify them more easily in this way or by shaping them with hand signals.

The child will hear several musical effects characteristic of the baroque period as he continues to listen to the "Sarabande." He will hear the melody elaborated by trills and added notes. The phrases become slower at cadences.

Related Activities: The child will enjoy listening to the other two dances composed by Corelli and later arranged by Pinelli in this simplified version of a baroque suite. The "Gigue" and "Badinerie" are typical examples of other dances of this period (BOL #63; MSB 78101). The older child will find the lives of the composers, especially of Bach and Handel, of particular interest. (Selected reading sources are listed at the end of this chapter.) Other baroque compositions may be compared with this "Sarabande" and with the other two dances in this suite. The following are appropriate and will give the child an opportunity to compare the different ways in which composers of this period used similar forms and dance styles:

Bach: "Badinerie," *Suite No. 2 in B Minor* (AIM–III–1)

Handel: "Bourrée" and "Minuet II" (AIM–III–2; MSB 78002), "Minuet I" (MSB 78002), *Royal Fireworks Music*

Other compositions representative of the baroque period are listed at the end of the chapter.

The examples of musical form that have been discussed are easy for the child to identify since each is closely related to his direct experiences with singing. The contrasts in variations on a theme are easy to recognize, and binary forms are often similar to songs because of their brevity.

Children should progress in their ability to recognize the form of compositions they hear. The ternary (ABA) form is an appropriate choice for their next experience with form recognition. This simple structure has been utilized by composers for many years and resembles the form of some songs children have learned to sing.

Many ABA-form compositions contain longer sections with several musical thoughts which are unified by a single mood. "Laideronette, Empress of the Pagodas," from the *Mother Goose Suite* by Maurice Ravel (BOL #57), is an example of this more complex form. The first A section contains several musical ideas and changes of orchestral tone color; yet there is a consistent mood throughout. The B section will be easy for the child to identify, since a stately procession is heard. The A section returns with slight changes and recalls the scurrying high sounds of the beginning.

This composition features a device often heard in music of the impressionist period. The pentatonic (five-tone) scale is used to create these distinctive, oriental-sounding melodies. The teacher may provide an introduction to this new scale by showing how the black keys of the piano provide one series of tone combinations which a composer of the impressionist period might use. The teacher should place small sections of the main themes on a board and play them or have a child find them on the piano or another melody instrument. The child should have several opportunities to hear these themes in order to become acquainted with the distinctive sound of the pentatonic scale.

The child will then easily identify these themes as he listens to the recording. He will also hear several familiar instruments.

The child will discover the ABA form of this selection as he hears the contrast between the A and B sections and then hears the A section return. He may also hear instruments that are new to him. Unusual percussion instruments such as the gong, celeste, and xylophone are introduced in addition to the harp.

The teacher may suggest after this form is recognized that the child compare the ways in which this composition is similar to a song in ABA form and the ways in which it is different. "Laideronette" *is* similar to ABA songs in its basic form. It is different since several melodies may be combined in one section. It is longer than any song the child has sung, and the contrasts in mood are more obvious than those in most songs.

The teacher should name the composition and briefly outline the story, *after* the child has listened to the music itself and discovered the formal structure. The child should realize that titles and stories have little specific relation to music. This understanding will be deepened if the teacher has added one more step before mentioning the composition's title. The child might be asked first what he feels as he listens to this impressionist selection. The many responses that may be made will further point up the fact that music has no specific descriptive meaning. Moods are expressed, but music does not tell a specific story!

Related Activities: This selection was also arranged for the piano by the composer. Children will enjoy comparing the piano version (MSB 78013) with the orchestral performance they have heard. Some characteristic sounds of impressionist selections will become obvious as the child experiments with techniques used by these composers. He will enjoy activities that involve creating pentatonic melodies using the black keys of the piano or chromatic resonator bells. The child will enjoy reading about impressionist composers and their new approaches to composition. Debussy was another major impressionist composer who also used *pentatonic scales, whole-tone scales,* and *chromaticism.* These terms are often used to describe techniques of the impressionist period. The child should hear compositions featuring ternary (ABA) form that are representative of other periods and styles. Several selections are listed at the end of the chapter.

One *rondo* form will be extremely easy for the child to recognize after he has had several opportunities to identify two- and three-part forms. This example of rondo form seems to be an extension of ABA form. The "Scherzo" from Beethoven's *Symphony No. 7* (BOL #62) will remind the child of the ABA forms he has already heard. He will discover some differences between rondo and ABA form as he participates in the following listening activities:

The themes should be thoroughly familiar before the child listens to this scherzo. They should be presented in large notation and either played by the teacher as the child follows the notation or sung by the child:

First theme

Second theme

As the child listens to this scherzo for the first time he will become aware of several musical effects. The whirling speed will at first be most obvious. He will also recognize the themes he has learned, although they will be performed much faster than he can sing or play them. The oboe will be easily recognized in a solo performance.

The child will hear the A section several times as he listens to the scherzo a second time. He will begin to understand that this is a characteristic of rondo form and he will further identify the sections of this particular rondo by participating in several additional activities: (1) Children may indicate the sections of the form on the chalkboard as they listen to the "Scherzo" and identify the appearances of the two themes. (2) They may develop movement responses that are expressive and that distinguish the two themes. These responses may be expanded in several ways. The class may decide to divide into two groups: one group will express the mood of the first theme while a second group will respond to the contrast of the second theme.

Related Activities: Beethoven substituted the scherzo for the minuet, which was the traditional third movement in earlier symphonies. A comparison of the minuet with this scherzo will show the similarities and the differences. The child should hear one of the following minuets and compare it to the Beethoven scherzo:

Haydn: "Minuet," *"Surprise" Symphony* (BOL #63)
Mozart: "Minuet," *Symphony No. 40* (BOL #62)

Differences in rhythmic accent and tempo distinguish the minuet from the scherzo. A minuet has three strong pulses in each measure, while a scherzo has a swinging or circular motion with one strong accent to a measure. A scherzo is generally much faster and more exciting than a minuet.

Polyphonic forms should also be identified by the older child. Polyphony, which means "many voices," refers to music that has horizontal motion and that seldom falls into the clear sections typical of the forms previously described. Polyphonic forms may be introduced in a very simple manner. The older child has become conscious of combinations of melodic lines as he has participated in part-singing activities. Many polyphonic compositions will remind him of the rounds and canons he has sung.

Polyphonic forms were featured in baroque and earlier musical periods. The child will become conscious of the extent to which these forms are still in use as he listens to the "Shepherds' Dance" from the opera *Amahl and the Night Visitors* by Gian-Carlo Menotti (AIM–IV–2; BOL #58). The first section of this contemporary composition features two oboes playing a round or canon. The second section is quite different, however, as a joyous peasant dance develops and whirls to an exciting climax.

> The teacher may place the theme for the first section on the chalkboard and show the child how the two entrances are combined in a manner similar to the rounds and canons he has sung. The class will enjoy singing these examples in two parts or playing them on simple melody instruments.

> The child should be very familiar with this style of orchestral writing because of his previous experiences with the singing of rounds. He will also recognize the oboes as they perform this duet.

> The mood of this first section may seem strange to the child. He should discover that the melody is neither major nor minor but is composed of tones found in the *mixolydian mode*. The child may find this new scale quite easily by playing a major scale with a lowered seventh scale step.

> The child should listen to the entire dance and compare the mood of the first section with the gradual increase in excitement as the dance itself gains full momentum.

> *Related Activities:* The child will enjoy listening to other portions of this opera (see "Introduction" and "March of the Three Kings," BOL #58). He will also enjoy reading the story of the opera during the Christmas season. These activities may also be used as a way to expand the child's listening horizons. He should become aware of musical resources in the community and on radio and television. *Amahl and the Night Visitors* is often performed during the Christmas season and is frequently presented on television.

Composers use other polyphonic techniques as well. The composer of the twentieth century continues to use a polyphonic device that was introduced hundreds of years ago. Two melodies are combined in a *contrapuntal* manner. John Philip Sousa used contrapuntal techniques as he embellished the Trio melody of "The Stars and Stripes Forever" (AIM–IV–2; BOL #54). The melody is heard first without contrapuntal accompaniment. The famous piccolo solo is then added as the first contrapuntal line. Later the equally familiar trombone melody provides a contrasting contrapuntal effect. The child will recognize these devices with delight as he listens to this popular patriotic favorite time after time.

Children should have additional opportunities to hear selections with polyphonic forms after they have learned to identify canonic repetition and counterpoint. Two examples of the baroque period are described in Chapter 5 (page 101).

The first theme of the third movement of Gustav Mahler's *Symphony No. 1* (BOL #62) is an example of the manner in which one late romantic composer used two polyphonic techniques. This slow section has both canonic and contrapuntal elements. Children will be fascinated from the beginning as they listen to this selection and identify a familiar song in an orchestral arrangement. They will also learn to recognize polyphonic effects more easily as they participate in these listening activities:

> Children will recognize a variant of "Frère Jacques" ("Are You Sleeping?") as they listen to this recording. They will realize, however, that the song they know is not quite the same as this theme. The teacher may show examples of both on the chalkboard.

Frère Jacques

Theme

A comparison of these two themes will show the child several distinct differences. The Mahler theme differs from the familiar song in the following ways:

1. It is in a minor rather than a major tonality.
2. The melodic outline is slightly changed and more elaborate.
3. The theme is performed at a much slower tempo than the song is customarily sung.
4. The theme is played by bass instruments at an extremely low pitch level.

The canonic entrances will remind children of rounds they have sung. The children will also identify a contrapuntal melody, as the oboe plays a counter-melody high above the repeated theme:

Children will enjoy playing the theme and counter-melody together. They will also understand contrapuntal effects more completely if they see the two melodies written as a two-part arrangement.

Repeated listening will help children discover the many elements of music that are combined by the composer to create a specific expressive effect or mood. The minor tonality, the choice of instruments (orchestration), the tempo, and the rhythmic pulse all contribute to the plaintive mood of this selection.

The low theme is played by several instruments that are seldom heard in solo performances. Children will enjoy identifying the unusual and distinctive tone colors of the string bass and tuba as they continue to listen to this selection.

Related Activities: Children who have participated in these activities will be able to identify polyphonic effects as they listen to similar compositions. Recordings of other polyphonic selections are listed at the end of this chapter. Children who have listened to the Mahler symphonic movement become aware of the ways in which he has transformed a simple melody. Some children will want to explore ways of changing other melodies. They should be encouraged to make arrangements of familiar songs. They may compose a descant or countermelody; change the expressive effect by a tonality change and by adding appropriate instrumental tone colors; or compose variations to a melody by changing harmonic, melodic, or rhythmic elements.

Older children will have developed more acute listening skills and a more receptive attitude toward listening after they have participated in the activities described here. They should be interested in other types of musical composition as they continue to enjoy listening to music of several periods and styles.

RELATED ACTIVITIES

The older child should be thoroughly familiar with orchestral music of several periods after he has participated in the activities described above and in Chapter 6. He should also become acquainted with the other instrumental and vocal media used by well-known composers. Orchestral music represents only one facet of our vast heritage of worthwhile music. Some composers have written beautiful compositions for chamber music groups, and others have composed musical settings for dramatic stories by creating operas and operettas. Many famous composers have considered the voice to be the most beautiful of all instruments. They have composed art songs, oratorios, and other works for solo voices or choral groups.

Chamber Music

Many composers have created outstanding music for smaller groups of instruments. The child should become aware of this more intimate type of instrumental music. Instruments with similar tone colors are generally combined in these smaller groups. String quartets and woodwind quintets are typical examples.

The string quartet consists of two violins, a viola, and a cello. The quartet has a consistent tone color since the instruments are played in the same manner and produce similar sounds. The woodwind quintet has a wider range of tone-color possibilities. Four basic woodwind instruments are joined by the French horn. This brass instrument blends well with the timbres of the flute, oboe, clarinet, and bassoon.

The second movement of the *Emperor Quartet* by Haydn (MSB 78042) provides an effective introduction to the string quartet. This selection has a musical form—theme and variations—that the child will readily recognize. The four string instruments will also be familiar. The child should learn to sing the melody or theme of this movement first as he participates in the following listening activities:

Children will enjoy singing the Austrian National Hymn as a prelude to listening. This famous melody by Franz Joseph Haydn is included in several of the basic music series. It appears under several titles: "Austrian Hymn," "Emperor's Hymn," and "Glorious Things of Thee Are Spoken." Performances of this famous quartet movement are also included in the recordings that accompany several of the basic series books.

The theme should be placed on the chalk, flannel, or magnetic board before the class listens to this selection. The four-part quartet notation is included in some of the basic series.

Children should recognize the theme immediately as they listen to this chamber-music selection from the classical period. They should be able to identify the different string instruments and recognize the variation form.

The composition contains some elements that are new, and the children will become aware of these as they continue to listen. A chamber-music composition has a more transparent texture than orchestral selections. The texture of the music changes in obvious ways as different instruments play the theme or an embellishing accompaniment.

Children will enjoy analyzing the changes Haydn has made in his variations on this theme. The composer has varied several musical ele-

ments with which the class is familiar. They will discover polyphonic techniques as well as melodic, rhythmic, and harmonic
variants as they continue to listen to this quartet movement.

Related Activities: Children should have the opportunity to listen to
other chamber music compositions. One romantic-period composition, the "Andantino" from the *Trout Quintet* by Schubert, also
employs a song melody as the theme. The composer has written
the movement in variation form. This quintet is performed by an
unusual combination of instruments. The composer has written
parts for the piano and the string bass as well as for the violin,
viola, and cello. This song, "The Trout," is included in several
of the basic music series, and recordings of the quintet movement
may be found in the collections that accompany several of the
series.

The child should become acquainted with woodwind quintet performances in a similar manner. He will enjoy listening to such compositions as Tchaikovsky's *Album for the Young* (BOL #68). He will
also discover that composers of the present century have written for
this instrumental combination in a fascinating way as he listens to
Three Compositions by Béla Bartók (BOL #68) and *Kleine Kammer-
musik* by Paul Hindemith. Sections of the latter work are included
in several of the basic series recordings.

Vocal and Choral Literature

Composed songs and choral and operatic works have been created
by well-known composers of every period. The child should become
acquainted with several representative examples of each.

The *art* song became an important part of music literature during
the nineteenth century. Composers of the romantic period created
hundreds of these charming songs. German art songs, or Lieder, are
considered by many musicians to be equal to chamber music compositions in their subtlety and musical effectiveness.

Examples of Lieder will be found in basic series books planned for
the older child. Songs composed by Schubert, Schumann, and Brahms
are most frequently included. The child will become aware of the
difference between composed art songs and folk songs as he listens
or sings. The complex and effective accompaniments that have been
added to underline the meaning of the text easily distinguish the art
song from a folk song.

"The Trout" by Franz Schubert is a typical example. The melody
itself is simple and comparable to the melodies of many folk songs.
The accompaniment, however, is complex and intensifies the meaning

of the text. (Teachers should compile a list of art songs [Lieder] by checking the classified indexes of their basic series books.)

While the teacher will have little difficulty finding examples of art songs in basic series books and accompanying recordings, other vocal and choral works are not so readily available.

Children should be introduced to *opera*. They will discover that operas are a fascinating combination of many types of music. Vocal solos, choruses, and instrumental effects are combined in a dramatic manner. Operas also include elements of other arts, since the staging and action are closely related to theater and since the scenery and costuming reflect the design of the artist. A study of opera excerpts should prove to be stimulating and instructive for the student.

Sacred choral works have been created by many composers. *Oratorios* are examples of this musical form. Children should have as many opportunities as possible to hear outstanding choral examples from oratorios and other sacred choral works. The music specialist and classroom teacher should be aware of any local performance of music of this type and prepare children for attendance. Many outstanding performances are often presented on radio, television, and in local churches during the Christmas and Easter seasons.

Contemporary Music

Composers frequently experimented with different musical effects in the past. The composer of today is experimenting with even more varied and interesting possibilities than his predecessors. The older child should become aware of some of these contemporary trends in composition.

The child will find the music of Schoenberg or Webern less strange as he begins to understand the terms "serial," "twelve-tone," "atonal." Composers of the past used familiar musical elements in different ways as they created music representative of a certain style. Atonal composers, however, have relinquished some of these traditional techniques. Their compositions may seem strange to the student at first because of the original manner in which the melodic tendencies and harmonic effects are created.

Atonal composers use traditional instrumental and vocal effects in their compositions. Other composers, however, have created musical efforts in new ways by using electronic sounds. Children should enjoy listening to recordings of these electronic experiments.

Contemporary experiments with new sounds are an important part of the total scope of music. The child should be as aware of new trends as he is of the varied heritage of music literature representing periods and styles of the past.

Music of Other Cultures

The child who has developed a receptive attitude toward listening to many types of music should also be introduced to ethnic music of other cultures. Examples of music of different cultures may be introduced both as a listening activity and as a way of correlating music with other parts of the school curriculum. The teacher will find examples in the recordings that accompany some of the basic music series. These selections are often included in classified indexes as music from another country.

The child will gain a heightened awareness of another culture as he listens to music indigenous to that culture. He will also understand the universality of music as he participates in listening activities involving ethnic music. Sources for ethnic recordings are included in the references at the end of this chapter.

The child who has participated in the listening activities described in this chapter will have developed a positive feeling toward music of many types and toward performances employing orchestral, chamber music, and vocal-choral combinations. He will be receptive to later listening activities in both the school and the community.

THE TEACHER'S ROLE

The description in Chapter 6 of the teacher's contribution to the listening program is equally appropriate for the teacher of the older child. Some additional factors should also be considered carefully as the teacher plans listening activities for the older child.

Repetition has been stressed elsewhere in this book as an important part of the music program. It is equally pertinent as the teacher presents listening activities. The child should have many opportunities to hear the same selection. At first he may hear only a few obvious effects as he listens. Later he will become aware of more subtle aspects of the music. Repeated listening also provides frequent opportunities to correlate listening activities with other aspects of the music program. The child may explore form and style through his expressive responses, he may use his heightened listening awareness in a creative manner, or he may become deeply interested in one period or type of music and continue to add to his knowledge through independent study.

Community resources should become a part of the listening program for the older child. The teacher should be aware of appropriate concerts in the area and prepare the child for attendance. Secondary-school choral and instrumental programs will provide many appropriate listening experiences for the older child.

The child must be helped to develop the habits and behavior that will prepare him for concert attendance. He should become consciously aware of the need for courteous, attentive behavior as he is part of the "audience" for classroom and school programs. He should attend many such programs as a listener and as an active participant.

Other resources will add richness to the listening program and help children transfer their listening skills to other situations. They should acquire the habit of reading to become informed about concerts in the community and on radio and television. A "Musical Current Events" bulletin board might become a feature of the classroom or music room. Children will find notices of future programs in local newspapers and in national magazines that list radio and television programs.

The alert teacher will find musical resources on radio and television. Those areas with an educational television station often have more varied programs of serious music.

Organization of music materials is a necessity if the listening program is to be effective. This factor is often neglected by the teacher, and the lack of organization seriously impedes the success and continuity of listening activities. Music specialists should prepare cross-indexed files of available recordings. The topics might include prominent instruments, form, style, and the other categories listed at the end of this chapter. The teacher who has organized recordings in this way will be able to select examples in an efficient manner. It is a simple matter to choose several additional selections featuring a certain instrument or a specific form from a well-organized file.

PROGRAM OBJECTIVES

The listening program for the older child should be based on specific and sequential objectives. Three categories of objectives describe the child's listening development in the areas of instrumental identification, form and style recognition, and awareness of several types of musical media.

Instrument Identification

The child's ability to identify instrumental tone colors is one important aspect of his listening and general musical growth. He should attain the following objectives as he develops this listening skill. He should:

> Recognize each instrument in the string section in solo performances and as each is heard in performances with other instruments.
> Identify a variety of other instruments. The bassoon, celeste, and harp are a few of the many instruments the older child should recognize.

Identify many instruments in a single composition with a more complex
texture and thereby demonstrate that he has developed greater
tone-color discrimination than children in early childhood classrooms.

Form and Style Recognition

The older child should be aware of form in music and of stylistic
differences after he has participated in the listening activities described in this chapter. He should:

Indicate his knowledge of the basic musical forms as he identifies them
in compositions he has not previously heard.

Demonstrate his awareness of stylistic differences as he compares musical examples of different periods.

Varied Musical Media

The older child will learn that composers have selected a variety of
combinations of instruments and voices to express their musical ideas.
He should:

Recognize the characteristic tone-colors of chamber music groups such
as the string quartet or the woodwind quintet.

Understand the difference between the composed solo song and folk
songs.

Develop an awareness of the many musical, dramatic, and art elements
that are combined in an opera.

Respond to the vocal and choral timbres in sacred choral compositions.

Develop a receptive attitude toward contemporary experiments with
unusual musical effects.

Become aware of the ethnic music of other cultures.

PROGRAM EVALUATION

Evaluation has been emphasized as a basic and necessary element
in all previous parts of the music program. The evaluation process
must be applied with equal care if the teacher is to determine the
extent to which the older child has achieved the goals of the listening
program.

The older child is accustomed to written tests, and these instruments
of measurement are appropriate as a means of evaluating some aspects
of the listening program. The child's ability to identify instruments,
musical forms, contrasting styles, and different musical media may be
measured through the administration of a test. These tests should be

simple in design and yet planned in such a way that they provide accurate evaluation. The test construction may feature possible answers requiring decisions from the child. Multiple-choice items are one possibility.

The child's ability to identify woodwinds may be measured as he listens to a recording and completes a written test. The teacher may select a recording similar to "The White Peacock" by Griffes (AIM–VI–1). The child should understand that he will hear some of the instruments listed on the test but that others will not be heard. He may listen first and identify the instruments that are featured. He may then listen a second time and indicate the order in which they are heard.

The teacher should periodically present tests of this type since additional listening activities must be selected with careful regard to the child's level of attainment. Recorded selections appropriate for testing purposes are listed at the end of the chapter. The teacher may simply select an unfamiliar example of a musical form or style to measure the child's ability to identify these musical elements. Instrument identification is featured in one category of these chapter references. The compositions listed there are outstanding examples of selections featuring several instruments.

Tests that measure the child's ability to identify instruments, forms, or stylistic contrasts will not measure the complete success of the listening program. The child's attitude toward listening and the extent to which he has developed positive listening habits are equally important and impossible to measure in a similar manner. Measurement of listening skills will, however, provide the teacher with information that is necessary to the child's development of listening skills, attitudes, and habits. The child's attitudes and habits are formed as the result of successful accomplishment in a stimulating environment. The teacher who has provided challenging listening activities selected through periodic evaluation of the child's ability to listen attentively has led him to the point where he wants to listen to many types of music because listening has become an extremely satisfying musical experience.

SUMMARY

The listening program may be considered a culmination of the older child's total musical growth. The child who listens attentively to a complex orchestral, choral, or chamber music recording reflects through his attention the success of the total music program. His interest in listening is the result of many years of comprehensive and successful experiences with music.

The activities described in this chapter will provide the older child with the specific listening skills he needs to develop his listening potentials as fully as possible. They are based also on the child's earlier experiences with music. He must acquire specific information concerning the way music is created and organized if he is to learn to listen in a sensitive and discerning manner. His developing awareness of tone-color, form, style, and media will give him the incentive to listen to music.

The listening program for the older child may also be considered as a bridge to further experiences with music. Older pupils and adults will experience music through listening more frequently than they will through active participation. The successful listening program for the older child will have provided a foundation for these continued experiences with listening. The quality of the experiences he has had and the intellectual knowledge he has gained provide him with a solid basis for the development of discriminating musical judgment.

QUESTIONS AND PROJECTS

1. Discuss the differences between the early childhood listening program and a program for older children. Are there distinct differences in emphasis? How can sequence and continuity be achieved?
2. Compare the listening activities and teaching suggestions included in two basic series books. Evaluate their relative effectiveness.
3. Examine the teacher's guides for a basic record series and list solo instrument performances appropriate for intermediate-grade classrooms. Use the criteria indicated in this chapter to make the selection, and compare your list with those below.
4. The basic record series emphasize instrumental performances. On the assumption that older children should experience a variety of performing media, find additional recordings that will assist you in presenting a comprehensive program of listening activities.
5. Prepare for a discussion of the topic, "What are the basic goals of the intermediate-grade listening program?"
6. Survey available literature to gather information about the value of music scores as children participate in listening activities.
7. Listening is sometimes assumed to call for a passive attitude and a lack of active involvement. What devices can be used to insure a high level of involvement on the part of intermediate-grade children?

REFERENCES

Recommended Readings

For the Teacher

The books listed at the end of Chapter 6 are also appropriate for the classroom teacher of older children. In addition, the following are recommended.

Baldwin, Lillian. *Music for Young Listeners.* 3 vols. (*The Blue Book, The Crimson Book, The Green Book.*) Morristown, N.J.: Silver Burdett Co., 1951.

Bernstein, Leonard. *The Joy of Music.* New York: Simon & Schuster, 1959.

For the Child

Bakeless, Katherine. *Story-Lives of Great Composers.* Rev. ed. Philadelphia: J. B. Lippincott Co., 1962.

Britten, Benjamin, and Holst, Imogen. *The Wonderful World of Music.* Rev. ed. Garden City, N.Y.: Doubleday & Co., 1968.

Buchanan, Fannie, and Luckenbill, Charles L. *How Man Made Music.* Chicago: Follett Publishing Co., 1959.

Goulden, Shirley. *The Royal Book of Ballet.* Chicago: Follett Publishing Co., 1964.

Mirsky, Reba Paeff. Biographies of Bach, Beethoven, Haydn, Mozart. Chicago: Follett Publishing Co., 1957–65.

Surplus, Robert W., ed. *Musical Books for Young People.* Minneapolis: Lerner Publications Co. (a series whose individual titles are devoted to music notation, the orchestra, conducting, specific families of instruments, etc.).

Wheeler, Opal. Biographies of and stories about Beethoven, Chopin, Handel, Schumann, and Tchaikovsky and, written with Sybil Deucher, Bach, Haydn, Mozart, and Schubert. New York: E. P. Dutton & Co.

Young Keyboard, Jr. New Haven, Conn.: Keyboard Publications, Inc. (a monthly magazine featuring enlarged thematics and pictures of composers, artists, instruments).

Audio-Visual Aids

Instrument Identification

The materials listed at the end of Chapter 6 are also appropriate for use with older children.

Britten, Benjamin. *The Young Person's Guide to the Orchestra* (several recorded performances are available).

Instruments of the Orchestra. Hollywood, Calif.: Capitol Records (teacher's book, two recordings).

Filmstrips

The following filmstrips have accompanying recordings. Additional filmstrip-record combinations are listed by Educational Audio Visual, Inc., Pleasantville, N.Y.

The Jam Handy Organization, Detroit, Mich.: *Great Composers and Their Music; Instruments of the Symphony Orchestra; Music Stories; Opera and Ballet Stories.*

Society for Visual Education, Inc., Chicago, Ill.: *The Story of Handel's* Messiah; *The Story of the Nutcracker.*

Ethnic Recordings

Folkways/Scholastic Records, New York, N.Y., and Englewood Cliffs, N.J., has an extensive collection of ethnic recordings. The listing headed "The People of the World–East to West" provides recordings for any classroom purpose.

2age 157

Basic Record Series

Adventures in Music. New York: RCA Victor Educational Sales.

AIM–III–1, Grade 3, Vol. 1
AIM–III–2, Grade 3, Vol. 2
AIM–IV–1, Grade 4, Vol. 1
AIM–IV–2, Grade 4, Vol. 2
AIM–V–1, Grade 5, Vol. 1
AIM–V–2, Grade 5, Vol. 2
AIM–VI–1, Grade 6, Vol. 1
AIM–VI–2, Grade 6, Vol. 2

Bowmar Orchestral Library. Los Angeles: Bowmar Records.

BOL #53, Pictures and Patterns
BOL #54, Marches
BOL #55, Dances, Part I
BOL #56, Dances, Part II
BOL #57, Fairy Tales in Music
BOL #58, Stories in Ballet and Opera
BOL #59, Legends in Music
BOL #60, Under Many Flags
BOL #62, Masters of Music
BOL #63, Concert Matinee
BOL #65, Music U.S.A.
BOL #67, Fantasy in Music
BOL #68, Classroom Concert

Musical Sound Books. Scarsdale, N.Y.: Musical Sound Books.

MSB 78000 series, For Young Listeners
MSB 78100 series, Music To Remember
MSB 78300 series, Tiny Masterpieces

String Instruments

Violin

Bach: "Jesu, Joy of Man's Desiring" (BOL #62)
Beethoven-Kreisler: "Rondino" (MSB 78312)
Brahms: "Hungarian Dance No. 1" (AIM–V–2)
———. "Lullaby" (MSB 78312)
English Folk Tune: "Greensleeves" (MSB 78311)
Grieg: "In the Hall of the Mountain King," *Peer Gynt Suite No. 1* (MSB 78029; AIM–III–2)
———. "Norwegian Bridal Procession" (MSB 78031)
———. "Wedding Day at Troldhaugen" (BOL #62)
Kabalevsky: "Gavotte" (BOL #55)
Mozart: "Menuetto," *Divertimento No. 17 in D* (AIM–V–2)
———. "Minuet," *Symphony No. 40* (BOL #62)
Rossini-Respighi: "Pizzicato," *The Fantastic Toyshop* (BOL #53)
Schubert: "First Movement," *Symphony No. 5* (AIM–V–1)
Strauss, R.: *Rosenkavalier Suite* (AIM–VI–1)
Welsh Folk Tune: "The Ash Grove" (MSB 78311)

Cello

Elgar: "Pomp and Circumstance No. 1" (BOL #54; MSB 78120)
Prokofiev: "March" (BOL #54)
Saint-Saëns: "The Swan," *Carnival of the Animals* (MSB 78314; AIM–III–2)
Wagner: "Song to the Evening Star" (MSB 78313)
————. "Walter's Prize Song" (MSB 78313)

String Bass

Handel: "A Ground" (BOL #53)
Mahler: "Second Movement," *Symphony No. 1* (BOL #62)

Other Instruments

Bassoon

Bartok: *Three Compositions* (BOL #68)
Ippolitov-Ivanov: "Cortege of the Sardar," *Caucasian Sketches* (BOL #54)
Mahler: "Second Movement," *Symphony No. 1* (BOL #62)
Pinto: *Memories of Childhood* (BOL #68)
Stravinsky: "Devil Dance" (BOL #68)
Tchaikovsky: *Album for the Young* (BOL #68)

English Horn

Borodin: "In the Steppes of Central Asia" (AIM–VI–1)
Debussy: "The Play of the Waves," *La Mer* (AIM–VI–2)

French Horn

Bartok: *Three Compositions* (BOL #68)
Pinto: *Memories of Childhood* (BOL #68)
Stravinsky: "Devil Dance" (BOL #68)
Tchaikovsky: *Album for the Young* (BOL #68)

Harp

Debussy: "The Play of the Waves," *La Mer* (AIM–VI–2)
Schumann-Glazounov: "Chopin," *Carnaval* (BOL #53)
Vaughn Williams: "Fantasia on Greensleeves" (AIM–VI–2)

Harpsichord

Bach: "March in D" (MSB 78039)
————. "Minuet in G" (MSB 78039)
Scarlatti: "Pastorale in D Minor" (MSB 78039)
————. "The Cat's Fugue" (MSB 78039)

Organ

Bach: "And Sheep May Safely Graze" (MSB 78316)
————. "Jesu, Joy of Man's Desiring" (MSB 78316)
Handel: "Awake, My Soul" (MSB 78317)
Haydn: "Glorious Things of Thee Are Spoken" (MSB 78317)

Piano

Beethoven: "Album Leaf" (MSB 78309)
———. "Minuet in G" (MSB 78309)
Bizet: *Children's Games* (MSB 78008–78009)
Chopin: "Polonaise in A Major, Op. 40" (MSB 78044)
———. "Prelude in D Flat, No. 15" (MSB 78044)
Copland: "Hoe-Down," *Rodeo* (BOL #55)
Debussy: *The Children's Corner Suite* (MSB 78036–78037)
Ibert: "The Little White Donkey," *Histoires No. 2* (MSB 78310)
Mozart: "Allegro in B Flat" (MSB 78307)
———. "Minuet in F" (MSB 78307)
———. "Minuet in G" (MSB 78307)
Ravel: *Mother Goose Suite* (MSB 78013–78014)
Schubert: "Scherzo in B Flat" (MSB 78308)
———. "Waltz in A Major" (MSB 78308)
———. "Waltz in A Flat" (MSB 78308)
Schumann: *Scenes from Childhood* (MSB 78006–78007)
Villa-Lobos: *The Baby's Family* (MSB 78310)

Musical Forms

Polyphonic

Bach, "Jesu, Joy of Man's Desiring," *Cantata No. 147* (AIM–V–1; BOL #62)
———. "Little Fugue in G Minor" (AIM–VI–1)
Mahler: "Second Movement," *Symphony No. 1* (BOL #62)
Menotti: "Shepherd's Dance," *Amahl and the Night Visitors* (AIM–IV–2; BOL #58)
Thomson: "Fugue and Chorale on Yankee Doodle," *Tuesday in November* (BOL #65)

Rondo

Beethoven: "Scherzo," *Symphony No. 7* (BOL #62)
Gottschalk-Kay: "Grand Walkaround," *Cakewalk Ballet Suite* (AIM–V–1)
Mozart: "Romanze" (AIM–IV–1; MSB 78004), "Rondo" (MSB 78004), *Eine kleine Nachtmusik*
Tchaikovsky: "Waltz," *The Sleeping Beauty* (AIM–IV–1; BOL #67; MSB 78108)

Variation

Anderson: "The Girl I Left Behind Me," *Irish Suite* (AIM–V–2)
Cailliet: "Pop! Goes the Weasel" (AIM–IV–1; BOL #65)
Copland: "Shaker Tune," *Appalachian Spring* (BOL #65)
Gould: "American Salute" (AIM–V–1; BOL #65)
Haydn: "The Emperor's Hymn," *String Quartet in C Major* (MSB 78042)
———. "Theme and Variations," *"Surprise" Symphony* (BOL #62)

Familiar Melodies

Cailliet: "Pop! Goes the Weasel" (AIM–IV–1; BOL #65; MSB 78114)
Copland: "Shaker Tune," *Appalachian Spring* (BOL #65; MSB 78152)– "Simple Gifts"

Copland: "Street in a Frontier Town," *Billy the Kid* (AIM–VI–1)—"Dogie Song"; "Old Chisholm Trail"; "Good-bye, Old Paint"

Gould: "American Salute" (AIM–V–1; BOL #65)—"When Johnny Comes Marching Home"

Grofé: "Desert Water Hole," *Death Valley Suite* (AIM–IV–1)—"Oh Suzanna"; "Old Folks at Home"; "Old Black Joe"

Mahler: "Second Movement," *Symphony No. 1* (BOL #62)—"Frère Jacques"

Thomson: "Fugue and Chorale on Yankee Doodle" (BOL #65)

Vaughan Williams: "Fantasia on Greensleeves" (AIM–VI–2; MSB 78151)

Periods and Styles

Baroque

Bach: "Ah Dearest Jesus, Holy Child," "How Shall I Fitly Meet Thee?" *Christmas Oratorio* (MSB 78041)

————. "Badinerie," *Suite No. 2 in B Minor* (AIM–III–1)

————. "Jesu, Joy of Man's Desiring," *Cantata No. 147* (AIM–V–1; BOL #62)

————. "Little Fugue in G Minor" (AIM–VI–1)

————. "March in D" (MSB 78039)

————. "Minuet in G" (MSB 78039)

————. *Suite No. 3 in D Major* (MSB 78040–78041)

Corelli-Pinelli: *Suite for String Orchestra* (BOL #63; MSB 78101); "Sarabande" (AIM–VI–2)

Handel: "A Ground" (BOL #53)

————. *Royal Fireworks Music* (MSB 78002); "Bourrée" (BOL #62); "Bourrée and Menuet II" (AIM–III–2)

————. *Water Music* (MSB 78001)

Lully: "Marche," *Ballet Suite* (AIM–III–2)

Scarlatti: "The Cat's Fugue" (MSB 78039)

————. "Non Presto," *The Good-Humored Ladies* (AIM–IV–2)

————. "Pastorale in D Minor" (MSB 78039)

Classical

Beethoven: "Scherzo," *Symphony No. 7* (BOL #62)

————. "Second Movement," *Symphony No. 8* (AIM–VI–1)

Boccherini: "Minuet," *String Quartet in E Major* (MSB 78019)

Haydn: "Andante" (MSB 78042), "Minuet" (BOL #63), "Theme and Variations" (BOL #62), "Surprise" Symphony

————. "Theme and Variations," *String Quartet in C Major* (MSB 78042)

————. *Toy Symphony* (MSB 78043)

Mozart: *Eine kleine Nachtmusik* (MSB 78004); "Romanze" (AIM–IV–1)

————. "Menuetto," *Divertimento No. 17 in D* (AIM–V–2)

————. "Minuet" (BOL #53)

————. "Minuet," *Symphony No. 40* (BOL #62)

Romantic

Bizet: "The Changing of the Guard," *Carmen Suite No. 2* (AIM–III–2)

————. "Farandole," *L'Arlésienne Suite No. 2* (AIM–VI–1)

————. "Minuetto," *L'Arlésienne Suite No. 1* (AIM–IV–2)

Brahms: "Hungarian Dance No. 1" (AIM–V–2)

————. "Hungarian Dance No. 5" (BOL #55; MSB 78110)

————. "Hungarian Dance No. 6" (BOL #62; MSB 78110)

————. *Liebeslieder Waltzes* (MSB 78105–78106)

Chopin: "Polonaise in A Major" (MSB 78044)
———. "Prelude in D Flat, No. 15" (MSB 78044)
Humperdinck: "Overture" (BOL #58), "Prelude" (AIM–V–2; MSB 78051),
    Hansel and Gretel
Mahler: "Second Movement," Symphony No. 1 (BOL #62)
Mendelssohn: Midsummer Night's Dream Music (MSB 78025–78028);
    "Scherzo" (BOL #57)
Respighi: "The Pines of the Villa Borghese," The Pines of Rome (AIM–IV
    –1)
Saint-Saëns: Carnival of the Animals (MSB 78010–78012); The "Swan"
    (AIM–III–2)
Schubert: "First Movement" (AIM–V–1), "Minuet" (BOL #62), Sym-
    phony No. 5
———. "Marche Militaire" (BOL #54; MSB 78005)
Schumann: Scenes from Childhood (MSB 78006–78007); "Träumerei" (AIM–
    IV–2; BOL #63)
Schumann-Glazounov: "Chopin," "German Waltz–Paganini," Carnaval (BOL
    #53)
Strauss, R.: Rosenkavalier Suite (AIM–VI–1)
Tchaikovsky: "Fourth Movement," Symphony No. 4 (AIM–VI–2)
———. Nutcracker Suite (BOL #58; MSB 78033–78035)
———. "Waltz," The Sleeping Beauty (AIM–IV–1; BOL #67; MSB 78108)
Verdi: "Triumphal March," Aida (BOL #62; MSB 78048)
Wagner: "Prelude to Act III," Lohengrin (AIM–VI–1)
———. "Ride of the Valkyries," The Valkyries (BOL #62; MSB 78049)

Nationalistic

Borodin: "In the Steppes of Central Asia" (AIM–VI–1)
Dvorak: "Slavonic Dance No. 1" (BOL #55; MSB 78111)
———. "Slavonic Dance No. 3" (MSB 78111)
———. "Slavonic Dance No. 7" (AIM–IV–2)
Grieg: "Norwegian Bridal Procession" (MSB 78031)
———. "Norwegian Dance in A (No. 2)" (BOL #63)
———. "Norwegian Rustic March," Lyric Suite (AIM–IV–1)
———. Peer Gynt Suite No. 1 (BOL #59; MSB 78029; MSB 78031); "In
    the Hall of the Mountain King" (AIM–III–2)
———. Peer Gynt Suite No. 2 (MSB 78030)
———. Sigurd Jorsalfar (MSB 78032)
———. "Wedding Day at Troldhaugen" (BOL #62)
Rimsky-Korsakov: "Bridal Procession," Le Coq d'Or Suite (AIM–IV–1)
———. "Dance of the Clowns," The Snow Maiden (MSB 78050)
Sibelius: "Alla Marcia," Karelia Suite (AIM–V–1)
———. "Finlandia" (BOL #60)
Smetana: "Dance of the Comedians," The Bartered Bride (AIM–VI–2; MSB
    78109
———. "The Moldau" (BOL #60)

Impressionistic

Debussy: Children's Corner Suite (BOL #63; MSB 78036–78037); "The
    Snow Is Dancing" (AIM–III–1)
———. "En Bateau" (BOL #53)
———. "The Play of the Waves," La Mer (AIM–VI–2)
Griffes: "The White Peacock" (AIM–VI–1)
Ravel: Mother Goose Suite (BOL #57; MSB 78013–78014); "The Conver-
    sations of Beauty and the Beast" (AIM–V–1), "Laideronnette, Empress
    of the Pagodas" (AIM–IV–2)

Contemporary

Bartók: "Bear Dance" (AIM–III–2), "An Evening in the Village" (AIM–V–2), *Hungarian Sketches*
———. *Three Compositions* (BOL #68)
Copland: "Circus Music," *The Red Pony* (AIM–III–1)
———. "Hoe-Down," *Rodeo* (AIM–V–2; BOL #55)
———. "Shaker Tune" ("Simple Gifts"), *Appalachian Spring* (BOL #65; MSB 78152)
———. "Street in a Frontier Town," *Billy the Kid* (AIM–VI–1)
Ives: "Last Movement," *Symphony No. 2* (BOL #65)
Kabalevsky: "Gavotte" (BOL #55)
———. "Intermezzo," *The Comedians* (BOL #53)
Khatchaturian: "Galop," "Mazurka" (BOL #55), "Waltz" (AIM–IV–2), *Masquerade Suite*
Kodály: "Entrance of the Emperor and His Court," *Háry János Suite* (AIM–IV–2)
Menotti: *Suite from Amahl and the Night Visitors* (BOL #58); "Shepherds' Dance" (AIM–IV–2)
Prokofiev: *Cinderella* (BOL #67)
———. *Classical Symphony* (MSB 78102–78103)
———. "March," *Love for Three Oranges* (BOL #54)
———. "Waltz on the Ice," *Winter Holiday* (AIM–III–2)
Shostakovich: "Polka," *The Golden Age* (MSB 78104)
Stravinsky: "Devil's Dance" (BOL #68)
———. "Infernal Dance of King Kastchei," *Firebird Suite* (AIM–V–2)
Thomson: "Fugue and Chorale on Yankee Doodle," *Tuesday in November* (BOL #65)
———. *The Plow That Broke the Plains* (BOL #65)
Vaughan Williams: "Fantasia on Greensleeves" (AIM–VI–2; MSB 78151)
Villa-Lobos: "The Little Train of the Caipira," *Bachianas Brasileiras No. 2* (AIM–III–1)
Walton: *Façade Suite* (BOL #55); "Valse" (AIM–VI–2)

Several Instruments (evaluation)

Bartók: "An Evening in the Village," *Hungarian Sketches* (AIM–V–2)—clarinet, flute, oboe, piccolo
Bizet: "The Changing of the Guard," *Carmen Suite No. 2* (AIM–III–2)—trumpet, piccolo, flute, cymbals
Charpentier: "On Muleback," *Impressions of Italy* (AIM–V–1)—pizzicato strings, flute duet, French horn
Copland: "Circus Music," *The Red Pony* (AIM–III–1)—trumpet, snare drum, triangle
Ginastera: "Wheat Dance," *Estancia* (AIM–IV–1)—violin, flute, French horn
Grieg: "In the Hall of the Mountain King," *Peer Gynt Suite No. 1* (AIM–III–2; BOL #59; MSB 78029)—violins, pizzicato strings, bassoon, cymbals
Griffes: "The White Peacock" (AIM–VI–1)—oboe, flute, clarinet, harp, celeste
Holst: "The Spirits of the Earth," *The Perfect Fool* (AIM–VI–2)—trombone, string bass, cello, viola, tympani
Kabalevsky: "Gavotte" (BOL #55)—violin, oboe, clarinet
Lecuona: "Andalucia," *Suite Andalucia* (AIM–IV–1)—tambourine, flute, cymbals
Prokofiev: "March" (BOL #54)—trumpet, cello, snare drum, cymbals
Ravel: "The Conversations of Beauty and the Beast," *Mother Goose Suite* (AIM–V–1)—woodwind solos, harp, cymbals

Smetana: "Dance of the Comedians," *The Bartered Bride* (AIM–VI–2; MSB 78109)—violin, oboe, clarinet, trumpet

Sousa: "The Stars and Stripes Forever" (AIM–IV–2; BOL #54)—piccolo, cymbals, trombone, trumpet

Tchaikovsky: "Arabian Dance," *Nutcracker Suite* (BOL #58)—woodwind solos

———. "Chinese Dance," *Nutcracker Suite* (BOL #58)—piccolo, glockenspiel, contra-bassoon

———. "March," *Nutcracker Suite* (BOL #58)—trumpet, flute, violin

———. "Waltz of the Flowers," *Nutcracker Suite* (BOL #58)—harp, woodwind solos, string solos

Villa-Lobos: "The Little Train of Caipira," *Bachianas Brasileiras No. 2* (AIM–III–1)—percussion, brass, flute

Walton: "Polka," *Façade Suite* (BOL #55)—trombone, woodwinds, brasses, percussion

Chamber Music

String Quartet

Haydn: "The Emperor's Hymn," *String Quartet in C Major* (MSB 78042)

Tchaikovsky: "Andante Cantabile," *String Quartet No. 1, Op. 11* (MSB 78019)

String Quintet

Boccherini: "Minuet," *String Quintet in E Major* (MSB 78019)

Woodwind Quintet

Bartók: *Three Compositions* (BOL #68)

Pinto: *Memories of Childhood* (BOL #68)

Stravinsky: "Devil Dance" (BOL #68)

Tchaikovsky: *Album for the Young* (BOL #68)

8

INSTRUMENTS IN
THE MUSIC PROGRAM

Children of any age love to play instruments. The older child will respond as quickly and eagerly to the opportunity to play an instrument as will the youngest child in an early childhood classroom. Melody and percussion instruments should be considered an important part of the music program for both younger and older children. The effective use of instruments will intensify many other aspects of the child's musical growth.

Instrumental activities will help children acquire basic performance skills. Young children will often develop singing ability more quickly and easily as they find song patterns on simple melody instruments. They will become more acutely aware of rhythmic elements that are produced on percussion instruments. Older children will become more conscious of the meaning and importance of notation as they read symbols and play instruments. They will also discover that melody instruments are often an effective aid to part-singing activities.

Children will learn to listen intently to various elements of music as they play simple instruments. The younger child will begin to identify instrumental timbres after he has experimented with the tonal possibilities of instruments he is able to play. He will acquire concepts of other musical elements through playing. The older child will add to his previous acquisition of concepts as he creates instrumental introductions, descants, or codas to embellish familiar songs. His musical experiments with instruments will help him become more aware of the element of form in musical composition.

The expressive qualities of music will be revealed to children as a variety of instruments are added to daily musical activities. The younger child will realize that some instruments convey the mood of a lullaby while others intensify the accented pulses of a faster, more rhythmic song. The older child will discover rich possibilities for orchestration as he becomes familiar with a greater variety of instruments.

Instruments should always be introduced for musical purposes. They should not be added to the program merely to keep the child occupied or introduced in the regimented, unmusical format of the rhythm band. Instrumental activities should always be complementary to other basic musical activities and should be considered a part of the total music program. Each instrument should be introduced to reinforce some aspect of the child's total musical growth.

The suggestions here are organized according to the age of the children for whom they are recommended. The teacher should, however, be quite flexible in selecting appropriate activities for a specific classroom. Some younger children will be able to participate successfully in activities that are generally more appropriate for the older child. The divisions are, nevertheless, carefully made in terms of children's experiences with music or their coordination and maturation level.

ACTIVITIES FOR THE YOUNG CHILD

The young child is fascinated by sound, and he will participate eagerly in activities involving instruments. The teacher should help him become acquainted with several types of instruments by adding them to other musical activities. Tuned bells of different types may be added to singing activities. Drums and other percussion instruments will intensify rhythmic activities. Autoharp and piano chords will provide a pleasing harmonic accompaniment, and the child should also be introduced to the melodic possibilities of the piano.

Simple Melody Instruments

Tuned bells provide an effective introduction to instruments in early childhood classrooms. While several types of bell sets are available, a set of resonator bells is the most flexible simple melody instrument with the most pleasing musical sounds. The bells are easy for young children to play because they have larger playing surfaces than other bell sets. They may be used in a variety of ways because each bell is separate.

The following activities will introduce children to resonator bells in an atmosphere of musical discovery that is directly related to the singing program:

Children should learn to sing "I Got a Letter" (page 249) in order to be prepared for the instrumental activities that follow.

The teacher should display the d' and f' bells [1] and tell the class that they will be able to play the "Oh yes" patterns on these two bells.

Each child should have the opportunity to find and play these tones. Children may sing the song repeatedly, substituting original words that they have made up for this melody, while each child plays the discovered bell tones. The teacher may decide to continue this activity on succeeding days instead of providing a turn for each child during one music period.

Related Activities: Children will enjoy discovering other song patterns in a similar manner. As they find two-tone patterns in the following songs, they will also improve in their ability to sing:

"Who's That?" c'-g' (page 251)
"I See a Girl," g'-c' (page 255)
"Three Pirates," c'-f' (page 277)

The child may gradually add other song patterns. He will enjoy activities involving three or more resonator bells. The melody patterns that the teacher selects for the child to find may include a sharp or flat.

The teacher may review a familiar song or introduce a few resonator bells to help the child learn phrases in an unfamiliar song. "Bye O, My Baby" (page 267) is an appropriate choice.

The child will see four bells in sequence. They will include the tones b, c-sharp', d-sharp,' and e'. He will realize that some of these bells may be played in a combination that will reproduce the first phrase of the song.

The teacher will sing the first phrase with the class. The children should then explore the tonal possibilities of the four bells to find the phrase outline.

The child will discover that the e', c-sharp', and b bells may be played to produce the phrase. Each child should be given the opportunity of playing and singing this phrase.

Children will also find that bells may be used as an accompaniment for this lullaby. The bells may be played very softly on these repeated phrases to reflect the quiet mood of this song.

Related Activities: Some children will be interested in finding a harmonic accompaniment to this lullaby by further experimentation with these bells. They will discover that the e' and b bells may be

---

[1] The system used to designate pitches is explained in Chapter 2 (page 17).

used to accompany the song. Children may find similar phrases in other songs they have learned. "Who Built the Ark?" (page 261) has a repeated melody pattern with the same tones.

Time should be devoted to letting each child find other simple song phrases on selected resonator bells. Some time should also be allowed for experimentation with other types of bells. A list of appropriate song patterns is included in the references at the end of this chapter.

Step bells and *chromatic melody bells* are also useful instruments in the classroom music program. Step bells help the child see and hear melodic intervals and patterns more easily than any other musical instrument. The instrument is constructed in a manner that enables the child to conceptualize melodic direction and interval distances with ease.[2] Chromatic melody bells include more tones and are similar to the piano in the arrangement of half steps and whole steps. A set of chromatic bells may be placed and played in a vertical position to help the child see and hear melodic patterns.

The child may learn to play these bells first as a transition from resonator bell performances to later keyboard activities. He may also experiment with these two types of melody bells to develop the following melodic concepts: (1) high-low; (2) ascending-descending; (3) same-different. He will further develop these concepts as the teacher helps him find melodic patterns that express each melodic element that he should learn to conceptualize. The songs for young children in the Appendix provide appropriate examples.

Melody bells may be added to the program in many other ways. These simple melody instruments are an effective addition to the singing program at any stage of the child's vocal development. He will sing *limited-range patterns* more accurately as he finds them on bells and sings at the same time. He will place *upper-range tones* more easily as he plays and sings. Several songs with patterns young children can play are listed at the end of this chapter.

Children may also be introduced to the harmonic element of music as they experiment with tuned bells. Some songs may be harmonized with one chord or a single resonator bell tone. "I Got a Letter" (page 249) is an example. The entire song may be harmonized with the d' bell. The child will discover this as he participates in these activities:

Children should take turns accompanying this song. They may decide to play just the d' bell tone. They may, instead, combine the d', f', and a' bells to provide a chordal accompaniment to the song.

---

[2] Some teachers build a step-like platform for resonator bells. By using this platform they can show children the distance between tones and the rise and fall of melody patterns. The platform is quite flexible for classroom use, since resonator bells may be replaced with others at any time a different pattern of bell tones is needed.

Three children may play this accompaniment together, each performing on one of the three bells.

Related Activities: The teacher may decide at this point to present the autoharp as an instrument for the child to play. At first the teacher may press the Dm button while each child strums the strings to produce the chord sound. Later, children may play the instrument without aid from adults. Preschool children are seldom able to select the chords and strum at the same time. Many children in the primary grades *will* be able to play a complete accompaniment. The child may find the three bell tones on the piano. The teacher will help three children find the d', f', and a' tones on the piano and later give other trios of children an opportunity to play these tones together as a harmonic accompaniment for "I Got a Letter."

Instruments with Harmonic Possibilities

The *autoharp* may be presented at this point as an instrument for children to play. Since the child has sung with autoharp accompaniment, he will enjoy exploring the musical possibilities of this simple instrument. He will also find that many of his favorite songs may be harmonized by alternating just two chord buttons. The following songs from the Appendix are examples (other appropriate songs are listed at the end of this chapter):

"Hop, Old Squirrel" (page 247)—D—A₇[3] "Who's That?" (page 251)—C—G₇ "Sandy Land" (page 269)—F—C₇.

The teacher may also introduce the child to the *piano,* an instrument with even greater melodic and harmonic possibilities. Any child in an early childhood classroom will find that melodic elements are exciting discoveries on the piano keyboard. Young children enjoy transferring to the piano keyboard the melodic patterns and the harmonic accompaniments they have discovered. They will have little trouble playing melody patterns at the piano, but they will need assistance from the teacher as they find chords. The following activities will help them make a transition from bell or autoharp accompaniments to the playing of chords on a piano keyboard:

The melody of "See That Rabbit" (Example 8–1) provides a simple introduction to piano chording, since it may be harmonized effectively with a single chord. Children should learn to sing this simple song before they proceed with the following activities.

The teacher will accompany singing with the e' and b' tones on the piano after children are able to sing the melody.

Children will then take turns finding these tones at the keyboard and

---

[3] The autoharp chords in this chapter are selected from the harmonic combinations of the Educators Model 15 Bar Autoharp.

Example 8–1

SEE THAT RABBIT⁴

American Folk Song

See that rab - bit, Oh yes!   See that rab - bit, Oh yes!

Eat - ing let–tuce, Oh yes!   Eat - ing let–tuce, Oh yes!

accompanying the class while they sing the melody again. The
teacher may decide to have younger children play a single tone at
first and choose pairs to play as the others sing. Older children
in early childhood classrooms will be able to play both tones with
ease.

Related Activities: Other songs may also be harmonized with a single
chord. "I Got a Letter" (page 249) and "Going Down to Cairo"
(page 283) are examples from the Appendix.

Expressive Qualities of Instruments

Young children should also become acquainted with the sounds of
rhythm or percussion instruments. Activities involving some of these
instruments have been discussed in other chapters as devices to help
the child develop rhythmic sensitivity and as a way to heighten the
child's listening ability as he learns to identify instruments. A varied
selection of percussion instruments will also help children become
aware of the ways in which simple orchestrations will heighten the expressive qualities of music.

Children should learn to explore the tonal possibilities of various
types of percussion instruments. They should play several different
drums and other frequently used instruments. They should also become acquainted with the varied timbres of tambourines, sand blocks,
and an assortment of instruments characteristic of Latin-American
music.

⁴ From *Discovering Music Together—Early Childhood* by Robert B. Smith and
Charles Leonhard. Copyright © 1968 by Follett Educational Corporation. Reprinted
by permission of the publisher. Adapted from Archive of Folk Song recording 3015
A2 ("Lucy Rabbit"), courtesy of The Library of Congress.

The child will enjoy activities that involve selecting one or more of these instruments to intensify the expressive qualities of a song. The following activities will serve as an effective introduction to the understanding of tone color and orchestration:

> Children will have learned to sing the delightful folk song, "When the Train Comes Along (page 281). The teacher may review this song and suggest that children find instruments that provide appropriate tone colors.
>
> A varied selection of instruments should be available as the child begins to experiment with different sounds to discover which instruments will convey the musical effect of the song.
>
> Children will often select sand blocks as an appropriate instrument with which to accompany the song. The teacher may suggest that they try to find another instrument which may be added as the song becomes louder. (Suggestions for performing this song as a *patrol* are included on page 280). Guiros, Spanish cabazas, shakers, or maracas may be chosen. Children will learn a great deal about basic tone-color effects as they participate in these activities. They will also thoroughly enjoy themselves.
>
> *Related Activities:* This orchestration activity with percussion instruments may be expanded to include other instruments the child has learned to play. Tuned bells may be added to play the train-whistle introduction to this song. Children will discover that the accompaniment for the first eight measures is easy to play on the piano. The entire song may be harmonized with two autoharp chords (G and D). Children will listen attentively as they discover the interesting ways a contemporary composer has orchestrated a similar musical theme and mood. They should have the opportunity to hear "The Little Train of the Caipira" from Villa-Lobos' *Bachianas Brasileiras No. 2* (AIM–III–1; BOL #64).

These activities are a few of the many possible ways in which teachers may add instruments to the music program for younger children. A variety of instruments the young child plays without difficulty will help him become more aware of melodic, rhythmic, harmonic, and expressive facets of the music program.

ACTIVITIES FOR THE OLDER CHILD

Older children should also have many opportunities to explore the tonal possibilities of several types of instruments. They will be able to play the instruments described above in more complicated and varied ways. They will also be able to play other instruments that are frustrating to the younger child.

Autoharp

The autoharp is one instrument the older child may use daily to accompany singing activities. He has become acquainted with this instrument as a younger child. The teacher has accompanied many songs with the autoharp, and the child has explored its tonal possibilities and produced a few simple harmonic effects.

The older child has the coordination and sufficient musical experience to play more complicated accompaniments. He will become increasingly aware of harmonic tendencies as he adds the IV chord and secondary chords to his repertoire.

The child will become aware of the ways in which added chords provide a richer and more appropriate harmonic setting as he participates in activities of this type:

> The teacher will have presented the song "Kum Ba Yah" (page 293) as a singing activity. The child may learn to harmonize this song with two autoharp chords in a simple, yet effective manner.

> The child will understand first that two chords may be used to harmonize this melody. He may have previously discovered chord roots in this key, and the teacher will explain that the F chord in this key represents the I chord and that C_7 is the V_7 chord. The child will find the following harmonization after the teacher tells him that a single chord may be used to harmonize practically every measure:

```
        F                    F            F                         C7
Kum ba | yah, my Lord, Kum ba | yah!   Kum ba | yah, my Lord, Kum ba | yah!

        F                    F            F   (C7)         F
Kum ba | yah, my Lord, Kum ba | yah!   Oh, | Lord, Kum ba | yah! ‖
```

> The teacher will introduce the B-flat (IV) chord at this point. Children should then experiment to discover the places where this chord is a more effective harmonic accompaniment. They will find that the B-flat chord is an appropriate accompaniment for d" and b-flat' in this song:

Kum ba yah, my Lord, Kum ba yah!   Kum ba yah, my Lord, Kum ba yah!

Related Activities: The child will enjoy creating a harmonic accompaniment for "Sarasponda" (page 309) in a similar manner. The song may be harmonized with the C (I) and G₇ (V₇) chords in C Major. The IV chord (F) is much more appropriate, however, as an accompaniment to portions of measures five and six. Children should have many other opportunities to harmonize songs with the primary chords in several keys. Songs that may be harmonized with these three basic chords are listed at the end of the chapter.

A recent autoharp model offers many harmonic possibilities that were not previously available with this useful instrument. The Educators Model 15 Bar Autoharp has an expanded system of chords. Teachers and children will be able to accompany songs in the following keys:

Major keys—C, F, G, B flat, D, E flat
Minor keys—A, D, G

The B-flat bar may be used as a V₇ chord in the key of E flat. The autoharp chords suggested in this chapter are based on the harmonic possibilities of this improved model. The additional keys will be extremely useful in the classroom. Many secondary chord substitutions are also possible.

Older children will be able to find and perform more complex autoharp accompaniments. They may discover the rich harmonic possibilities of secondary chords [5] as they participate in these activities:

The child should learn to sing "I Love the Mountains" (page 303). He should recognize some harmonic elements in this song as he sings his part in a round and performs the final phrase as a chant while the other children sing the melody.

He should learn to accompany this song by selecting the three primary chords in this key to accompany certain phrase sections. He will discover that the following chord sequence may be used to accompany each phrase in this song:

F   Bb | C7   C7
I love the moun-tains. | I love the roll-ing hills. |

F   Bb | C7   C7
I love the foun-tains. | I love the daf-fo-dils. |

The teacher may then introduce secondary chords. The child should listen to several secondary chords in the key of F major, later experimenting with these chords to discover which is appropriate

[5] Primary and secondary chords are defined in the Glossary under *harmony.*

for accompanying a portion of this melody. He will find that the
II Chord (G Minor) is an effective addition to the harmonic accompaniment:

F   B♭   Gm   C7
I love the moun-tains. │ I love the roll-ing hills. │

He may also discover, if the teacher isolates the third round entrance,
that another secondary chord will be more appropriate than the IV
chord (B-flat) for accompanying the entire song. The third phrase
is composed of the following tones:

F   (Dm)   Gm   C7
I   love   the fire - side   when ___   the lights are low,

The tones that accompany the word "Fireside" suggest a secondary
chord which is also an appropriate accompaniment for "mountains"
and "fountains." The VI chord (D Minor) is an effective substitution for the B-flat chord:

F   Dm   Gm   C7
I love the fire–side │ when the lights are low. │

The child should become aware of these harmonic possibilities and
study the autoharp accompaniments suggested in the basic series books.
He will discover that secondary chords are frequently added to accompany the songs he sings.

Piano

The piano is appropriate for a variety of melodic and harmonic
instrumental activities. The older child will learn to play familiar
melodies easily if he is introduced first to the black keys of the piano
and learns to play pentatonic melodies.

The teacher may introduce these activities by having children find
three-tone songs they learned in early childhood classrooms. "Hop,
Old Squirrel" (page 247) is a song that may be played on three adjacent black keys.

The child will also enjoy finding two- or three-note chants or des-

cants to familiar melodies. "Swing Low, Sweet Chariot" is a pentatonic song that may be accompanied in this simple manner. The child
will enjoy his introduction to keyboard experiences as he discovers and
plays one of the following added parts while other children sing this
familiar spiritual: [6]

Children will also discover that a few songs may be played in one
of two positions combining the groupings of two and three black keys.
Songs in the first position may be played and sung easily by any child:

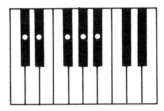

Songs in the second position are equally easy to play. They will often
be more difficult for many children to sing:

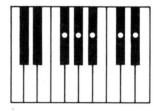

Many song melodies may be played on the black keys of the piano
by combining the above positions. "There Was a Shepherdess" ("*Il
était une bergère*," Example 8–2) is one example. Older children will

[6] From *Discovering Music Together,* Book 4, © 1966 Follett Publishing Company.
Used by permission.

Example 8–2

THERE WAS A SHEPHERDESS

There was   a shep-herd - ess___ ,   Who played her drum, rum, tum, tum, tum, tum,

There was   a shep - herd - ess___ ,   Who watched her sheep and drummed, tum, tum,

Who   watched her sheep and   drummed .

discover how simple this song is to play on black keys as they analyze
it and practice it in this manner:

Children should learn to sing this song first. They should then understand that most of the song may be played in the first position
and that some of the song is higher, requiring the second black-
key position.

The teacher may introduce the actual playing of the song by suggesting that the child find the "rum, tum, tum, tum, tum" pattern first.
He will find the pattern without difficulty after he has been shown
the two adjacent black keys.

He should then discover two identical patterns in the first position.
He will find that measures one and two, and measures five and
six may be played in this position.

The child will then play the first six measures several times, combining
the phrases he has learned to play in the proper order.

The final phrase requires the second black-key position. Children may
sing this phrase and then discover the note sequence that is
necessary in order to play measures seven through ten. The child
will find that the top key in this position is not necessary as he
plays this phrase.

Each child should have several opportunities to play the complete
melody. Several children may perform at the piano at the same
time while others finger the phrases on practice keyboards or on the
keyboards included in some basic series books.

Children should also learn to play this melody on adjacent white keys.
The teacher may suggest first that the song be played on the white
keys to the left of the black key positions. The child must be
aware of the fact that several keys are not to be played as he trans-

fers the melody to this new position. He will not play e′ as he finds the first six measures in this new position. He will not play b′ in the higher position. He should also learn to play the song on the white-key combinations to the right of the black-key positions. The teacher may explain the principles of transposition after these playing activities have been completed. Children will discover that they have played this song in three different keys and will begin to understand how melodies are transposed to different keys.

Many songs may be played on the black keys of the piano. Other examples are listed at the end of this chapter.

Older children should also learn to play harmonic accompaniments on the piano keyboard. Some children may have learned to play a few simple chords in primary-grade classrooms. They should also have learned to harmonize as they participated in the autoharp activities described above. Piano harmonization should be introduced with a few simple activities, such as those described on page 168. After successful practice in accompanying a song with a single chord, children will want to continue this type of activity. They should experiment with ways to accompany songs that require the alternation of two or more chords.

"Tirra-lirra-lirra" (page 339) may be harmonized with two basic chords in the key of C Major. The child should easily hear the harmonic changes as he learns the following chords and harmonizes this song at the keyboard:

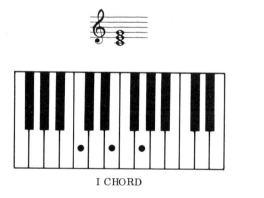

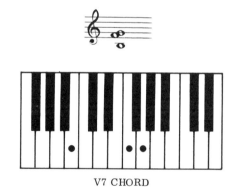

I CHORD   V7 CHORD

Tirra-lirra-lirra, | spring is here, | All the birds are singing |
I   I | I   V7 | V7   V7 |

loud and clear, | I would like to join them | with my song, |
V7   I | I   I | I   V7 |

Tirra-lirra-lirra, | all day long. ‖
V7   V7 | V7   I

Many songs in this text may be harmonized with two piano chords. Examples are listed at the end of the chapter. The teacher will also find appropriate examples in basic series books.

The teacher may introduce other chords at the keyboard. Children will enjoy selecting chords to harmonize "There Was a Shepherdess" in F Major.

> These activities may be preceded by harmonizing this song with the autoharp, since the child is already familiar with the harmonic possibilities of this simple instrument. He will discover that this song may be harmonized with the F (I), B-flat (IV), and C₇ (V₇) chords.

> The teacher may then show how these chords are related to the key of F Major and to the F-Major scale. The class should understand that these are the basic or *primary* chords in this key:

> They will then see these chords in a simplified version and find them on the piano keyboard:

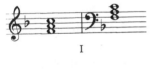

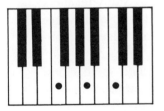

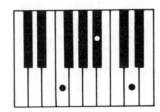

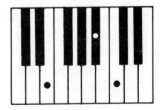

> Children will easily find these chords as they play a harmonic accompaniment while other children sing or play the melody of this French folk song.

> Many other songs may be harmonized with these same three chords. Examples may be found at the end of this chapter and in all basic series books.

The child should also learn to play basic chord patterns in other keys. He should become familiar with the I, IV, and V_7 chords in C, D, and G Major, and in other keys as well if time permits. He should, in each case, understand the harmonic relationship of these chords to the key in which he is finding and playing them. He will find that the pattern he has discovered may be easily transferred to these other keys.

Related Activities: Some children will become intensely interested in this activity. They will enjoy playing the melody and the chord accompaniment together. This type of coordination requires more time than is available in many classrooms. The child will practice at other times and pursue this combined activity through individual study and practice. Children who learn to play both the melody and the accompaniment may enjoy serving as accompanist while the class sings familiar songs. This type of activity should be encouraged as much as possible.

Small Wind Instruments

Small winds are extremely useful instruments for classroom instruction. The recorder has the widest range and the most pleasant tone quality. It is also the most difficult of the small winds to play, and it is more expensive than those instruments that have been developed to introduce children to the basic techniques required to play wind instruments. The modern small wind instruments (e.g., the tonette, song flute, and flutophone) do not have the tone quality and flexibility of the recorder. They are, however, easier to play and are often used for group instruction in classrooms with older children.

Teachers who have had experience playing the recorder should consider selecting this instrument for group instruction. Many teachers will introduce one of the other small winds instead because they are easier to play and the child will more quickly develop playing technique.

The teaching suggestions that follow may be applied in teaching children to play any of the small winds. They are as appropriate for the recorder as they are for any simplified plastic or metal substitute.

The class should begin to play small wind instruments by practicing left-hand fingerings. The melody "Winter, Goodby" (Example 8–3) provides an ideal introduction to left-hand fingerings.

The child should first learn to play the three tones that comprise the first four measures of this song. The tones are fingered in the following way on all small winds:

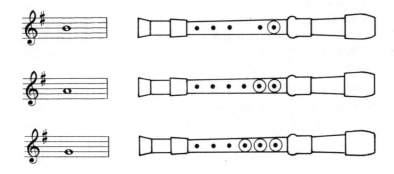

The thumb hole must also be covered on the recorder and other small winds as the child plays these tones.

The child should practice fingering these tones in sequence several times without attempting to play the instrument. He will have previously experimented with fingering and playing each of these tones.

He will then practice playing this first phrase. The teacher will indicate the tempo of the performance by conducting or by tapping out the meter.

The child will then scan the notation to discover these familiar tones in other song phrases. He will find several phrases in which

Example 8–3

WINTER, GOODBY!

they appear again and will see that the final phrase is composed entirely of these three tones.

The child should be helped to discover the fingering for the other two tones in this song. The teacher will introduce the fingering chart for the instrument that has been selected, and the child will practice c″ and d″ before he attempts to play those phrases that require the two additional tones.

The teacher then will have the child practice and play measures 9 through 12. These measures should be introduced next because the child will play the added tones easily and then return to the three tones he has previously played in the same sequence. The same procedure should be followed. First the child should finger the tones in the new phrase as he names the notes. He should then play the phrase.

Measures 5 through 8 should be practiced in a similar manner. The playing of these phrases should be delayed because more complicated fingering changes are required.

The entire song should be practiced in the order in which the phrases appear. The song should be practiced first as a finger drill. Then the child should play the entire melody.

The learning sequence described should be followed as the child learns to play other new tones on a small wind. He should learn each tone in the following manner and then add it to a phrase:

He will discover the fingering for the new tone on the fingering chart that accompanies each small wind instrument.

He will practice playing the new tone until he produces the correct sound.

He will practice the new fingering together with familiar fingerings as he names notes but does not play.

He will then play the phrase with the new tone.

Children should play several other melodies involving familiar tones before they are faced with a new learning and playing problem to solve. They will enjoy playing harmonic accompaniments on small winds. "Winter, Goodby!" may be harmonized in a very simple manner as children participate in these playing activities:

Children should be introduced to the harmonic possibilities of small winds by learning to play simple two-part chords. They may learn to play the simple forms of the I and the V_7 chords in G Major by playing both parts of the following chords:

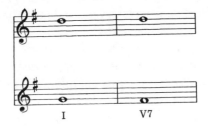

The teacher will then suggest that these chords be played to harmonize the melody of "Winter, Goodby!" Children will find one chord that may be used to harmonize each measure. The chords are indicated below the notation for this song (page 179).

The children should then be ready to find a more complicated accompaniment. The V_7 chord is appropriate on the third metrical pulse of some measures:

They will also enjoy playing chords in three parts after they have participated in some or all of the above activities. The I and V_7 chords in G Major sound more complete if they are played in the following manner:

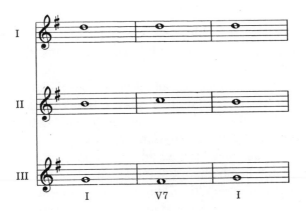

Children should play the melody and harmony together after they have learned to play two- or three-part chord accompaniments. The class may be divided into three or four groups for this activity. Every child should have several opportunities to play the melody as well as each harmonic part.

The child begins to acquire facility on an instrument and to become aware of the possibilities of more complicated melody instruments as he participates in small-wind playing activities. His knowledge and ability in other areas of music are also reinforced. Small-wind playing activities will transfer to other parts of the music program in several ways:

> Children often learn to sing more accurately as they see and feel intervals between tones. The older child who has had little singing experience as a younger child will often sing much better after he has learned to play a small wind instrument.

> Children learn to read notation easily as they develop small-wind playing facility. They must read melodic and rhythmic notation symbols if they are to play melody notes and rhythmic patterns correctly. There is a direct transfer between this type of reading practice and other classroom music reading activities.

> Many children will be motivated to study other instruments after they have successfully learned to play a small wind instrument. Woodwind instruments will be quite interesting to the child at this time. He will also have developed a general interest in instrumental instruction and should be helped to decide which of several instruments he may study through class instruction.

Percussion Instruments

While older children will enjoy playing percussion instruments as much as the child in an early childhood classroom, they should not continue to play them on the same level. Percussion instruments may be used for many challenging activities in the classroom. The older child has sufficient coordination to play subtle rhythmic effects. He will be delighted with his ability to maintain one rhythmic pattern as other children play different rhythmic effects.

Latin American songs are highly rhythmic, and their rhythmic patterns may be heightened by instrumental accompaniments that will challenge the older child. "Tinga Layo" is an example with strong repeated rhythms. Several versions of this song may be found in the basic series books. The rhythmic pattern of this song consists of several contrasting rhythmic phrases:

One syncopated pattern is repeated throughout the song. This pattern will often be selected by children as an appropriate accompaniment to play a percussion instrument:

Other patterns may also be selected. The following are equally appropriate:

Children should learn to sing the song first and then listen carefully in order to select those patterns that will provide an appropriate accompaniment. They should also decide which instruments should be used to play each pattern. A Latin American song generally has rather complicated syncopated patterns. Several types of instruments playing one pattern may obscure the rhythmic pulse. The child will discover this and often decide that one type of instrument should be selected for a specific accompaniment pattern.

The following instruments are examples of the many Latin American instruments suitable for these activities:

maracas	shakers
bongo drums	conga drums
guiros	claves

Older children will discover that they can create rhythmic accompaniments for other songs in a similar fashion. They will enjoy solving some of the problems involved in selecting instruments to accompany songs that represent different ethnic cultures. Suggestions are included in the basic music series.

Expressive Possibilities

Children who have learned to play the various instruments described in this section should continue to play them during classroom music activities and should gradually become aware of the expressive possibilities of each instrument.

The autoharp has expressive as well as harmonic possibilities. The child will find that sweeping glissandos are possible and that the instrument may be played in several other ways as well. Children may strum softly, strike percussively, or use soft mallets to produce still other expressive sounds.

The piano has an even larger range of expressive tonal possibilities. It is an instrument upon which the child may produce practically any tone-color effect that is possible on other instruments. Piano accompaniments may be varied in several expressive ways. Simple chords may be transformed into an accompaniment appropriate to the mood of a song as the child softly arpeggiates chords to accompany a lullaby or arranges chord tones in patterns to heighten the mood of another song. A simple chord accompaniment may become more interesting as the syncopated patterns of a calypso song are added.

The small wind instruments are more limited in terms of their expressive possibilities because they must be played with uniform breathing to produce accurate tones. Extreme contrasts of loudness and softness are therefore impossible to produce. Small winds may be played in an expressive manner, however, as the child becomes aware of the importance of phrasing and legato-staccato effects. These instruments may be added to the vocal program in a variety of ways. Children may play melodies and harmonic parts as others sing; they may harmonize the melody to accompany singing; and they may add introductions, codas, and other effects. Small winds may also be used effectively in listening activities. Children should learn to play themes that are within their level of playing ability before they identify the theme in a recording. As they compare their performance with the recorded version, they will become more conscious of the expressive effects professional musicians can produce after years of study.

Percussion instruments are so varied in the sounds they produce that the child will discover many expressive possibilities as he experiments with different percussion timbres. A single instrument may be played in different ways to produce a variety of expressive effects. A drum produces one sound when it is played near the rim and quite a different sound when the center of the head is struck. Different types of mallets and different ways of hitting the drum head with the hand produce still other effects. As the child acquires skill in playing percussion instruments, he will discover that each instrument has several tone-color possibilities.

SUMMARY

Activities involving instruments will add an important musical dimension to the child's music education. Children of any age quickly discover that instruments add excitement to the music program, and their experiences with instruments help them develop performance skills and acquire a deeper understanding of musical elements.

Instrumental activities will affect the musical development of children in early childhood classrooms in several different ways. Young children will often sing more accurately as they find melodic patterns on bells or at the piano keyboard. They become more aware of harmonic elements as they play simple accompaniments on bells or on the autoharp. Their understanding of tone color and expressive qualities of music are heightened as they experiment with varied rhythm instruments.

Older children will respond with equal enthusiasm to instrumental activities, and experiences with instruments will be reflected in their musical growth. The older child can successfully complete activities that are too difficult for most children in early childhood classrooms. He will develop harmonic competency, performance skills, and facility with the expressive elements of music as he participates in selected activities with a variety of instruments.

Classroom activities involving instruments should not be considered a separate part of the music program. Instruments ranging from tom-toms to the recorder will make a significant contribution to the child's music education.

QUESTIONS AND PROJECTS

1. Analyze a primary-grade basic series book and list those songs that may be accompanied by one or two chords. Arrange the songs in an approximate order of difficulty, considering the sequence in terms of helping children learn to play simple harmonic accompaniments.
2. Find two- and three-tone patterns in songs appropriate for either early childhood groups or for older children. Develop a lesson plan for introducing these patterns as a means of helping children learn to play simple melody instruments.
3. Select a pentatonic song and create short patterns that may be repeated as an accompaniment. Play these accompaniments on bells or at the piano (perhaps with the assistance of several others) while the class sings.
4. Acquire basic playing skill on a small wind instrument. Choose the recorder, if possible, since a large repertoire of solo and ensemble literature is available for this instrument.
5. Compare the teaching approaches of two instruction books (several methods books are available for the autoharp and for the small wind instruments). Select those teaching approaches that seem appropriate for intermediate-grade children and arrange them in an appropriate sequence.
6. Assume that you will teach in an elementary school in which no instruments are available. How would this lack of equipment affect the overall musical development of children? What procedures would you use to overcome this handicap?
7. Discuss in class the ideal relationship between instrumental activities in the general music program and those that introduce children to band or orchestra instruments through specialized programs. Invite a specialist in instrumental music to serve as a resource person for this discussion if possible.

REFERENCES

Classroom Instruments

Suppliers of the commonly used classroom instruments are listed at the end of Chapter 4. The following firms are somewhat more specialized:

Harmolin, Inc., La Jolla, Calif. (resonator bells, melody and harmony stringed instruments for the young child)
Jensen Manufacturing Div., The Muter Co., Chicago, Ill. (soprano recorders and instructional material)
George Kelischek Workshop, Atlanta, Ga. (recorders, ancient instruments, Orff instruments)
B. F. Kitching & Co., Inc., La Grange, Ill. (mallet-played instruments)
Magnamusic-Baton, Inc., St. Louis, Mo. (Orff instruments)
Magnamusic Distributors, Inc., Sharon, Conn. (Orff instruments)

Bell and Piano Melody Patterns

Two-tone patterns

"I Got a Letter" (page 249)   "Little Bird" (page 257)
"Who's That?" (page 251)   "Three Pirates" (page 277)
"I See a Girl" (page 255)   "Riding in a Buggy" (page 279)

Three-tone patterns

"Who Built the Ark?" (page 261)
"Sing with Me" (page 253)
"Bye O, My Baby" (page 267)

"Hoosen Johnny" (page 273)
"Going Down to Cairo" (page 283)
"Eliza Jane" (page 343)

Upper-range patterns

"Sandy Land" (page 269)
"Going to Boston" (page 271)
"Hoosen Johnny" (page 273)

"When the Train Comes Along"
  (page 281)
"Going Down to Cairo" (page 283)
"Eliza Jane" (page 343)

Autoharp and Piano Harmonizations

One chord

"I Got a Letter" (page 249)
"Going Down to Cairo" (page 283)
"The Lone Star Trail" [7]

"Frère Jacques" ("Are You
  Sleeping")
"Canoe Song"

Two chords

"Hop, Old Squirrel" (page 247)
"Who's That?" (page 251)
"I See a Girl" (page 255)
"Little Bird" (page 257)
"Sandy Land" (page 269)
"Going to Boston" (page 271)
"Savez vous?" (page 275)

"Going Down to Cairo" (page 283)
"Blow the Winds Southerly"
  (page 285)
"Kum Ba Yah" (page 293)
"Deaf Woman's Courtship"
  (page 311)
"Tirra-lirra-lirra" (page 339)

Three chords

"Sing With Me" (page 253)
"It Rained a Mist" (page 259)
"Hoosen Johnny" (page 273)
"Riding in a Buggy" (page 279)
"When the Train Comes Along"
  (page 281)

"Kum Ba Yah" (page 293)
"Masters in This Hall" (page 295)
"Sarasponda" (page 309)
"Hush, My Babe" (page 318)

Pentatonic Songs

(The songs are listed in approximate order of their difficulty as piano compositions.)

"Hop, Old Spirrel" (page 247)
"I Got a Letter" (page 249)
"See That Rabbit" (page 169)

"There Was a Shepherdess (Il etait
  une bergère") (page 175)

The following pentatonic songs are included frequently in basic series song collections:

"Old Dan Tucker"
"Cotton-Eye Joe"
"Willow-Bee"
"Goodbye, Old Paint"
"Toodala"

"The Farmer in the Dell"
"Scotland's Burning"
"Mary Had a Baby"
"Little David, Play on Your Harp"
"Swing Low, Sweet Chariot"

[7] Songs without page numbers are included in several of the basic series books.

9

THE CREATIVE MUSIC PROGRAM

The title of this chapter should not lead to the conclusion that creative approaches to music teaching are confined to these pages alone. The program described in earlier chapters of this text contains a constant creative element. The many teaching suggestions included in descriptions of singing, moving, playing, and listening situations emphasize flexibility at all times on the teacher's part and a creative use of music by children. Creative uses of music are therefore not presented as a separate facet of the total music program. Instead, creativity should permeate any situation involving music in the classroom.

Some teachers consider creativity to be a term implying an original creation. A definition of this sort is seldom applicable in the classroom, since the child bases his creative uses of music upon his past experiences. The definition is equally inadequate when it is applied to the many art works that are a part of our aesthetic heritage. Most works of art are based in part upon the discoveries and techniques of other artists. Few artists have ever developed a completely new style of artistic creation.

The definition of creativity implied in other parts of this text and emphasized in this chapter is quite different. Creativity is not a unique and distinct part of the music program, and the child does not have to create something completely original to be involved in a creative experience. The child is making a creative contribution and undergoing a creative experience whenever he uses familiar musical elements in a different manner. Creative activities in the classroom may also be defined as problem solving which is completed in an extremely musical way. The younger child is involved in the solution of a musical problem as he finds a simple accompaniment for a song. The older child is equally involved in problem solving through creative activities as he writes an original melody in rhythmic and melodic notation.

Young children should be involved in a variety of creative uses of music each day as they participate in the music program. The young child experiences music in a creative manner as he suggests new words for a song, moves expressively, or finds a simple accompaniment on melody bells. The older child will also find many creative ways to use his developing musical skills and his knowledge about music. Spontaneous creativity is less often found in classrooms with older children, possibly because the child's imagination, curiosity, inventiveness, and critical thinking are not sufficiently challenged by a flexible and diversified program.

The preschool child who has spontaneously created a new text for a familiar song is as creative for his level of musical growth as is the older child who has composed an original melody for voices or instruments. The teacher should challenge every child to discover more ways to combine musical elements in a creative manner. The door to the creative uses of music should always be open during the classroom music program: the child should continually find new ways to use his musical skills, concepts, and understanding in a creative way.

Teachers should always emphasize the creative *process* rather than the creative *product*. Songs that are "manufactured" as a class activity are not necessarily creative; they are often as much a result of teacher direction as they are the result of original ideas from children. A group activity emphasizing creative ways to manipulate music is therefore an activity stressing the creative process.

The creative product itself is dependent upon the way individual children make use of these techniques they have discovered together with other children. Some children will show great interest in combining musical elements in an original way, while others will exhibit more interest in other parts of the music program.

Every child should have experiences with the creative process. Recent experiments with contemporary music at the elementary school level have shown that young children become absorbed in simple composing techniques. (Sources that describe these experiments are listed at the end of this chapter.) The experiments have been concerned exclusively with creativity in relation to understanding trends in contemporary music. Children will be equally interested in discovering ways to "make music" in other musical styles as well.

Creativity in the music program should always be thought of as an integral part of both the teacher's presentation and the child's participation. The creative teacher will develop a classroom atmosphere that will help every child develop his creative capacities.

CREATIVE ACTIVITIES FOR THE YOUNG CHILD

Young children make creative responses as soon as they encounter the delightful sounds of music. The child often chants unconsciously as he plays or works. He responds spontaneously with his body as he hears exciting rhythmic patterns, and he is eager to experiment with any interesting sound. Little guidance is needed as teachers first provide opportunities for children in early childhood classrooms to experiment with music. Every child will participate eagerly as singing, movement, and other activities are presented in a flexible manner.

There are some differences in the abilities of preschool and primary-grade children as they become involved in creative activities. The nursery-school or kindergarten child has limitations in his creative uses of music. He does not have the physical coordination of older children and is therefore limited in the extent to which he can use musical elements in an original manner as he plays simple classroom instruments. He is equally hampered in his coordination as he creates expressive movement responses. His level of vocabulary development will often lead him to make simple word substitutions rather than those involving longer phrases.

The preschool child also has one distinct advantage over older children as he is introduced to the creative uses of music. He has boundless enthusiasm for new activities involving exciting sounds and will often make a spontaneous response as soon as an activity is presented. The atmosphere of many preschool classrooms is also a great help to the teacher who is encouraging creative responses. Many other activities during the school day have a similar focus, and the general "play" atmosphere provides an appropriate setting.

The teacher in a preschool classroom may often stimulate creative responses most effectively by simply being alert to children's unconscious responses to activities. The child will begin to develop his creative potential as the teacher helps him realize that he is "making music" through calling attention to his responses and thus reinforcing them.

The primary-grade child will need more careful and thoughtful assistance to stimulate his creative use of musical elements. His environment may be less appropriate for chanting and other spontaneous responses than the preschool classroom with its larger percentage of free play time.

The primary-grade teacher, and many teachers of younger children as well, may introduce creativity during the music period by reminding children of the ways they use music while playing. Children often chant and use vocal calls as they play. The teacher who listens carefully will hear examples that may be recalled during the music period.

Children must become conscious of this aspect of music if they are to realize their creative potential. Some chant, explore interesting tone colors, and create expressive movement patterns without guidance. Many others do not discover the delights of such activities without assistance from their teacher.

Young children will discover the excitement of using musical elements in a new way by creating:

New words to familiar songs   Expressive movement responses
Original melodies   Music with instruments

All young children will become conscious of the creative possibilities in music as they participate in introductory activities of the types just listed. Primary-grade children should, in addition, have many opportunities to repeat each type of activity and to develop more complex creative responses to music.

Creating New Words to Familiar Songs

The child may be introduced to the creative uses of music in a simple and delightful manner by creating new word-phrases to sing with a familiar melody. His first efforts should be immediately successful and therefore consist of single word substitutions or of very short phrases. Many of the songs in the Appendix are appropriate for this introductory activity. "Riding in a Buggy" (page 279) will provide the child with repeated opportunities to substitute original words for the song text:

The child should learn to sing this delightful song first with the words that accompany the melody.

The teacher may introduce creative word-changes by suggesting that children think of some other way to ride. Children will find that the entire song is transformed as one word is substituted for "buggy."

This simple but satisfying activity may be varied in several ways. Children will also enjoy substituting other names for "Mary Jane." They may designate some other child in the classroom, the teacher, or members of their family.

Creating new words will become slightly more complicated as the child finds a new word-phrase to substitute for "We're a long way from home." Children may have difficulty constructing an appropriate phrase and may need some assistance from the teacher at first.

Many experiences with the creation of word-phrases will lead the child to the point where he creates phrases and sentences with ease.

Other songs may be transformed in this simple manner. Songs in the Appendix that are particularly appropriate for these activities have teaching suggestions emphasizing word-substitution activities.

Children will exhibit great pride in these transformed songs. The song becomes partly the child's own creation, and children often refer to the song with original words as "our song." One nursery-school group felt this way about a new verse two boys created to the melody of "Three Pirates" (page 277). These children retained a few of the original word-phrases but transformed the song entirely with these changes:

Three ghosts came to London Town, Woo-hoo, woo-hoo,
Three ghosts came to London Town, Woo-hoo, woo-hoo,
Three ghosts came to London Town to see the king put on his crown,
Woo-hoo, you spooks,
Woo-hoo, you spooks,
Woo-hoo, woo-hoo, woo-hoo! [1]

The teacher did not initiate this creative activity with words. The children in this preschool group had transformed songs in this manner for several months. One of the two boys simply suggested that it would be fun to sing about "ghosts" rather than "pirates" and sang the first two phrases with this simple change. A second boy suggested the "woo-hoo" substitution, the two children changed the final phrase during free play, and they then completed the song in this way on another day.

These new words involved the class in a problem-solving situation with other musical elements. The children decided they should perform the new words in a different manner and became more aware of the importance of dynamics, tempo, and accent as they developed a different interpretation. The "ghost" words seemed to demand a softer dynamic level, a slower tempo, and more subdued accents.

Many creative word changes that the child volunteers will lead to similar music problem-solving situations. As children find new word combinations describing a different event, a seasonal change, or some other happening, they may need to make musical decisions concerning possible ways to interpret the transformed song.

Creating Melodies

Young children should be encouraged to create original melodies. Chants are often heard as children play and sing in the classroom or on the playground. The most common chant involves the descending

[1] By Rusty and John, members of the four-year-old group, Child Development Laboratory, University of Illinois.

minor third, the ascending perfect fourth, and another descending minor third:

The teacher may begin this activity by reminding children of chants they have sung while playing. The following activities will help the child realize that he has created a short melody and show him possible ways to extend and to complete original melodies:

A chant the teacher has heard on the playground or in the classroom will serve as an introduction to these activities. The perceptive teacher will hear many examples as children play.

The teacher will sing the chant, reminding children that they often sing in this way as they play. After explaining that this is one way to make music, the teacher may compare the chant to other songs the class has learned to sing. Two songs in this text have phrases similar to simple chants the child sings: "Little Bird" (page 257) and "What Shall We Do?" (Chapter 10, page 214).

The child should realize that a chant is the equivalent of one phrase in other songs. He will notice that other phrases in these two songs are similar to the first but repeated in a slightly different way. He will also become aware of the fact that the final phrase in each song is quite different from the chant-like beginning:

a) Little Bird

First phrase–

Final phrase–

b) What Shall We Do?

First phrase–

Final phrase

The teacher may then explain in a simple way how melodies are constructed. Songs the child has sung consist of scale-step motion, chord outlines, or a combination of the two types of melodic motion. The final phrases of these two songs combine chord-outline and scale-step motion.

At this point children should experiment with different ways to find a final phrase for the chant. They may play several examples on melody bells or sing them and then decide which provides an appropriate ending.

The activities will reveal aspects of the creative process to children, since they actually solve a problem involving the extension and completion of a melody phrase. The *product* itself may not be as creative, however, since the teacher has participated in these activities to a large extent. Every child in the classroom will gain a heightened understanding of the way melodies are created. Some children will show through their spontaneous singing that these experiences have helped them create longer and more complete melodies.

This introduction to the creation of melodies may be continued in several ways. The teacher will show that the child's original songs are interesting and appropriate for the class to hear. The class may find them so interesting that they want to sing them.

Other activities will also contribute to every child's understanding of the way melodies are created. The following will provide an interesting and creative problem-solving activity:

An unfamiliar melody may be selected and played or sung without the final phrase. The children will realize first that this is a game and that they are to find a phrase to complete the melody. Songs similar to the following example should be selected for this activity. The melody should sound incomplete without the final phrase:

Children should learn to sing or play this example, or others with similar characteristics. The child may find a final phrase quite easily as he experiments with ways to complete the melody by singing or playing. The teacher may help the class find an ending by placing the following phrases on the board and playing each as a final phrase:

original ending

The teacher should be flexible and permissive as children select an ending for this melody. The fact that the teacher is aware of the actual ending to the song should not be an element in the selection of a final phrase. Children may decide that another ending is equally effective. The decision in this creative process should be made by the children.

Creating Expressive Movement Responses

While some children do not chant or use melodic phrases in a unique manner, all young children *do* respond to exciting sounds with body movement, and their responses should be defined as creative expression through movement. The stages of expressive movment described in Chapter 4 are necessary, however, if the young child is to develop creative responses. Children must learn to use their body in an expressive manner if they are to react creatively to complex musical examples. The child must also acquire a singing and playing vocabulary if he is to make creative responses in these other areas of the music program.

The expressive movement program described in detail in Chapter 4 will provide creativity through movement appropriate for every young child. One additional type of activity may be added if children are intensely interested in creativity through body movement.

Children who show great interest in movement will enjoy creating original dances. They may create their own dances and accompany them with instruments as they participate in the following activities:

The teacher will introduce these activities by explaining to the class that their expressive movement responses are a type of dance. Children may review the many ways they have moved expressively at this point, recalling through movement their vocabulary of foot patterns and arm and body responses.

Children will then explore ways to combine these varied movements. They will show their original movement combinations or dances to the class.

These original dances may be accompanied by instruments. The child who has created the dance may have definite ideas concerning appropriate instruments. This situation often becomes a group problem-solving activity, with the class analyzing the dance patterns to determine which types of instruments will provide an effective accompaniment for different portions of the dance. This creative activity will become an extremely interesting musical experience for both the individual child and the entire group. Each child will use his past experiences with expressive movement in a new and original manner. The class will add a new dimension to their understanding of music as they identify the musical elements the child is expressing through movement and then develop an effective instrumental accompaniment.

This creative movement activity developed in the following way in one classroom:

> The children had experienced music through expressive movement every day for a period of eight months. They had developed a large vocabulary of expressive movement responses and thoroughly enjoyed movement activities.
>
> They were told that the many ways they moved were also a type of dancing and were then asked to create a dance using some of the many ways they had moved.
>
> Many children immediately asked if they might show their dances. A few of the original dances were quite interesting, and the group decided they all wanted to dance "David's dance." The dance was quite simple, consisting of a rhythmic pattern expressed by alternating two hops on one foot with two hops on the other. Each hopping pattern was ended with a twirling motion involving large arm movements.
>
> This dance became a classroom favorite, and instruments were later added as an accompaniment. The class experimented with many instruments to find those that were appropriate for either the hopping section or the twirl. They found that many simple percussion instruments provided an effective accompaniment for the accented hopping. An instrumental accompaniment appropriate for twirling was more difficult to select. Tambourines and maracas were chosen to accompany this portion of the dance.

Creating Music with Instruments

Simple classroom instruments provide an ideal medium for creative experiments with music. The young child loves to play instruments, and he will be eager to join any activity involving instruments.

Many children will enjoy the process of creating melodies on bells and other instruments. The child who may not sing with sufficient confidence to create melody phrases through song will experiment much more readily with instruments. The activities described on pages 191–94 are equally appropriate for creative experiments with simple melody instruments. Every child will enjoy finding chant phrases and final phrases for incomplete melodies on these instruments.

The creative use of simple instruments is suggested in other parts of this text. Several activities described in Chapter 8 will help the child develop creative facility through playing. He will become thoroughly familiar with bells and other simple melody instruments after he participates in the activities described on pages 165–69. His solution of musical problems involving these instruments will easily expand in a creative direction with little guidance. The child will also become aware of the creative possibilities of simple orchestrations after he has completed the activities described on pages 181–83.

The creative possibilities of simple melody instruments are also described in the teaching suggestions accompanying five of the songs included in the Appendix. Each suggested use may be expanded with additional creative possibilities.

Other types of instruments may also be played by the young child in a creative manner. He will discover the basic harmonic possibilities of the autoharp and piano through other activities described in Chapter 8 and in the Appendix. Accompaniments may be developed in an original and expressive manner.

Some children in early childhood classrooms will show an unusual interest in the creative possibilities of music. These children often possess exceptional ability in this area and should be guided as the gifted child is helped in other ways. Several activities described in the following section for older children will be appropriate for this smaller percentage of younger children in a classroom.

Every young child will thoroughly enjoy these activities which emphasize the creative process. The child will expand his musical horizons in many ways as his concepts about music are further developed by his original manipulation of musical elements and materials.

CREATIVE ACTIVITIES FOR THE OLDER CHILD

Creative activities should be an equally important part of music programs planned for the older child. The older child's creative potential is expanded by his increased maturation and by his previous experiences with music. He is capable of accomplishing challenging and satisfying activities involving musical creation.

Teachers of older children must create a flexible atmosphere with a strong element of curiosity and exploration if the child is to continue to develop his creative potential. The teacher need not be a trained musician to develop an appropriate environment. The ideal classroom setting for creative growth simply involves a situation in which the teacher and the class work together to discover the many ways in which musical elements may be manipulated in a flexible manner.

An Introduction to Creativity

Older children who have had many experiences with the creative possibilities of music will continue to show interest in activities with a creative focus.   Children who have not experienced the many flexible possibilities of music should be introduced to this aspect of their music education in an exploratory and interesting manner.

The teacher may introduce creative possibilities in sound by making the child aware of the many sounds in his environment. A project may be developed in which the child is to find tonal possibilities in the surroundings that are a normal part of his home or school life. Teachers will often be amazed at the inventiveness older children display as they complete the following activities:

> The class should begin this creative experiment as an individual search for sound. They will understand that they are to find musical sounds in equipment that they use every day and that their discoveries should be brought to the classroom or described.
>
> A time will be specified for the demonstration of these discoveries. The child may describe the sounds he has found at home or at play. He may also demonstrate the tonal possibilities of the equipment he has explored.
>
> The class will be fascinated by these demonstrations, and they will begin to realize that musical possibilities exist in their surroundings. The following discoveries may emerge from these demonstrations of musical sounds in their environment: (1) Some sounds are primarily melodic. Tones produced on glasses, bottles, and metal that vibrate at a specific pitch are examples. (2) Other sounds are percussive or rhythmic. The possibilities are endless.
>
> The class will discover that some sounds seem to belong together. They will also realize that these tonal discoveries can be combined in a musical way, since there will be strong contrasts of dynamics, tone colors, and other musical elements.
>
> They will experiment with different combinations. The teacher may decide to divide the class into smaller groups for this further exploration and base the division on the types of sounds that have been discovered.
>
> The teacher will find that the older child is often fascinated with this type of activity. A composition may be created by these smaller groups.
>
> A tape recorder should be added to the sequence of activities at this point. Children will delight in performing and then in listening to a tape recording of their discoveries.
>
> This activity may be requested time after time by the class. They will experiment further and find other ways to combine the sounds they have discovered. The extent of these activities will largely depend upon the child's previous experience with musical elements.

The child's interest in exploring and combining sounds in his environment may lead the teacher to suggest further exploration with

musical instruments. Children are well acquainted with the basic
sounds of several instruments they have used in the classroom. They
will be challenged as they are asked to find new sound possibilities on
the piano, autoharp, and other basic instruments.

Creating Songs and Other Melodies

Activities described in other chapters will have provided children
with experiences in the creation of short melodies. These situations
should be continued and expanded as the older child uses his knowledge of music in a creative manner. Teachers will stress the analysis
of familiar songs first as the children show that they are ready to create
a song. Several activities will help the child develop the ability to
compose complete songs:

> The child should be helped to analyze songs of different types to dis-
> cover how composers use melodic elements to create songs. He will
> find that many songs consist of combinations of chord outlines and
> scale-step motion. "Sarasponda," "The Ash Grove," "Tum Balalaika,"
> and "Kum Ba Yah" are a few of the many songs in this text that
> may be analyzed to show the child techniques of composition.

> The teacher may continue the process of introducing the child to the
> creation of an entire song by having him experiment with chord
> outlines in an attempt to find an interesting theme. It is often
> helpful to suggest at first that the child find a theme that sounds
> like a march, a bugle call, or some other thematic idea with which
> he has had experience. The class may then listen to these themes
> and select the most interesting for further development. The
> teacher may introduce the idea of sequence at this point and show
> how some composers repeat a phrase in a slightly different loca-
> tion. "I Love the Mountains" (page 303) and "Die Musici" (page
> 321) are two examples included in this text. A musical form with
> which the child is familiar may be introduced to show ways to ex-
> tend the theme or to provide contrast within a composition. Two-
> or three-part song forms are suitable choices. The child may be
> asked to find a B section featuring scale-step motion to contrast with
> the chord-outline patterns emphasized in the A section.

Poems or short examples of literature may also be used as a prelude
to song composition. The mood of a poem, descriptive words, and the
rhythmic pattern will be helpful to the child as he creates a musical
setting. These activities will help the child create a song:

> Children will select a favorite short poem. They will read the poem
> aloud, discovering the rhythmic pattern underlying the word-
> combinations. They will then find the rhythmic symbols that ex-
> press these patterns.

The poem will then be studied for descriptive words or moods that may be expressed in a musical way. The word-phrases may describe a situation or express contrasts that suggest melodic outlines.

The child should have an opportunity to find his own melody to part or all of the poem. Children will listen to these original melodies and decide which one reflects the feeling of the poem in the most effective manner.

Creating Accompaniments

Older children will find many ways to create harmonic accompaniments as they discover some of the techniques used by composers of different periods. The teacher may help the child become aware of several harmonic possibilities by presenting the following activities:

A theme should be selected as an introduction to these activities. The theme may be one a child has created or a portion of a familiar song. Themes based on the pentatonic scale are ideal for this purpose since they may be harmonized in several different ways. The following pentatonic theme is presented as an example (familiar songs based on the five tones of the pentatonic scale are listed at the end of Chapter 8):

This melody may be played quite easily by either the teacher or the child on the black keys of the piano or on chromatic resonator bells. The black keys immediately to the left of the printed notes provide a simple pentatonic position.

Black Key Position (G♭ Major)

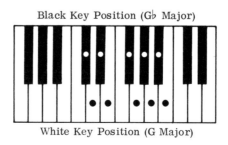

White Key Position (G Major)

The child might discover first the way composers of the classical period often harmonized themes. He will find it easy to play the following accomapniment:

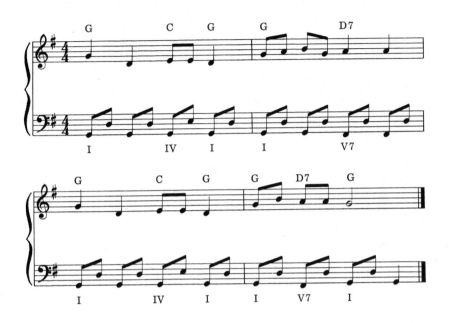

The entire accompaniment, with the exception of one tone, may be played on the black keys of the piano. The lower tone of the simplified V_7 chord will be easy for the child to play since it is immediately to the left of the grouping of three black keys. Few accompaniments of the classical period are as simple as this example. *Alberti bass* accompaniments are slightly more difficult to play but easy for the child to recognize as a harmonic setting characteristic of this period. The class may be divided into pairs

as children experiment with these accompaniments. One child may play the melody while another plays the accompaniment. Some children will enjoy adding accompaniments of this type to other songs. Every child will understand this harmonic style more thoroughly after he has completed these activities. The child will enjoy listening to a recording that features an accompaniment of this type. The "Romanze" movement from *Eine kleine Nacht-musik* by Mozart (AIM–IV–1; MSB 78004) is an appropriate choice.

Children will discover a completely different way to create an accompaniment as they are introduced to some techniques developed by composers of the impressionist school. The use of *pentatonic, whole-tone,* or *chromatic scale* passages will expand the child's creative vocabulary and provide a contrast to accompaniments in a classical style. The child should be introduced to these three different scales before he attempts to create an impressionistic accompaniment:

Pentatonic scale—

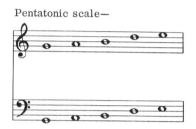

There are many ways to arrange the tones of a pentatonic scale. The example above is one the child will easily find on the black keys of the piano.

Whole-tone scale—

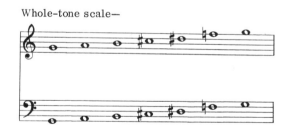

Chromatic scale—

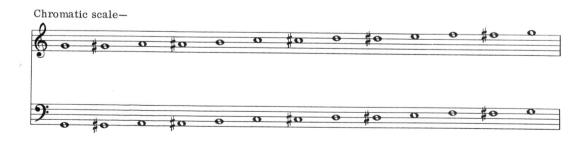

As the child sees and hears these three scales he will find several ways in which they are different from the major and minor diatonic scales he has previously heard. The number of tones within an octave is one obvious difference. The lack of a feeling of tonality is another. None of the three scales seems to be in a specific key. The child should experiment with the accompaniment possibilities of each scale. He may accompany a familiar theme first in a very simple manner by simply repeating a pattern he has selected. The following is one obvious example which may be played on the black keys:

The child will find other fascinating accompaniments as he experiments with these impressionistic techniques of composition. He may add interesting effects by using some additional techniques:

(1) The right pedal of the piano may be used to produce the shimmering sounds often heard in impressionist compositions.

(2) The accompaniment the child has created may be played in different locations on the keyboard. Accompaniments using tones in one of these three scales often sound as appropriate high above the melody as they do when they are played lower than the theme.

(3) Other instruments may be added to the accompaniment. The autoharp may be played without using the chord buttons to produce a sweeping glissando effect which is characteristic of the chromatic scale. Bells may be added to accompaniments to highlight the exotic quality often heard in impressionist works. The child will develop an interest in the sounds of impressionistic music after he has experimented with these tonal possibilities. He will also develop further understanding of creative techniques as he listens to one or more of the compositions included in the *Mother Goose Suite* by Ravel (AIM–IV–2; AIM–V–1; BOL #57; MSB 78013–78014).

Contemporary techniques will interest children as they continue to experiment with ways to create accompaniments. The child will discover another creative possibility with pentatonic effects as he accompanies a melody with *tone clusters*. A simple harmonic effect will result when five black keys are played together.

The accompaniment will be slightly dissonant and yet effective. Children may decide to find different clusters to provide a more varied effect. *Polytonality* is another contemporary technique the child may use to create an accompaniment. He will find dissonance in contemporary music more understandable as he plays a theme in one key and an accompaniment in another. A C-Major accompaniment for a theme played on the black keys will be similar to polytonal effects created by some contemporary composers:

Accompaniments of this type are often more effective if they are separated from the theme by at least an octave. They are fascinating to play and hear if the child adds an Alberti bass effect characteristic of the classical period. The resulting sounds will be quite similar to effects created by contemporary composers who have written compositions in a neoclassic style. Children should have the opportunity to hear one of these works after they have created this type of accompaniment. The *Classical Symphony* by Prokofiev (MSB 78102–78103) is a neoclassic example in which the composer has used polytonal effects.

Children will thoroughly enjoy these creative experiments. They will find it easy to create accompaniments in different styles. They will also learn a great deal about different types of music as they solve these musical problems.

Creating in Several Musical Forms

The older child will be intensely aware of form in music through many activities described in other chapters. He will have learned to identify several song forms described in Chapter 3. He will have experienced varied forms through the expressive movement activities included in Chapter 5. The listening activities in Chapter 7 will have helped him learn to analyze music and to identify formal elements. He will also enjoy creating music in different forms. His creation of songs will involve simple two- and three-part forms. Variation and rondo forms are also appropriate for creative activities.

The teacher may introduce several activities to help the child discover original ways to apply *variation form* to musical composition. The class will begin by creating a simple theme. They will enjoy experimenting with simple melody and rhythm instruments at this point. The theme they select may be performed on melody bells, while rhythm instruments are used to intensify the rhythmic pattern and other familiar instruments are added as a harmonic accompaniment.

The child should then begin to understand the manner in which variations are composed. Several musical elements may be changed to provide variations of a theme. Rhythmic patterns may be changed as a march theme is transformed into a waltz by substituting a pattern in groupings of three for one emphasizing patterns of twos. The melody itself may be changed in many ways. Harmonic changes provide still another variation possibility. A theme in a major key is often transformed completely when it is repeated in a parallel minor key. Children will understand how composers of one period created variations as they listen to a composition from the classical period. The "Andante" movement from the *"Surprise" Symphony* by Haydn (BOL #62; MSB 78042) is an appropriate selection. Haydn's variations of this familiar theme clearly show how musical elements are varied in this musical form.

Rondo form will be equally easy for the child to understand and to use in creating longer compositions. The child may be introduced to this form by recalling a song in ABA form he has created or sung. The teacher may then compare this familiar song with a composition in rondo form or explain that a simple rondo form is similar to ABA form but that at least two sections are added (ABACA is a typical rondo form).

Children may begin to use rondo form by transforming and extending a familiar song. They will create a contrasting C section and end the song with a third performance of the familiar first section. They will then be ready to compose a complete composition in this form, creating two contrasting sections to alternate with the first theme. They will also enjoy reviewing the compositions in this form that are described in Chapters 5 and 7.

Creating in Other Ways

There are other exciting ways for the child to develop his creative capacities. The work of Carl Orff offers many possibilities for the teacher who is thoroughly familiar with the educational theories of this prominent German composer and music educator.[2] Orff's principles of musical growth will help the child use musical elements in a flexible and original manner from the very beginning. He will develop rhythmic facility as he recites interesting speech patterns and produces them by clapping, stamping, and playing instruments.

He will learn to create melodies easily as he experiments with the wealth of pentatonic material emphasized in some parts of *Music for Children*.[3] Accompaniment possibilities are provided by "bordums," "ostinatos," and "roving Borduns." The musical forms and improvisations described by Orff will further develop the child's creative capacities. Canons and rondos are understandable and immediately adaptable to the child's own uses. Improvisation is structured, and the child learns many techniques that he may use in his own compositions.

The Orff instruments provide a further dimension for the child's creative experiments. A wide range of musical sounds may be produced, and the instruments are designed in such a way that problems of performing technique are minimal. The first two volumes of Orff's *Music for Children*, as adapted by Doreen Hall and Arnold Walter, contain many ideas that are appropriate for creative activities in classrooms with younger or older children. Teachers will also discover that many suggestions involving instruments Orff has designed may be played on familiar classroom instruments.

Grace Nash, a prominent American music educator, has adapted and amplified the Orff principles to suit the needs and capacities of children in American classrooms. This program, with a creative emphasis and a sequential structure, consists of films, recordings, and seven books of instructional material.[4]

Every older child will gain valuable knowledge concerning compositional techniques after he has participated in the activities described above. Harmonic, melodic, and formal characteristics of different periods and styles of composition will become more meaningful. Some children will use these techniques as they continue to create

---

[2] Orff's theories are discussed in Chapter 5 (p. 111) and Chapter 11 (pp. 238–39).

[3] Carl Orff and Gunild Keetman, *Music for Children*, adaptation by Doreen Hall and Arnold Walter (New York: Associated Music Publishers, 1960).

[4] Grace Nash, *Music with Children* (Scottsdale, Ariz.: Swartwout Enterprises, 1965–67).

original music compositions. Other children will benefit equally from these experiences even if they do not show such an intense interest in creating music. They will have become increasingly aware of the many ways composers have created musical works, and they will identify these techniques as they listen to music.

SUMMARY

Creativity should be present in any classroom music activity. Teachers should be as creative in their presentation of music as children will be in their responses. A child's response to music should be considered creative whenever he makes a flexible use of musical elements, not merely when he creates something unique.

The child in an early childhood classroom will make a variety of spontaneous responses to music. His creation of new words and short melodies is a facet of his creative growth. His responses involving expressive movement and his original manipulation of melody and rhythm instruments are equally creative.

The older child will continue these activities and will develop his potential further by his flexible and original use of even more elements of music. He will create longer melodies and compose musical settings for poems. He will analyze the techniques of composers of different periods and apply these discoveries to his own compositions. He will be able to complete creative activities that are too involved for younger children.

The creative *process* should be emphasized as children make creative discoveries. Each selected activity should feature the solution of a musical problem. Every child will benefit from activities with a creative focus, and some children will continue to use this vocabulary of discoveries to create music.

QUESTIONS AND PROJECTS

1. One major issue in education concerns the extent to which creativity can be taught. How do authorities on creativity approach this problem? What are the dominant trends in current educational practice?
2. Is creativity a general quality which enables a person to behave creatively in a variety of endeavors or is it specifically related to a given activity? What is the weight of authoritative opinion regarding this question?
3. Assume that you wish to emphasize the creative possibilities of music in a classroom. Select one or more of the approaches described in this chapter, select your own materials, and develop a lesson plan with a specific grade level in mind.

4. Prepare a list of songs from a collection that may be used for creative word substitutions. Your selection should be based on the capacities of a specific age group.
5. Select a pentatonic song ("Little David, Play on Your Harp" is an excellent example) and create short melody patterns that may be repeated as an accompaniment.
6. Examine the instrumental arrangements of Carl Orff or Grace Nash as examples of the types of accompaniments children might create.
7. Experiment with the accompaniments included in this chapter (pages 199–204), selecting a folk song first as the melody you will accompany. Choose the style of accompaniment most appropriate to convey the musical effect of the melody. Your choice may also be influenced by the meaning of the text.

REFERENCES

Orff Instruments

George Kelischek Workshop, Atlanta, Ga.
Magnamusic-Baton, Inc., St. Louis, Mo.
Magnamusic Distributors, Inc., Sharon, Conn.

Recommended Readings

Experiments in Musical Creativity. Washington, D.C.: Contemporary Music Project/Music Educators National Conference, 1966.
Fitzgerald, R. Bernard. "Creative Music Teaching in the Elementary School." *NEA Journal* 53, no. 9 (December 1964).
Flagg, Marion. "The Orff System in Today's World." *Music Educators Journal* 53, no. 4 (December 1966).
Fowler, Charles B. "Discovery Method—Its Relevance for Music Education." *Journal of Research in Music Education* 14, no. 2 (Summer 1966).
Nash, Grace. *Music with Children.* 7 teaching manuals. Scottsdale, Ariz.: Swartwout Enterprises, 1965–67.
Nye, Robert Evans, and Nye, Vernice Trousdale. *Music in the Elementary School—An Activities Approach to Music Methods and Materials,* chap. 9, "Responding Creatively." 2d ed. Englewood Cliffs, N.J.: Prentice-Hall, 1964.
Orff, Carl, and Keetman, Gunild. *Music for Children.* Adaptation by Doreen Hall and Arnold Walter. Vols. 1–2. New York: Associated Music Publishers, 1960.
Pierce, Anne E. *Teaching Music in the Elementary School,* chap. 10, "The Young Composer." New York: Holt, Rinehart & Winston, 1959.
Schubert, Inez, and Wood, Lucille. *The Craft of Music Teaching in the Elementary School.* Morristown, N.J.: Silver Burdett Co., 1964.
Snyder, Alice M. *Creating Music with Children.* New York: Mills Music, 1957.

Audio-Visual Aids

Music for Children. Hollywood, Calif.: Capitol Records (examples of the Orff approaches to music education).
Music with Children. Scottsdale, Ariz.: Swartwout Enterprises (four films showing the teaching techniques of Grace Nash).

10

MUSIC IN SPECIAL EDUCATION PROGRAMS

The contents of this chapter emphasize those aspects of music that are suitable for children with special needs. The focus will be somewhat different from that of previous chapters. While each musical activity *will* develop the child's musical capacities and help fulfill his musical needs, the functional aspects of music will receive major consideration.

Functional aspects of music are extremely important in the education of the *disadvantaged child*. Educators are convinced that carefully planned early educational experiences will overcome many of the environmental deprivations that interfere with the child's progress when he enters elementary school. The disadvantaged child has several inhibiting characteristics which may be at least partially overcome by a functional music program. These characteristics have never been described adequately in musical terms; such a description is a major purpose of this chapter.

The education of the *gifted child* is often included within the broad category of *special education*. Musically gifted children have been virtually ignored in music curriculum planning although they are enrolled in many classrooms. The musically gifted child should receive classroom assistance in order to develop his unusual capacities. Suggestions are included in this chapter.

One additional aspect of special education is also described in musical terms. While some *mentally handicapped children* have musical capacities similar to those of normal children, music has unique contributions to make to the handicapped child's education, and the function of music in the education of educable and trainable children is considered here.

Two important areas of special education are not discussed here. Music as one facet of adjunctive therapy is widely used in connection with *emotional disturbance*. Music for the emotionally disturbed child is a highly specialized field. The teacher who requires information concerning this aspect of special education will find sources listed in the chapter references. Children with *physical handicaps* should also participate in musical activities. The child with partial sight, partial hearing, or an orthopedic handicap will participate in music to the extent that his physical limitations permit. Detailed suggestions for an appropriate music program are not included here, however, due to the extreme range in physical capacities and because many of these handicapped children are included in the activities in normal classrooms as frequently as possible.

One point must be emphasized before proceeding further. All children respond to many aspects of music in a similar manner. The disadvantaged child responds to the excitement of rhythmic pulses as does the child with no learning disabilities. The mentally handicapped child may experience the joy of singing as fully as do other children. The suggestions that follow are considered in these terms. Teachers should present an effective music program in any classroom and also be aware of the specialized needs of individual children.

One music specialist expressed this philosophy well after teaching mentally retarded children for the first time. She remarked that they had enjoyed a comprehensive music program and had made excellent musical progress. She then added that she might not have presented so challenging a program if she had been fully aware of the limitations that might be considered in presenting an educational activity for the mentally handicapped.

MUSIC FOR THE CULTURALLY DISADVANTAGED

The preschool or elementary-school disadvantaged child shares many musical interests with other children. He is fascinated by rhythmic pulses, he loves to sing, and he is captivated by exciting tone colors. Disadvantaged children also exhibit some characteristics that will lead to music programs with a special emphasis. The child often has either a negative or an inadequate self-concept. He may also have little experience with the necessity to express his feelings or needs through words and therefore be deficient in language development.

Disadvantaged children often show that they have an inadequate social adjustment and that they have not developed attentive listening habits.

A music program planned for the disadvantaged child should emphasize activities to improve these cultural deficiencies. The child will feel more secure in his environment and develop a more realistic self-concept after he participates in some of these activities. His language development and his ability to listen will improve as other music activities are presented. Music should be an important part of the curriculum when the young disadvantaged child first enters school. His first experiences with music will make him eager to participate in other activities planned for his compensatory education.

Self-Concept

Many preschool children enter compensatory classrooms with an inadequate self-image. Some have received little attention from parents or other adults. A few do not even seem to respond to their names. Young disadvantaged children need some type of individual reinforcement as they attempt to adjust to new situations.

Musical activities will help the child learn to adjust to adults and other children in the classroom. Music may be unique in the way it permits the child to be easily drawn into a group and still feel a heightened sense of individuality. The disadvantaged child will become a part of the group and also receive individual attention as the teacher introduces a special type of song at the beginning of the school year. This type of song features the child's name and the clothing he is wearing.

The child will become aware of several things as songs of this type are sung. He will be happy to realize that he is recognized as an individual. He will also understand that other children must be recognized as well, and he will begin to realize the importance of sharing with others. His knowledge of colors and of names for articles of clothing will be expanded.

Two songs included in this book are appropriate for this activity —"Look Around the Room" (Chapter 2, page 19) and "I See a Girl" (Appendix, page 255). Several others are listed at the end of the chapter.

Disadvantaged children will benefit from this simple but satisfying activity in several ways:

> Each child will begin to sing. These easy songs will be repeated a number of times with few word changes as the teacher and the other children sing to each child.

> Each child will receive personal attention in a group atmosphere. This will strengthen his self-concept.

The child will begin to share with others in a pleasant atmosphere. He will also become aware of the other children in the group and begin to learn their names.

He will begin to identify colors and the names for articles of clothing.

This listing of accomplishments may seem at first too simple and basic to be considered a part of the child's education. Teachers must realize, however, that many disadvantaged children first enter classrooms with severe learning deficiencies. Activities of this type are immediately rewarding and are an important preparation for other aspects of the child's emotional and educational development.

Name songs should be repeated at intervals throughout the school year. The child may be rewarded by having the teacher sing to him after he has successfully completed an activity. Songs in this category should be used to bring the group together again after a school holiday or vacation.

The teacher must be aware of one fact concerning songs about a child's name or his clothing. Children receive great satisfaction as these songs are introduced, and they will constantly ask that they be repeated on subsequent days. The teacher should, however, gradually replace these songs with others. Several other aspects of music are equally important to the child's musical and general growth.

Language Development

Many young disadvantaged children have not developed an adequate vocabulary of meaningful words and phrases. Some speak in a dialect that is difficult to understand and limited in expressive possibilities. Other disadvantaged children have simply never learned to communicate with words. The child must develop a larger vocabulary of words in common usage. Music may be used in a pleasant and effective manner to help him acquire facility with words and phrases. Songs chosen for this specific purpose should have simple, repeated word-phrases. They should also have texts that suggest the possibility of word-substitutions.

These word substitutions should be introduced in a way that will actively involve the disadvantaged child in the singing activity. Some young children hesitate to participate in activities when they first enter the classroom. Every child must be actively involved in singing if he is to develop language facility in this delightful way.

Songs that include animal or nonsense sounds prove irresistible to any child, and he will happily participate. "Skip to My Lou" (Example 10–1) has several folk verses with sounds of this sort.

The teacher will transform this singing activity into a language-development situation after the children have all begun to sing. The

Example 10–1

SKIP TO MY LOU

Happily   American Game Song

Flies in the sug-ar bowl, shoo, shoo, shoo! Flies in the sug-ar bowl, shoo, shoo, shoo!

Flies in the sug-ar bowl, shoo, shoo, shoo! Skip to my Lou, my dar - ling.

Cows in the pasture, moo, moo, moo! (3 times)
Skip to my Lou, my darling.

child should learn to identify the animals he is singing about. Pictures may be used. Trips are often planned to expand the horizons and understanding of disadvantaged children. One of these trips might be a visit to a farm or a zoo.

The song may be used in another way to accelerate the child's verbal development. He may be asked to think of other animals to sing about, perhaps after a visit to a farm. He will also discover that he may use this same melody to sing about other things or events.

Other folk songs suggesting simple word-substitutions should then be introduced. "Little Bird" (page 257) is an excellent choice. The song will be easy for the child to vary by substituting new words, since only one word need be replaced. The child may first substitute "big" for "little" and learn something about size comparisons as he sings. He may think of birds of different colors and acquire knowledge about colors and their names. As he suggests the names of different birds, he will also add to his general knowledge and expand his word vocabulary in a meaningful way.

The teacher should expand each of these situations involving simple word-substitutions and provide the child with additional opportunities to understand the meanings of the words he has used. Concepts of large and small may be practiced in several ways, and relative size comparisons should be presented in a visual way. The child must also see colors as he identifies them. Pictures of the different birds he has sung about will make these names and categories more understandable.

Songs with directions may be presented to expand the child's understanding and use of language. "Sing with Me" (page 253) is an example. The words may be changed to involve children in actions that will increase their understanding of many words. The following are a few examples:

"Lean to the left, all together"
"Point to the right, all together"
"Reach up high, all together"
"Bend down low, all together"

Question songs will help the child learn to construct longer word-phrases. "Who's That?" (page 251) is an appropriate choice for the first activity in which the child answers a musical question through song. The child's answer will involve a simple rearrangement of the phrase.

"What Shall We Do?" (Example 10–2) and similar songs require complete phrases as answers. Children will thoroughly enjoy these

Example 10–2

WHAT SHALL WE DO?[1]

With spirit

American Folk Song

mf C   C   G7   C

What shall we do when we play in-side, play in-side, play in-side?

C   C   G7   C

What shall we do when we play in-side? When we play in-side to-day?

singing question-and-answer games, and the song may be changed to suit many situations. Questions that suggest a variety of possible answers as children continue to sing this song are: "What shall we do when we play outside?" "What shall we do on a rainy day?"

The child will be highly motivated as he develops language facility through singing. Teachers should consider the following important points in planning this musical aspect of compensatory education:

Every child must be actively engaged in the singing activity if he is to benefit from these learning situations.

[1] From *Alamance Play Party Songs and Singing Games* by Fletcher Collins, Jr., Mary Baldwin College, Staunton, Va. Used by permission.

Songs should be selected with careful consideration for the child's level of verbal development. These activities should begin with single word-substitutions and gradually involve more complicated phrases.

Learning To Listen

The disadvantaged child often enters school with poor listening habits and an inadequate attention span. He may never have learned to listen to others because of lack of contact with adults. Some children do not listen attentively because they have learned to "tune out" unpleasant events in their environment.

The child must learn to listen attentively if he is to participate successfully in any activity in the classroom. Teachers must capture the child's attention and plan situations that will make him *want* to become an attentive listener. Musical activities provide an effective way to help the child develop the habit of attentive listening. Singing and rhythmic activities will capture the interest of the child who may have ignored unpleasant happenings by simply not listening.

Several techniques will help the child develop the ability and the desire to listen. *Musical guessing games* may be introduced. The teacher will hum, whistle, or play familiar song melodies without words. The child will then identify the familiar sound. The child's first guesses will often prove to be inaccurate, and he will simply name songs he likes. As the game is continued, more children will prove that they are listening well. The teacher should gradually be more selective in rewarding careful listening.

The guessing game approach should gradually become more complicated. The teacher will play or hum short sections from the middle or end of longer songs. Children may find songs on simple melody instruments and play them for each other as variations of the guessing game. The teacher may continue to help the child develop listening skills by tapping or playing the rhythmic pattern of a song.

Rhythmic activities are another aspect of the music program that will help the child learn to listen. The general approach is described in Chapter 4. A few additional comments will help the teacher present effective rhythmic activities in classrooms for the disadvantaged.

The disadvantaged child is often overly stimulated by the excitement of rhythmic activities. He will react, sometimes violently, to exciting loud sounds. The teacher who introduces expressive movement activities by providing loud, fast music may find that the movement activity has degenerated into chaos. The child will not learn to listen in such a situation.

The teacher who introduces soft rhythmic patterns first will often be more successful in attracting the child's attention and in preparing him for attentive listening as he responds. The child should form the habit of listening first before he makes an active response. Patterns played softly on a drum or on other rhythm instruments will capture his attention.

More stimulating patterns may then be introduced. The child should continue to sit and listen first, however, before he makes an expressive movement response.

The Teacher's Role

Few teachers of disadvantaged children have begun their teaching career in compensatory classrooms. Many have previously taught older children or young children with more adequate home environments. These teachers must beware of attempting to use approaches or materials that may have been appropriate for other children. Finger-play songs are one example of the type of music that is generally not appropriate for preschool disadvantaged children. These songs require fine coordination and careful attention on the child's part if they are to be successfully completed. The disadvantaged child is often frustrated by such activities and will show his frustration through disturbing behavior.

The teacher who is aware of the importance of helping these children develop their capacities to the fullest will realize that music is more than a recreational activity. Music may be planned in such a way that musical activities will play an important part in the child's education.

Music is a delightful activity for any young child, and the disadvantaged youngster will immediately respond to the magic of this subject. He will be easily drawn into a group activity and achieve success because he is ready to learn to sing and to make expressive responses. His musical learnings and accomplishments will contribute greatly to the success of other parts of the preschool and primary-grade compensatory education program.

MUSIC FOR THE GIFTED CHILD

Some children display unusual musical capacities at an early age. Gifted children should be helped as they are in other subject-matter areas. The music program should be planned to provide opportunities for the development of their potential. Many of the activities in this text will provide appropriate experiences for the child who shows unusual talent and an intense interest in music. The gifted child will want to complete the *related activities* which are featured in several chapters.

As a young child he will delight in the discovery of original melodies, and he may compose introductions and accompaniments through experimentation with simple instruments. These and other related activities are described in Chapter 2. He will be equally fascinated by activities included in Chapters 4 and 6. Some of the instrumental and creative activities suggested for the older child in Chapters 8 and 9 may also be appropriate for the younger child with an unusual interest in music and with obvious musical gifts.

Older gifted children will benefit to an equal extent from the related activities described in Chapters 3, 5, and 7. The older child with musical talent will also respond to the more advanced instrumental and creative suggestions in Chapters 8 and 9. The following activities provided by school systems will help the gifted child develop some aspects of his potential:

> Special school or school-system choruses will be appropriate for the child with musical gifts who exhibits an unusual interest in singing.
>
> The gifted child will often be eager to enroll in the class study of an instrument. Woodwind, brass, string, and percussion instruction will interest these children. The gifted child often makes rapid progress and should have further opportunities to play his selected instrument.

Some children with musical gifts prefer to fulfill their intense interest in music by individual study and practice. They may become interested in one era of music and want to learn more about the period and the lives of composers. They will often want to listen to additional recordings after a listening activity has been presented. Some gifted children become absorbed in composition, analysis, or making musical arrangements for voices or instruments.

The Teacher's Role

Classroom teachers and special music teachers should attempt to help the musically gifted child whenever possible. This is often a difficult goal to achieve in the classroom, but teachers who are aware of the capacities and needs of these children will find ways to challenge their potential.

The younger child with musical gifts may develop his capacities within the group as teachers suggest additional activities that are related to the musical materials selected for the class. Teachers *do* need to be aware of the reactions of other children in these situations.

The child may be considered to be a "teacher's pet," since he is receiving more attention at times.

The older child will often receive more assistance geared to his needs through instrumental or choral activities. Some children will also need individual guidance from the classroom teacher or the music specialist as they show a desire to explore one area of music in more depth.

The gifted child who is enrolled in an elementary school in which a music specialist presents all aspects of the daily music program will be helped primarily by the specialist. Many schools are not provided with this amount of specialist assistance, however, and classroom teachers and music teachers must share the responsibility. The classroom teacher will identify the gifted child and mention his abilities to the music specialist. Activities geared to his capacities may be planned in a cooperative manner and added to the classroom music program.

MUSIC FOR THE MENTALLY HANDICAPPED

Children with mental limitations are grouped in one of two categories as they are enrolled in school. The *educable mentally handicapped child* has many of the capacities of other children in preschool and primary-grade classrooms. He may even be enrolled in classrooms with normal children in smaller school systems. The *trainable mentally handicapped child* has severe limitations and requires a special basic education program.

Musical activities are appropriate for both the educable and the trainable child. Some aspects of music must be planned, however, in terms of the child's special capacities and needs.

Activities for the Educable Mentally Handicapped

Many aspects of a music program planned for educable children should be similar to the music program presented in normal classrooms. The suggestions in this section reflect the results of experimenting by the author with both materials and teaching approaches in classrooms for the educable.

The music program described in Chapters 2, 4, and 6 is equally appropriate for the educable child. He should be able to complete successfully those activities described for other preschool and primary-grade children. He will also enjoy and benefit from the activities for the younger child presented in Chapters 8 and 9.

The younger educable child will participate in these parts of the music program as much as other children. Teachers may find, however, that educable children progress more slowly and that more repetition is required if the child is to develop his musical capacities. Specific teaching techniques will depend upon the range of mental capacities to be found in each classroom.

The older child in classrooms for the educable mentally handicapped needs special consideration as music activities are planned. Many activities planned for older children in normal classrooms are beyond his capacities. He should often continue to sing songs of the type described in Chapter 2. His expressive movement responses will be similar to those described in Chapter 4. The older child's interests may have progressed further than his performance capacities. He should continue to sing simple songs since he will be frustrated by longer phrases and more complicated word-combinations. He may not be interested, however, in many of the songs appropriate for the younger child. The teacher will need to find songs appropriate for the child's interests which also have characteristics similar to those described in Chapter 2. Songs should have the following characteristics: (1) The song should reflect the interests of the older educable child. (2) Each song should have repeated word- and melody-phrases.

Some songs are appropriate for children of any age. "Going Down to Cairo" (page 283) is an example. This river song has limited-range phrases which are appropriate for the youngest child and the least experienced singer. The subject, sailors singing as they leave one port and travel to Cairo, is interesting to the older educable child. Repetition is characteristic of both the melody and the words.

Teachers will find many other songs of this type by analyzing the basic series. The third- and fourth-grade books will generally provide the most suitable songs for older educable children. Outstanding examples are "Roll On, Columbia," "Down the River," and "Marching to Pretoria." Other songs with these characteristics are listed at the end of the chapter.

Teachers should consider one additional criterion in selecting the singing repertoire for children in educable classrooms. These children thoroughly enjoy fast, rhythmic songs. The following songs were chosen as favorites in one classroom with children in the age range from eleven to sixteen years of age: "Walking at Night" ("Stodole pumpa"), "Sarasponda" (page 309), and "Zulu Warrior."

Activities involving expressive movement will be a constant source of satisfaction for children in classrooms for the educable mentally handicapped. The younger child will enjoy the basic movement activities described in Chapter 4. Older children should continue with these basic movement activities. Since the age range in these classrooms is often much wider than in a classroom with normal children, teachers should consider an additional type of activity for older children. These children participate willingly in circle and square dances. The songs and dance patterns for these activities should be chosen with great care. The child should never feel that he is involved in an activity that is more suitable for children in early childhood classrooms. The simple action songs and dances listed in the chapter references for trainable mentally handicapped groups are not appropriate.

Pupils in classrooms for the educable mentally handicapped also enjoy activities involving simple instruments. The varied activities in this text described for early childhood groups are appropriate. The child will often create a musical effect as he plays an instrument that provides him with a positive feeling of accomplishment.

Activities for the Trainable Mentally Handicapped

Children in classrooms for the trainable mentally handicapped will also benefit from participation in music. Singing, rhythmic, and listening activities should be presented frequently, although several differences in emphasis are necessary as teachers plan a music program for these children.

Songs should be selected with great care. Limited-range songs and those with repeated limited-range patterns should be emphasized (see Chapter 2, pages 17–19), for a description of these song categories). The teacher may observe at first that some children do not actively participate in singing activities. The introduction of a few songs similar to those mentioned on pages 211–13 will generally lead the child into active participation. Teachers will also discover that songs with texts emphasizing simple verbal directions will prove helpful to other portions of the classroom program.

A few children in a classroom for the younger trainable mentally handicapped may be in a preverbal stage as the school year begins. Teachers should emphasize a singing repertoire with a variety of simple and repeated "nonsense" sounds if this is the case. The child may produce his first verbal utterances as he is motivated to join the singing activity.

The above suggestion for helping the preverbal child is directly related to another teaching technique which should be employed during singing activities with children in classrooms for the trainable mentally handicapped. Songs should be selected and activities should be planned to provide for a variety of types of participation. Some children will actively participate in singing as school begins. Others should first have the opportunity to perform simple actions or to play basic classroom rhythm instruments. The child should never be frustrated by the fact that he is not yet able to speak or to sing.

Instruments are frequently added to music programs for these children to facilitate the child's physical coordination development. Teachers must select instruments with care in order to provide situations in which the child is able to explore the tone colors and rhythmic possibilities of simple melody and rhythm instruments. Some instruments will prove extremely frustrating to the child. Large drums, dowel-rod sticks,[2] and individual resonator bells are appropriate.

The trainable child enjoys activities involving movement. The teacher will often discover, however, that movement activities must be introduced in a flexible way, since some trainable children are quite lethargic while others are extremely hyperactive. The phlegmatic child will be encouraged to participate, while extremely active children may respond better to the teaching suggestions described for the young disadvantaged child who has not yet learned to listen (pages 215–16).

Action songs and singing games have received little attention in other parts of this book. The young child who attempts to use his hands or body while he sings seldom is able to perform in both ways at the same time. Singing games that involve movement around the room are not basically musical, since they involve verbal directions rather than musical cues. Activities of this type are more appropriate for children in trainable classrooms. The young trainable child will find satisfaction in simple songs involving a physical response. He will also improve his physical coordination and learn to listen carefully to the directions in the song. "If You're Happy" (Chapter 4, page 83) is an excellent song for introducing physical activity through song.

Patterned dances are described in Chapter 5 (page 112). Circle dances, square dances, and dances of other cultures have not been emphasized as an important aspect of the child's rhythmic development. They are described instead as one way in which music can contribute to the child's understanding of a period in history or to his awareness of another culture. Patterned dances may be emphasized more as a part of the music program in classrooms with trainable children.

The older trainable child will enjoy patterned dances. Simple circle and square dances may be added to the music program to improve his coordination, increase his attentive listening ability, and help to lengthen his attention span. Patterned dances appropriate for the

[2] Commercial rhythm sticks are often difficult for younger children to handle. Dowel rods one inch in diameter may be cut into twelve-inch lengths and sanded to provide a more adequate instrument. The larger diameter makes the stick easier to grasp. The instrument often produces a more musical sound than thinner commercial sticks.

older trainable child should be relatively simple. The following dances are described in several of the basic series:

Bow to Your Partner	London Bridge
Round and Round the Village	Old Brass Wagon

The Teacher's Role

Teachers must be fully aware of the child's capacities and of the many possibilities of music if they are to present music activities suited to the needs of mentally handicapped children. There are many ways in which the child's experiences with music will develop his musical capacities and also contribute to other aspects of his growth.

Educable children are capable of achieving many of the objectives listed in Chapters 2, 4, and 6. The teacher should present the child with activities that have challenging possibilities and not merely consider music as a play activity. The child's pride in his musical accomplishments will often contribute to his desire to participate in other activities and lead to a relaxed yet purposeful classroom atmosphere.

Trainable children have more limitations which the teacher must consider in planning the music program. The distinction between trainable and educable children is often an arbitrary one, however, and some children will develop musical skills in a normal manner. The child may begin the school year by participating little or not at all as music activities are presented. He will not show a similar lack of response at the end of the year if an effective music program is presented.

A music program serves several purposes in classrooms for the mentally handicapped. The mentally handicapped child will often find success in his musical experiences more easily than in other areas of the curriculum.

SUMMARY

Music assumes a different role as activities are planned for children in special education programs. Most exceptional children have musical capacities, and a music program should be planned to develop these capacities. Music should also be added to the classroom program in a functional manner to assist in the child's total educational development.

The disadvantaged child has learning deficiencies which may be overcome in part by an effective music program. Children with unusual musical ability need individual attention as their specific talents are recognized and teachers plan ways to help them reach individual musical goals. Some mentally handicapped children will develop musical capacities as fully as children in normal classrooms, while others are limited in their ability to respond.

One important point cannot be overemphasized in regard to planning a music program for children in special education classrooms. Every child has musical capacities which should be developed as fully as possible. The perceptive teacher will understand that successful experiences with music will have a positive effect on the child's general motivation and on his attitude toward other aspects of the school curriculum.

QUESTIONS AND PROJECTS

1. Criticize the following statement: "A music program that is appropriate for the average pupil will be equally appropriate for a child in a special education program."
2. Prepare for a class discussion of the place of music in the education of exceptional children. Choose a specific area of special education and do appropriate outside reading. Reading sources should be concerned with the general educational aims of the area chosen.
3. Observe a class of exceptional children and interview the classroom teacher, if possible, to discover the educational objectives of the program. Prepare a short report relating the functional uses of music to this curriculum.
4. Assume that you will have one or more children with unusual musical ability in a classroom. Evaluate the listings of activities in this book to select those that will be appropriate for the gifted child at the grade level you have chosen.
5. How can the services of a music specialist be justified in a specific special education program? What unique contributions can a person with special music preparation make to the program?

REFERENCES

Supplementary Song Collections

Coleman, Jack L.; Schoepfle, Irene L.; and Templeton, Virginia. *Music for Exceptional Children.* Evanston, Ill.: Summy-Birchard Co., 1964.
Smith, Robert B., and Leonhard, Charles. *Discovering Music Together—Early Childhood.* Chicago: Follett Educational Corp., 1968.

Recommended Readings

Alvin, Juliette. *Music for the Handicapped Child.* London: Oxford University Press, 1965.
Dobbs, J. P. B. *The Slow Learner and Music.* London: Oxford University Press, 1965.
Gaston, E. Thayer. "Functional Music." In *Basic Concepts in Music Education,* 57th Yearbook of the National Society for the Study of Education, edited by Nelson B. Henry, chap. 12. Chicago: University of Chicago Press, 1958.

Ginglend, David R., and Stiles, Winifred E. *Music Activities for Retarded Children.* Nashville, Tenn.: Abingdon Press, 1965.

Robins, Ferris, and Robins, Jennet. *Educational Rhythmics for Mentally and Physically Handicapped Children.* New York: Association Press, 1968.

Taba, Hilda, and Elkins, Deborah. *Teaching Strategies for the Culturally Disadvantaged.* Chicago: Rand McNally & Co., 1967.

Usdan, Michael, and Bertolaet, Frederick. *Teachers for the Disadvantaged.* Chicago: Follett Publishing Co., 1966.

Music as Adjunctive Therapy:

Long, Nicholas J.; Morse, William C.; and Newman, Ruth G. *Conflict in the Classroom: The Education of Emotionally Disturbed Children.* Belmont, Calif.: Wadsworth Publishing Co., 1965.

Music Therapy, Proceedings of the National Association for Music Therapy (annual). Lawrence, Kans.: Allen Press.

Audio-Visual Aids

Learning as We Play. New York and Englewood Cliffs, N.J.: Folkways/Scholastic Records.

Let's Learn To Sing. Champaign, Ill.: Let's Learn Productions (three recordings).

More Learning as We Play. New York and Englewood Cliffs, N.J.: Folkways/ Scholastic Records.

Music for Exceptional Children. Evanston, Ill.: Summy-Birchard Co. (two record albums).

Songs for Children with Special Needs. Los Angeles: Bowmar Records (three record albums).

Two Albums for Exceptional Children. Los Angeles: Bowmar Records ("Basic Concepts Through Dance"; "Simplified Folk Dance Favorites").

Other Aids

Rohrbough, Lynn. *Handy Folk Dance Book.* Delaware, Ohio: Cooperative Recreation Service, Inc.

————. *Play Party Games.* Delaware, Ohio: Cooperative Recreation Service, Inc.

Songs and Dances for Special Education Programs

Songs for the Culturally Disadvantaged Child

Songs followed by page numbers appear in this book The remainder appear in the kindergarten, first-grade, or second-grade books of at least two of the basic music series (see list at the end of Chapter 2). Some of the songs may be used in more than one category. Songs that feature names often include references to color and clothing. Nonsense or animal sounds may be included in the texts of songs that are also appropriate for word substitutions.

Names

"Bow, Belinda"

"Hey, Betty Martin"

"I See a Girl," page 255

"Look Around the Room," page 19

"Pawpaw Patch"

"Riding in a Buggy," page 279

"Walk Along, John"

"Who's That?" page 251

Colors

"I See a Girl," page 255
"Look Around the Room," page 19

"Mary Wore a Red Dress"
("Mary Was a Red Bird")

Question Songs

"What Shall We Do?" page 214
"Who's That?" page 251

Nonsense and Animal Sounds

"Barnyard Song"
"(I) Bought Me a Cat"

"Old McDonald Had a Farm"
"Toodala"

Word Substitutions

"The Allee Allee O," page 265
"Bluebird, Bluebird"
"Ha, Ha, Thisaway," page 263
"Little Bird," page 257

"Riding in a Buggy," page 279
"Sing with Me," page 253
"The Wheels of (on) the Bus"

Songs for the Older Child with a Mental Handicap

These songs have been selected because of their appeal to older children in classrooms for the mentally handicapped. Each is included in two or more of the basic music series books.

"Aydi Bim Bam"
"Come Rowing with Me"
"Deaf Woman's Courtship"
"Down the River"
"Goodby, Old Paint"
"Kum Ba Yah"
"Marching to Pretoria"

"Mi Chiacra" ("My Farm")
"Roll On, Columbia"
"Sarasponda"
"Tinga Layo"
"We Are Good Musicians"
"We're All Together Again"

Action Songs and Simple Dances

These songs, with repeated actions or simple dance patterns, have been selected from the kindergarten, first-, and second-grade books of the basic music series.

"Bow, Belinda"
"Bow to Your Partner"
"Clap Your Hands"
"Here We Go Round the
    Mulberry Bush"
"(Here We Go,) Santy Maloney"

"London Bridge"
"Looby Loo"
"Old Brass Wagon"
"Round and Round the Village"
"Stamping (Clapping) Land"
"We'll Hop and We'll Jump"

11

THE PROGRAM
IN ACTION

Previous chapters have described in detail a complete and comprehensive music program for every child. The capacities of children in early childhood classrooms as well as those of pupils in the upper grades have received equal attention. The program has structure and definite objectives. The activities involve far more than simple recreational uses of music, and they will challenge children and teachers as well.

This program of sequential and varied activities is appropriate for any school. A complete implementation of this program, however, requires careful consideration of the practical possibilities that exist in a specific school or school system.

This chapter describes a variety of practical considerations that are extremely important to the success of the music program. Current practices in the administration and implementation of music are surveyed; new trends are discussed and their applicability to music education is defined; directions in teacher training are evaluated, and suggestions are made for improving the existing situation; detailed suggestions are made to increase the effectiveness of music in the classroom; and the role and responsibilities of school administrators are discussed.

THE CURRENT SITUATION

A survey of school music programs in all parts of the country leads to the conclusion that there are practically as many ways to present music as there are school systems. Music specialists and classroom teachers present aspects of the music program in a variety of ways and combinations; great diversity is found in the way materials are utilized; different musical goals are evident. These extreme differences are to be expected in comparing and contrasting music programs at the preschool and elementary-school level. The differences are almost equally great at the same grade level in different school systems.

The Preschool Music Program

Preschool music education programs are the most varied. Some kindergartens are included in public school systems, while many others are administered by parent groups, churches, or private operators. A recent survey revealed that only fifty-eight per cent of the children who have reached the appropriate age level are enrolled in kindergarten.

An even smaller percentage of preschool children attends nursery school. Some nursery schools serve as observation facilities for human development courses in colleges and universities. Many others are operated as profit-making ventures, and still others are day-care centers for the children of working mothers. A few nursery-school classrooms are now administered by school systems, since the extreme importance of early education is beginning to be recognized.

The music program reflects the diversity of direction and administration in preschool classrooms. Special music teachers are seldom scheduled at the kindergarten level, and few trained musicians present nursery school music. The classroom teacher often does not have the minimum training in music required of many elementary-school classroom teachers. The few college courses that do include preschool music often combine this subject with the other arts as a survey of methods and materials.

Some teachers of preschool children present daily musical activities and involve every child. Other teachers consider music to be an activity appropriate only for the child who displays unusual interest. In many preschool classrooms there is no music at all, with the exception of a few recordings played while the child rests.

The importance of early experience with music has been a constant underlying theme in other parts of this text. The preschool child develops basic musical skills easily and has reached a stage of readiness for singing, moving, and listening activities. Music should be a daily event in every preschool classroom. At present it is not, and those teachers who do include music are seldom aware of the child's capacities.

One recent development in preschool education holds promise for innovations in the general preschool program. Federal programs for the preschool culturally disadvantaged include curriculum areas that are also appropriate for other preschool children. The effect of these programs is becoming apparent throughout the country. These new emphases may exert an influence on preschool education in general as the new educational directions prove worthwhile.

The Elementary School Music Program

Music programs at the elementary-school level are planned and implemented in a variety of ways. The following are descriptions of the most common types of programs:

Some school systems provide one music specialist for every large elementary school. The specialist is acquainted with each child, teaches frequently in every classroom, and is available for conferences and planning sessions with classroom teachers.

In other school systems fewer specialists are hired, but their contact time is scheduled in a similar manner. The special music teacher visits each classroom an equal number of times during the school year. He travels from school to school and has little time for conferences and other contacts with classroom teachers.

Some systems utilize the services of the special music teacher in a different way. The music specialist is *on call* to help any classroom teacher who requests assistance. This assistance may involve several aspects of the music program. One classroom teacher may request appropriate musical materials for a special unit, while another may need help in planning a part of the program with which he is unfamiliar. Many classroom teachers will request classroom demonstrations of varied types.

A few systems provide practically no assistance from music specialists. The system with a very low ratio of specialists to the number of elementary classrooms must define the role of the special music teacher in a very different way from the systems previously described. The music teacher will be a resource for program planning, for selection of musical materials, and for general coordination of activities. He will have little or no direct contact with either the child or the classroom teacher.

Some systems attempt to overcome a shortage of qualified music personnel by utilizing the special competencies of classroom teachers. One teacher with more training in a specific subject-matter area will present activities in that area to several classes on one or more grade levels. Principals and elementary supervisors attempt to select new teachers with special competencies in order to provide a balance of these specific abilities in each elementary school.

Implications

One important fact emerges when preschool and elementary-school music programs are evaluated throughout the country. The trained music educator seldom presents all aspects of music through direct contact with the child. Classroom teachers have the responsibility for the majority of musical activities in the classroom. At least eighty per cent of the music program is handled by classroom teachers in elementary schools, and virtually all music is conducted by the classroom teacher in preschool classrooms.

Many classroom music programs, at both the preschool and the elementary-school levels, reflect the need for more qualified teachers. The classroom teacher studies some subjects in depth through college training, but music is not a major area of training. One or two basic courses are offered at best, and some states do not require courses in music as a prerequisite for teaching in the elementary school. Many teachers feel completely inadequate when they are faced with the responsibility of presenting music unless they have developed their abilities through private study.

Educators disagree at times concerning the balance of specialists and classroom teachers in several subject-matter areas. Some feel that special teachers are able to present certain subjects more effectively because of their depth of knowledge in the area. Others are convinced that classroom teachers are more successful in any situation because of their knowledge of each child's ability and their contact in the classroom.

This question is not pertinent regarding the classroom music program. Administrators need not concern themselves with the question of who *should* teach music. Who *does* teach music is a much more practical consideration. Classroom teachers are faced with this responsibility in practically every situation, and their training in this area needs careful consideration if they are to become effective teachers of music.

PREPARATION FOR TEACHING CLASSROOM MUSIC

College instuctors who train the prospective classroom teacher to teach music will consider the following points in planning appropriate courses:

> Every child has musical capacities. These capacities will be developed most effectively through a comprehensive music program presented in the school classroom.

> Prospective classroom teachers are effective in the presentation of music activities only if they feel confident and at ease in this area of the child's education. They will develop positive attitudes toward their role as a teacher of music if they develop basic music skills and acquire knowledge concerning the child's musical needs and the methods and materials that will develop his capacities.

Many college students have made a decision concerning the level of elementary education that most interests them before they enroll in basic music courses for classroom teachers. A course that will prepare the prospective teacher to present an effective music program for the older child will not necessarily develop the skills and understandings that he must acquire to present music to the younger child.

The ideal college course would include some basic activities necessary to the musical development of any student and also provide training for different levels of the child's music education. This is a rare situation in current college-level courses, but a few institutions *are* reorganizing this aspect of teacher training in this practical manner.

The most efficient organization of such a course requires some sectioning. While every student should participate in lectures and laboratory experiences emphasizing basic musicianship, methods and more advanced basic skills are presented more efficiently if the total class enrollment is divided into early childhood and intermediate grade sections. This division leads to the most effective teaching-learning situation and the most comprehensive presentation of goals, levels, and techniques.

Training the Teacher of Young Children

Teachers of children in early childhood classrooms must have a variety of basic music skills in order to present music activities in an effective way. They must sing tunefully, accompany classroom singing by playing an instrument, and be able to present rhythmic and listening activities. The prospective teacher should also acquire knowledge concerning the young child's musical capacities and how they may be developed in the classroom.

The following goals are important in the basic music education of these college students:

> Students must develop basic music performance skills. They will learn to sing accurately in a range appropriate for younger children. They will develop keyboard facility and become acquainted with other instruments such as the autoharp for later classroom use.
>
> Students will learn to read music and will demonstrate this ability by singing and by playing the piano and other instruments.

They will develop the ability to transpose simple melodies and to transcribe easy melodic and rhythmic patterns through dictation.

The student will develop listening skills. He will demonstrate the ability to identify the characteristic tone colors of different instruments. He will also become acquainted with different types of music, and he should have frequent opportunities to attend concerts.

Students will acquire knowledge concerning both the general characteristics and the musical capacities of the young child. They will acquire a repertoire of vocal, rhythmic, and listening materials and methods that will develop the child's musical capacities.

Students will develop confidence in their ability to teach music by successfully presenting musical activities to a group. Practice teaching should take place with groups of children if possible; other students will serve as substitutes if necessary. College teachers who do not have groups of children available for practice teaching purposes should investigate the possibilities in the community. Nursery schools or private kindergartens may welcome the opportunity for additional music activities. Students may be organized as teaching teams and cooperatively plan and present a sequence of music activities over a period of several weeks.

These goals may be expanded in many ways. These defined skills, methods, and materials require a comprehensive college course involving far more than a superficial survey of music texts and varied teaching methods.

Training the Teacher of Older Children

Training in music is equally important for the prospective teacher of older children. Music specialists visit classrooms with older children more frequently, but in many systems the classroom teacher presents at least half of the music activities in a daily program. In others practically all music is the responsibility of the classroom teacher.

College students expecting to teach at this level should develop some of the competencies and understandings described above for the teacher of young children. Their training should involve, in addition, some facets of music that are particularly appropriate for the older child. The following goals should be achieved by the student who will present music to older children:

Students will develop basic vocal ability. They will also acquire confidence in their ability to maintain a part as choral arrangements are performed, and they will understand the manner in which children develop part-singing ability.

The student will acquire knowledge concerning the way children learn to read music as he develops melodic and rhythmic reading skills.

Listening activities will help the student become aware of form and style in music. He will also acquire a knowledge of a repertoire of compositions that will help the older child develop appropriate listening skills.

The student will add to his knowledge and performing ability on instruments by learning to play a small wind instrument and by becoming acquainted with other instruments that are appropriate for older children.

Many other activities are appropriate for prospective teachers of older children. The goals described emphasize the specific skills and understandings that the student should acquire before presenting music to older children.

Practical Considerations

Differences in emphasis are often difficult to include in a single course for classroom teachers. Students should nevertheless participate in special activities suited to their future classroom needs.

Some college instructors are unable to present courses with sufficient depth for several reasons. The course may not meet often enough to provide practice in basic skills. Too many students may be enrolled in one section so that activities such as group piano instruction are difficult to present. Facilities and equipment may not be available for adequate group instruction. These and other problems often reduce the effectiveness of a basic music course for classroom teachers. The goals described represent an ideal situation for college teaching as well as a careful consideration of students' needs.

The student who completes such a course will enter a classroom with confidence in his ability to teach music. He will have acquired the necessary skills, and he will thoroughly understand the teaching approaches and materials that are needed to develop the child's musical potential.

THE EFFECTIVE CLASSROOM MUSIC PROGRAM

Music activities may be presented in a variety of ways. A realistic appraisal of the current educational situation shows that there are too few teachers for too many classrooms. This is also true in special subject-matter areas. There are more positions available than there are trained music specialists.

There are many ways to increase the effectiveness of the classroom music program. Special music teachers may be utilized in several different ways. Audio-visual aids offer exciting possibilities for improving the program. In-service training programs and cooperative teaching schedules offer additional opportunities for improving the presentation of music in the classroom. A combination of these approaches will be necessary in many instances. All children should experience music in some manner every day. The fullest use of the suggestions below will help teachers provide daily activities with music.

Effective Scheduling of Music Teachers

Some school systems do not use the services of the music specialist in the most effective manner. The specialist visits all classrooms the same number of times and therefore assists the classroom teacher with musical competence as frequently as the teacher with little training or self-confidence in music. This type of schedule is appropriate if specialists present all music in the classroom. Such programs do exist in systems that employ a special music teacher for each elementary classroom building. The approach is not appropriate for systems with fewer music teachers.

In many situations the teaching of the specialist should be scheduled in a more flexible manner. Two types of schedules are possible:

The specialist may be *on call*. Classroom teachers request a visit when they need assistance with some aspect of classroom music. These requested visits may involve either consultation or demonstration teaching.

The specialist schedules classroom visits and conferences after information is gathered concerning each teacher's music training and teaching experience. New teachers in the system often receive the major portion of the specialist's professional assistance at the beginning of the school year. Later, a flexible schedule is planned which provides direct classroom assistance for those teachers who are least able to present effective music activities.

The second of these two approaches is generally more effective. The specialist who is on call will often find that teachers who are conscious of the importance of music in the child's education will request assistance more than others. This may occur in spite of the fact that they possess musical competence. The second approach assesses the musical capacities of all teachers, and assistance is provided for those most in need of help.

There are a few school systems in which classroom visits by special teachers are virtually impossible. The system that assigns a special music teacher to a large number of schools should consider him a *resource person*. The resource music teacher will schedule in-service training for classroom teachers, suggest a general sequence of music activities, and select materials to improve the effectiveness of classroom music.

One important point should be stressed, regardless of the number of music specialists or the types of schedules they maintain. The classroom teacher should always be present when music teachers present activities in the classroom. A new and necessary trend in education—*released time* for elementary classroom teachers—has led to the hiring of additional teachers in special subject areas to give the classroom teacher more time for planning and conferences. This additional staff does help teachers find time for other activities. They should not leave the classroom, however, when a new educational activity is presented by a specialist. The classroom teacher who leaves the room as the specialist enters is often completely unaware of the activities presented. Continuity is impossible under such circumstances. The child should experience music every day, and the teacher in the classroom should continue and reinforce the specialist's teaching through daily repetition.

The classroom teacher with little competence in music may assist the specialist in many ways. The teacher will be an observer and a recorder as the child's musical capacities are evaluated at the beginning of the year. The specialist may introduce the evaluation devices described in other chapters while the teacher takes notes concerning the ability of each child. Similar activities will be repeated later in the school year.

Classroom teachers may assist the specialist in a variety of other ways. They will observe carefully and be prepared to repeat activities on subsequent days.

The Use of Teaching Aids

Many aids are available to help teachers present more effective classroom music. Some of these aids are particularly suited to the needs of the classroom teacher with little assistance from music teachers. Other aids will make musical experiences more meaningful to the child as he participates in more challenging aspects of music.

Radio and television music programs are available in most geographical areas. Teachers and administrators should be aware of the broadcasts in their area. Colleges and universities often broadcast radio and television series that have been approved by the National Association of Educational Broadcasters in Washington, D.C. Larger school systems frequently have the facilities with which to transmit radio and television series. Music specialists and committees of classroom teachers should audition available programs to determine their effectiveness and applicability to the needs of a specific system.

National Educational Radio, an affiliate of the National Association of Educational Broadcasters, will send complete audition tapes to members of this association to help in the selection of appropriate programs.

Radio and television programs are classroom teaching aids that originate outside the classroom and over which the teacher has little or no control. Other audio-visual aids may be used in the classroom to increase the effectiveness of music. A great variety is available. They range from theme charts to complex electronic devices. Many of these aids will help the teacher present music in a more effective manner. Recordings, charts, filmstrips, and other aids should be carefully selected in direct relation to the objectives of the music program. Some systems should purchase audio-visual instructional material to aid the classroom teacher who needs help in presenting basic musical activities. Other systems with more specialist assistance may give first priority to those visual aids that will help the music reading or listening program.

The music specialist should consider it an obligation to be thoroughly informed concerning the latest advances in these classroom aids. New devices appear each year, and they must be evaluated in terms of their possible effectiveness in the classroom music program. Sources for these audio-visual devices are listed at the end of this and appropriate preceding chapters.

In-service Training Programs

Some classroom teachers have little confidence in their ability to teach music because their training has been so limited. Other teachers have developed their musical skills to such an extent that they may serve as music teachers in a cooperating teacher plan. The range of competencies due to teacher preparation, training, and background leads to problems as special music teachers attempt to plan and present a uniformly effective program in every classroom.

It is often necessary to plan in-service training for the teacher in the system. In-service programs may have several purposes:

Workshops may be planned for new teachers in a system. The new teacher will be introduced to the goals of the music program and brought to understand the extent to which the classroom teacher is involved in music. The music specialist will acquire useful information concerning the competencies of new teachers by conducting such a workshop. This information may be used later to plan further in-service training suited to the needs of these teachers.

In-service programs are planned for teachers who need more training in certain musical skills. The sessions may stress a single skill (e.g.

piano facility). Skill-centered programs may also emphasize a variety of activities that will lead to more effective classroom teaching.

The in-service training of classroom teachers may have another emphasis. The adoption of new materials in a school system may involve a change of direction in the music program. Basic text adoptions, a new series of recordings, or other changes in music materials may lead to an in-service training program for classroom teachers. The teacher will be introduced to the new music resources and will be instructed in appropriate techniques for presenting these materials in the classroom.

In-service training programs are planned for varying lengths of time and at different times during the school week. Some programs require only a few days of workshop activity stressing a survey of the curriculum or of materials. Other programs may be scheduled for a full semester or more. Classes in basic musical skills are an example.

Some systems schedule in-service programs after school, and enrollment depends upon teacher interest. The classroom teacher often has little energy for personal study, however. This type of scheduling is less effective than other, more realistic methods. Some systems require each teacher to show evidence of professional growth at designated intervals. Training programs administered by personnel in the system may be chosen to satisfy these requirements. Other systems have developed an effective approach for encouraging the classroom teacher to enroll in courses or in-service training programs to acquire more knowledge or additional skills. *Released time* is provided for the teacher who pursues further study. A specified amount is provided away from the classroom routine for preparation for courses or for other aspects of professional training. A variety of administrative procedures is employed in this approach to the professional growth of the classroom teacher.

Teachers have varied obligations. Few teachers feel fully qualified to direct all aspects of the child's education when they first enter a classroom. Many experienced teachers discover that new approaches to teaching require further study. In-service training is an effective way to improve the musical competence, knowledge, and teaching techniques of classroom teachers.

Cooperative Teaching

Systems with little or no assistance from music specialists may emphasize *cooperative* or *team teaching* in the elementary school. The cooperative teacher has more training in one subject-matter area and teaches this subject in several classrooms, while other classroom teachers instruct the child in areas in which they are more competent. Some elementary schools attempt to achieve a balance of these competencies as teachers are employed. One may be competent in music while others have more knowledge of science, mathematics, or art.

The cooperative or team-teaching approach represents one attempt to solve curriculum problems in school systems that lack sufficient assistance from special teachers. Cooperative teaching will often result in improved classroom instruction. Few classroom teachers, however, have sufficient training in a specific subject-matter area to take the place of a qualified specialist.

A Consistent Direction

The suggestions for improving the effectiveness of the classroom music program described here have a consistent orientation. The child has musical capacities which he will develop through daily group instruction. He should therefore have the opportunity to participate in effective music activities in the classroom.

It is difficult to define the role of the classroom teacher and the music specialist as they teach in a cooperative manner. The specialist should have more knowledge and skills in the area of music. The classroom teacher will, in many cases, have a more complete awareness of the child's personality and capacities.

The above suggestions for effective teaching will strengthen any elementary music program. The music specialist's time must be scheduled in a way that is appropriate for the needs of a specific system. Classroom teachers exhibit a wide range of musical competencies and often need additional training. Audio-visual aids will be helpful in promoting successful teaching in many classrooms.

NEW TRENDS

Classroom teachers, music specialists, and administrators must be fully aware of recent developments in the field of elementary music education if they are to develop an effective music program. Several trends should be carefully evaluated as materials are selected and programs are planned.

New trends are evident in the recent basic music series. Several series are structured in terms of the child's general musical growth. The concepts he should acquire are suggested in a sequential progression geared to his development. Specific musical skills are carefully organized and involve much more than the acquisition of a repertoire of recreational songs. Varied aspects of music are presented in such a way that a general music program is carefully defined at the elementary school level.

Another new trend in elementary music education will begin to exert an influence on the musical materials available for classroom use. The *Juilliard Repertoire Project* has enlisted the aid of prominent musicians to analyze music of all periods for use in school classrooms. These experts have chosen the literature which has been subsequently tested in classrooms throughout the country. The repertoire that results from this careful selection and evaluation will add a new and richer dimension to music literature for children.

The *Contemporary Music Project,* administered by the Music Educators National Conference and supported by a grant from the Ford Foundation, is another dominant new trend in elementary music education. Centers have been established to help young children experiment with the creation and understanding of music involving contemporary techniques of composition. Some of these experimental situations have also involved the classroom teacher and music specialist in workshops featuring the approaches experimentally developed with children. Children *and* teachers have responded in a very positive way to these experiments with creativity. Additional curriculum experimentation is planned, and the results will influence trends in music education and help to define the place of contemporary music in the child's education.

Carl Orff, in his dual role of composer and music educator, is certainly not a new arrival on either the composition or the education scenes. His views concerning the child's music education, however, are being considered more widely in this country each year.

Orff's principles of musical growth may be incorporated in a selective manner in education programs. His definition of *elemental music* offers exciting possibilities in activities planned to involve the child in the making of music. His fascinating uses of instruments and his structured presentations of melodic possibilities, rhythmic patterns, basic forms, and accompaniments are also fully applicable to the American elementary classroom.

Music for Children,[1] a series of publications that illustrates Orff's principles, is not, however, a complete music program in itself. The first two volumes have much to offer, although many American folk songs have more enduring and worthwhile pentatonic melodies. The other volumes are less useful in the classroom. The vocal ranges are often impossibly high, and the arrangements demand much of both child and teacher. The American music educator should examine these methods and materials with care. *Music for Children* should

---

[1] Carl Orff and Gunild Keetman, *Music for Children,* adaptation by Doreen Hall and Arnold Walter (New York: Associated Music Publishers, 1960).

not be considered a comprehensive music education program that will develop all the capacities and meet all the musical needs of every American child.[2]

The influence of *Zoltán Kodály* is responsible for another trend in music education in this country. This famous Hungarian composer was actively involved in music education in his own country for many years, and his principles of education have spread widely of late. The translations and distribution of his choral method are one major reason for the dissemination of his influence.

Twelve volumes in the Kodály Choral Method[3] are currently in English editions, and others are in preparation. Some of this vocal and choral material is suitable for use in American classrooms. The following descriptions indicate possible uses:

Fifty Nursery Songs features pentatonic melodies with a total range of not more than five notes. The ranges are similar to the *limited range* described here in Chapter 2, and the composer has shown his understanding of the vocal needs of the younger child through his consistent use of repeated melody phrases. The texts are more complicated, and teachers will often need to simplify them before teaching the songs to young children.

Let Us Sing Correctly demands a great deal of the older child. The 101 intonation exercises emphasize unaccompanied two-part singing and syllables. Some of the exercises may be used to improve the intonation of special school choruses.

Bicinia Hungarica (four volumes) is the most comprehensive collection of two-part choral arrangements ever assembled for elementary school children by a major composer. The vocal ranges are extremely practical and are consistent with those for the older child described here in Chapter 3. While the arrangements are generally much more difficult than those included in the basic music series published in this country, several of the songs are appropriate for elementary school special choruses.

The remaining volumes in this series will be of interest only to the trained choral director. Excellent sight-singing and part-singing exercises are featured in several volumes. Kodály's belief that singing should always be the central focus of any music program is exemplified throughout. The American music educator is generally more concerned with the child's total musical growth and considers singing

---

[2] See Grace Nash, *Music with Children* (Scottsdale, Ariz.: Swartwout Enterprises, 1965–67). This adaptation of the Orff principles of music education provides materials more suitable for elementary classrooms in this country. Some of Mrs. Nash's original melodies will become classroom favorites. Her adaptations of the Orff instrumental arrangements are also outstanding.

[3] Zoltán Kodály, *Choral Method* (Oceanside, N.Y.: Boosey & Hawkes, 1957–64).

to be only one of a number of activities that should be emphasized in the classroom.[4]

The inexperienced music specialist must beware of "hopping on the bandwagon" merely because a popular new approach to teaching appears. This criticism has been leveled at the field of elementary music education for many years. New developments often sweep the country in a superficial way and are then quickly forgotten. New trends in music education must be carefully evaluated in terms of their applicability to the musical direction in a specific school system. The new basic music series are an example. Each series has a slightly different orientation, and one may well be more appropriate than another in a given situation. The new trend of a structured program, developing in a sequential manner from kindergarten to the sixth grade, is an important innovation in the field and one that will strengthen many music programs.

Other innovations must be carefully evaluated in terms of their suitability for improving certain aspects of the music program. Special music teachers should keep informed concerning the progress of the Juilliard Repertoire Project, since the results may add both depth and breadth to the song literature currently available for children. The first report of the Contemporary Music Project should also be studied for ideas concerning the presentation of contemporary music in the classroom; the teacher will also need to analyze future reports as they are published.

Some portions of both the Orff and the Kodály approaches to music education are appropriate for American classrooms but neither system is completely effective. Each stresses a few aspects of music and neither develops all the skills, concepts and understandings that are considered necessary in an American music education program suited to the needs of every child.

THE IMPORTANCE OF ADMINISTRATION

The music program will not be effective at any preschool or elementary-school level unless administration of several types is considered to be a vital part of the program. The music specialist is often an administrator as well. Principals must be fully cognizant of the objectives of the music program if this subject is to be a recognized part of the curriculum. Other administrators, e.g. the superintendent

---

[4] See also Mary Helen Richards, *Threshold to Music* (Palo Alto, Calif.: Fearon Publishers, 1964). Mrs. Richards has adapted some of Kodály's basic approaches for the American classroom. She features American folk songs and a clearly presented, structured approach to rhythmic and melodic reading.

and curriculum coordinator, must be aware of the benefits of music if this subject is to receive administrative and financial support.

The music specialist may be involved in administration as fully as he is in curriculum planning and direct classroom contact with children. He will supervise the acquisition and distribution of musical materials. He will also perform an administrative function as he establishes communication with other administrators and with classroom teachers. He may direct the teaching activities of other music specialists.

Elementary school principals must be convinced of the values of music if this subject is to attain its proper place in the school day. The principal must be fully cognizant of goals for each level of music education and realize the importance of facilities and equipment in the realization of these goals. Other administrators must be aware of the intrinsic value of music in the child's education. Superintendents and curriculum specialists will help provide facilities for music when they recognize the need for group music instruction in every classroom.

SUMMARY

Music for every child becomes more than a phrase as a music program is planned and implemented through the practical suggestions described in this chapter. These practical considerations are absolutely necessary if the challenging objectives presented in other chapters are to be attained by every child in the classroom.

Teachers and administrators must assess the effectiveness of their present program and cooperatively plan ways to improve classroom music activities. Scheduling, the training of the classroom teacher, and the selective introduction of audio-visual devices should be considered as instruction is planned and implemented.

New trends in music education must be evaluated in terms of the goals of a particular system. Administrators must be fully aware of the value of music if adequate facilities are to be provided for the child's music education.

Music should be an exciting and stimulating part of the child's life in school. A program that combines the practical approaches of this chapter with the sequential activities described in other parts of this text will bring music to every child.

QUESTIONS AND PROJECTS

1. Interview an elementary music specialist or classroom teacher to discover what problems interfere with the presentation of an effective music program.

2. Discuss the varied arrangements for teaching music described in this chapter. What are the advantages and disadvantages of each arrangement?
3. Consider the problems of sequence and continuity in the child's music education. What procedures will ensure the greatest amount of continuity from one grade level to another?

REFERENCES

Recommended Readings

"Administrative and Supervisory Problems." In *Music Education in Action*, edited by Archie N. Jones, chap. 7. Dubuque, Iowa: Wm. C. Brown Co., 1965.

Buechner, Alan C. "Team Teaching in Elementary Music Education." *Music Educators Journal* 50, no. 2 (November–December 1963).

Cheyette, Irving, and Cheyette, Herbert. *Teaching Music Creatively in the Elementary School*, chap. 11, "The Music Teacher as Supervisor and Resource and Unit Consultant." New York: McGraw-Hill Book Co., 1969.

Contemporary Music Project. *Experiments in Musical Creativity*. Washington, D.C.: Music Educators National Conference, 1966.

Flagg, Marion. "The Orff System in Today's World." *Music Educators Journal* 53, no. 4 (December 1966).

Hartsell, O. M. *Teaching Music in the Elementary School: Opinion and Comment*. Washington, D.C.: Association for Supervision and Curriculum Development, National Education Association, 1963.

Hermann, Edward J. *Supervising Music in the Elementary School*. Englewood Cliffs, N.J.: Prentice-Hall, 1965.

Kodály, Zoltán. *Choral Method*. 15 vols. Oceanside, N.Y.: Boosey & Hawkes, 1957–64.

Nash, Grace. *Music with Children*. Scottsdale, Ariz.: Swartwout Enterprises, 1965–67.

Nye, Robert Evans, and Nye, Vernice Trousdale. "Responding Creatively." In *Music in the Elementary School*, 2d ed., by Nye and Nye, chap. 9. Englewood Cliffs, N.J.: Prentice-Hall, 1964.

Orff, Carl, and Keetman, Gunild. *Music for Children*. Adapted by Doreen Hall and Arnold Walter. New York: Associated Music Publishers, 1960.

Palisca, Claude V., ed. *Music in Our Schools: A Search for Improvement*, Report of the Yale seminar on music education. Washington, D.C.: Office of Education, U.S. Department of Health, Education, and Welfare, 1964. (See Chapter 7, "Aids to Teaching," and Chapter 8, "Teacher Training and Retraining.")

Richards, Mary Helen. *Threshold to Music*. Palo Alto, Calif.: Fearon Publishers, 1964.

Sándor, Frigyes, ed. *Musical Education in Hungary*. Translated by Balogh, Horne, and Járbányi; revised by Cynthia Jolly. Budapest and London: Corvina Press, in cooperation with Barrie & Rockcliff, 1966 (distributed in the U.S.A. by Boosey & Hawkes, Oceanside, N.Y.).

Snyder, Keith D. *School Music Administration and Supervision*. Boston: Allyn & Bacon, 1959.

Thomas, Ronald B. "Innovative Music Education Programs." *Music Educators Journal* 53, no. 9 (May 1967): 50–52.

Audio-Visual Aids

Film Guide for Music Educators (ed. Donald J. Shetler), Music Educators National Conference, Washington, D.C.

National Association of Educational Broadcasters, Washington, D.C.

  Educational Television Services, Indiana University, Bloomington (television programs for elementary schools)

  National Educational Radio, University of Illinois, Urbana (radio series for elementary schools)

Appendix

SONGS FOR EVERY CHILD

The songs and teaching suggestions included in this Appendix are closely related to the contents of Chapters 2 and 3. This song collection has also been referred to frequently in the remaining chapters. The first section, Songs for Early Childhood (pages 246–83), contains those songs most appropriate for children between the approximate ages of three and eight. The second section contains songs related to the vocal and rhythmic program for older children described in Chapters 3 and 5. The songs and teaching suggestions included from page 284 through page 327 pertain directly to the vocal program, while the contents of pages 328–43 are closely related to the program of rhythmic activities.

SONGS FOR EARLY CHILDHOOD

Hop, Old Squirrel

Characteristics

"Hop, Old Squirrel" is suitable for the beginning singer at any pre-school or primary-grade level.

The song has a *limited range* of three tones, and there are many repetitions of the tone f-sharp'.[1]

Teaching Suggestions

No specific teaching techniques are necessary. The song is short and delightfully simple.

The young child will generally begin to sing the "eidledum" phrase first. These four repeated sections may be suggested as the child's special part of the song if "Hop, Old Squirrel" is introduced early in the school year. This technique will be effective in involving the shiest child in active participation.

This song provides an ideal opportunity to introduce melody instruments that the child will be able to play. A single resonator bell may be introduced and played first by the teacher as the child sings the "Hop, Old Squirrel" pattern. The child will easily play this part and will later enjoy finding the entire song on three bells.

Line notation may be introduced after this song is learned. The many repeated tones and the scale-step progression make this an excellent first example to direct the child's attention to the relationship between visual notation and melodic direction.

---

[1] An explanation of the markings designating tones in specific octaves is provided in Chapter 2 (page 17).

HOP, OLD SQUIRREL[2]

Well accented

Negro Folk Song

Hop, old squirrel, ei-dle-dum, ei-dle-dum, Hop, old squirrel, ei-dle-dum, dum.

Hop, old squirrel, ei-dle-dum, ei-dle-dum, Hop, old squirrel, ei-dle-dum dee!

2. Hide, old squirrel, eidledum, eidledum, ...

3. Peek at me, eidledum, eidledum, ...

Reprinted by permission of the publishers from Dorothy Scarborough, *On the Trail of Negro Folk Songs.* Cambridge, Mass.: Harvard University Press, Copyright, 1925, by Harvard University Press, 1953 by Mary McDaniel Parker.

[2] The autoharp chords selected to accompany the songs in this text are based on the harmonic possibilities of the Educators Model 15 Bar Autoharp.

I Got a Letter

Characteristics

"I Got a Letter" is particularly suitable for the beginning singer and for the child who is beginning to develop basic lower-range singing ability.

This song is in the key of D Minor. The child will be introduced to minor melodic and harmonic effects as he sings.

Teaching Suggestions

The teacher should introduce this song with an accented and syncopated performance.

The pattern "Oh yes, Oh yes" will help the slowest beginning singer. Every child will be able to sing this pattern after the song is repeated several times.

Mood contrasts may be introduced later by singing such words as "I didn't get a letter this morning, Oh no, Oh no" in a slower and less accented performance. The child will become aware of interpretation and contrasting moods as he sings these two texts in two different ways.

The song may be harmonized with a single tone or chord. The child will begin to develop harmonic concepts as he adds a D resonator bell to the melody line. He should not be told when to play the bell. The rhythmic groupings of this strongly accented song will help him select appropriate places. The child will later enjoy a richer harmonic sound as he substitutes an autoharp chord for the resonator bell.

I GOT A LETTER

Happily

mp

I got a let-ter this morn - ing—, Oh yes—, Oh yes—,

I got a let-ter this morn - ing—, Oh yes—, Oh yes—!

Adapted from *Birchard Music Series,* Book Two. Copyright © 1962, Summy-Birchard Company, Evanston, Illinois. All rights reserved. Used by permission.

Who's That?

Characteristics

While this is an extremely easy song to sing, every child will enjoy performing it since it provides a delightful setting for a "name" game.

The repeated pattern "tapping at the window—knocking at the door" will be helpful to the beginning singer.

This song may be repeated to evaluate individual singing ability. Children will participate eagerly in the musical guessing game, and the teacher will use this opportunity to evaluate individual vocal progress.

Teaching Suggestions

After the song is learned, a number of variations may be introduced. Children's names may be added to answer the musical questions. A guessing game may be introduced. One child may turn away from the group and sing the question. The teacher will designate another child to answer. The child who sang the question will then attempt to guess which child sang the answer.

WHO'S THAT?

Reprinted by permission of the publishers from Dorothy Scarborough, *On the Trail of Negro Folk Songs*. Cambridge, Mass.: Harvard University Press, Copyright, 1925, by Harvard University Press, 1953 by Mary McDaniel Parker.

Sing with Me

Characteristics

Every child between the ages of four and eight will enjoy singing this song. Some three-year-olds will be unable to sing the bottom tone.

"Sing with Me" is particularly appropriate when the teacher discovers that the child is ready to develop lower-range singing ability.

Teaching Suggestions

This song is an effective choice to begin the daily music period.

The song features a simple, repeated limited-range pattern:

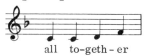

all to-geth-er

Word substitutions will help involve the child in beginning rhythmic activities. "Lean with me," "clap with me," and other activity suggestions will encourage rhythmic participation.

The many word-substitution possibilities will show the young child one way to use songs in a creative manner.

The limited-range pattern may be repeated to give the child additional opportunities to play simple melody instruments. The three tones are easy to find and play as a melodic accompaniment.

SING WITH ME

R.B.S.   American Singing Game

Sing with me, all to-geth-er, Sing with me, all to-geth-er, Sing with me, all to-geth-er, Won't you be my hon - ey?

2. Lean with me, all together....

3. Clap with me, all together....

I See a Girl

Characteristics

This song is appropriate for every child between the ages of four and eight.

It will give the teacher another opportunity to evaluate lower-range singing ability. The answer to the question, "Who are you?" will show the child's ability to sing between g' and c'.

Teaching Suggestions

This song provides an effective way to become acquainted with children at the beginning of the year. The many repetitions necessary as the teacher and other children sing to each child will never become boring. There are often many "blue shirts" or "black shoes" in each room, and suspense is maintained until the child is chosen at the end of the "Who are you?" phrase.

The importance of singing an answer to this happy question should be emphasized as much as possible. An example may be provided quite easily as the children sing to the teacher first.

The child will become aware of the element of rhythm and begin to develop basic rhythmic concepts and a foundation for later rhythmic reading as rhythmic activities are added to this song. These activities should be introduced first through direct participation. The teacher will help each child feel the underlying meter by clapping or tapping while he sings. The contrast between metrical groupings and the rhythm of the song melody may be shown first as children clap the meter and the teacher adds the rhythmic pattern. The child will develop further understanding of this rhythmic activity if both meter and rhythm are then displayed in line notation:

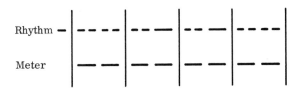

Some teachers prefer to proceed directly to actual rhythmic notation. This is particularly appropriate if the child has had many previous prereading experiences.

I SEE A GIRL

R.B.S.

German Folk Song

Happily

I see a girl whose dress is blue, dress is blue, dress is blue, I

see a girl whose dress is blue, Who are you?

Little Bird

Characteristics

This song is a favorite of any child and of many adults. Only one tone, the final c', moves out of a five-tone range from d' to a'.

The repeated limited-range pattern, "through my window," will be helpful to the child who first matches tones a little higher than most beginning singers.

Teaching Suggestions

This song is an ideal example of the type that should be presented to show the child how to change words in a flexible way. One word change is all that is necessary to transform "little bird" into a red bird, black bird, or eagle.

LITTLE BIRD

American Folk Song

Playfully

Lit - tle bird, lit - tle bird, go through my win - dow, Lit - tle bird,

lit - tle bird, go through my win - dow, Lit - tle bird, lit - tle bird, go

through my win - dow and buy mo - las - ses can - dy.

From John A. Lomax and Alan Lomax, *Our Singing Country.* Copyright 1941, Ludlow Music, Inc. Used by permission.

use names of towns

It Rained a Mist

Characteristics

Every child who is developing lower-range ability will enjoy singing this folk song.

Teaching Suggestions

The teacher's first performance of this song should emphasize those musical features that make it such a contrast to most American folk songs. The slow tempo, the minor tonality, and the wistful quality should be emphasized. The child will be captivated immediately by the haunting feeling that results from an effective performance.

The song will be requested and performed many times as weather changes suggest word substitutions. "The sun will shine," "the wind did blow," and many other replacements will be suggested after the child has learned to sing this folk song.

The teacher will help the child sing this song more accurately by showing the similarities and differences in two phrases. "It rained all over the town, town, town" is very similar to "it rained all over the town," but the melodies are slightly different. The teacher may underline these differences by hand signals or line notation:

It   rained all   o – ver   the   town, town, town,

It   rained_____   all   o – ver   the   town.

AM "19 —
(1st 2nd 3 times in
minor)

IT RAINED A MIST

Quietly

Folk Song from Virginia

It rained a mist, It rained a mist, It rained all o - ver the town, town, town, It rained_ all o - ver the town_____.

Reprinted by permission of the publishers from Arthur Kyle Davis, *Traditional Ballads of Virginia*. Cambridge, Mass.: Harvard University Press, Copyright, 1929, by the President and Fellows of Harvard University, and 1957 by Arthur Kyle Davis, Jr.

Who Built the Ark?

Characteristics

The child who is developing an *extended lower range* will learn to sing this song with ease.

The song also includes tones that are helpful to the child who begins to sing by matching extremely low pitches. Repetitions of the first melody pattern will help him begin to match tones.

Teaching Suggestions

This syncopated song sells itself. An effective first presentation, fast and well accented, will lead to immediate participation by the child.

The song provides the teacher with another opportunity to evaluate vocal ability. The refrain consists of a repeated question and answer. Two children should be selected for this evaluation activity. One will sing the question and the other the answer. The procedure may then be reversed. By providing each with a chance to sing both patterns, the teacher will obtain an accurate evaluation of lower-range singing ability.

As the child sings the refrain of this song he will become aware of dynamic contrast. This section should be sung first in a loud and robust manner and then repeated as an echo.

The entire song may be accompanied by a single E tone on a melody instrument. The teacher may later introduce a B tone and encourage the child to find places where it is an appropriate accompaniment. Measures 3, 4, and 7 may be harmonized with this tone.

This three-part song will give the child an opportunity to identify ABA contrasts in musical form.

WHO BUILT THE ARK?

From *Rolling Along in Song*, edited and arranged by J. Rosamond Johnson. Copyright 1937 by The Viking Press, Inc., copyright © renewed 1965 by Mrs. Nora E. Johnson. Reprinted by permission of The Viking Press, Inc.

Ha, Ha, Thisaway

Characteristics

The song is appropriate for the child between four and eight years of age who has had previous singing experience.

One repeated pattern in the B section is suitable for the beginning singer:

When   I   was   a   lit - tle girl,

Teaching Suggestions

This song should be presented in a soft but well-accented performance by the teacher. The song will tend to become raucous and too loud unless the child hears a softer model first.

The song text implies many word substitution possibilities. Different ages may be substituted, and the B section may easily become a birthday celebration song. The child will also enjoy singing about different people in addition to "girls" and "boys." The teacher's question, "What (Whom) else can we sing about?" will be answered in many ways. One favorite with the young boy is:

When I   was   a   cow - boy,   rid - ing my horse on the range.

Other word substitutions will make this song suitable for holidays. "Witches," "jack-o-lanterns," and valentine subjects are a few of the many possibilities. The child will have repeated opportunities to sing this happy song as he suggests appropriate word changes to suit holidays or other occasions. He will also further develop his creative abilities.

This is another song in three-part form. The child should recognize this if he has previously identified form contrasts in other songs.

The two sections of this song also contain strong rhythmic contrasts. The child may be singing and hearing a dotted rhythmic grouping for the first time. It will be appropriate to show him the difference visually between ♩. ♪ and the even eighth-note groupings in the B section. He will sing the two types of rhythmic groupings more accurately after he has seen and clapped or tapped each. He will also develop an understanding of rhythmic notation in a meaningful way.

HA, HA, THISAWAY

Happily   Huddie Ledbetter

Ha, ha, this-a-way, ha, ha, that-a-way, Ha, ha, this-a-way,

Fine

then, oh then. When I was a lit - tle {girl, boy,}

D.C. al Fine

lit-tle {girl, boy,} lit-tle {girl, boy,} When I was a lit-tle {girl, boy,} _____ years old.

Collected and adapted by John A. Lomax and Alan Lomax. Copyright 1936 and renewed © 1964, Folkways Music Publishers, New York. Used by permission.

The Allee Allee O

Characteristics

The child who has learned to sing "Ha, Ha, Thisaway" easily will also sing this New England boat song without difficulty.

Two of the phrases lie between e' and b'. They will be helpful to the few children who first sing higher tones.

Teaching Suggestions

This is a spirited song, and the first presentation should be lively and full of fun.

The child will enjoy singing about other types of boats and subjects connected with the water. As he sings about big boats—little boats, whales—guppies, or any other pair contrasting in size, he should be encouraged to sing in an appropriate manner. The child will often decide that he should sing softly as he substitutes such words as "rowboat" or "guppy." As he makes these musical decisions he is beginning to understand principles of interpretation.

This is an excellent "boy" song. The teacher should always consider a balance in song repertoire and choose songs that will appeal to as many children as possible. Every child will enjoy this happy chantey.

THE ALLEE ALLEE O

With spirit   Massachusetts Song

O, the big ship's a-sail - ing through the Al - lee Al - lee O,   the

Al - lee Al - lee O,   the Al - lee Al - lee O,   O, the

big ship's a-sail-ing through the Al - lee Al - lee O,   Hey,   ding dong day.

From Richard Chase, *Singing Games and Playparty Games* (New York: Dover
Publications, 1949).

Bye O, My Baby

Characteristics

Every child will find at least one melody pattern he can sing easily in this Scottish lullaby.

The beginning singer who matches very low tones first will find singing success as he repeats the first melody pattern.

Teaching Suggestions

The teacher's first presentation of this soft lullaby should feature a legato, flowing vocal line. Songs of this type are often introduced most effectively after a rhythmic activity. The child will become quiet and attentive as he hears this soothing melody.

The child will also enjoy humming a repetition of the lullaby.

Children will learn to sing this melody more easily if the teacher introduces hand signals after the first presentation. Practically every phrase begins on e'. The child should listen to each and then show the shape of the phrase with hand signals. He will demonstrate that he is developing concepts of melodic direction as he participates in this activity.

The teacher may then show the rise and fall of several patterns by placing them on a chalk or flannel board in line notation:

— – —

— —

BYE O, MY BABY

Bye o, my ba - by, bye o, my ba - by,

Bye __ o, my ba - by, bye o, my lamb,

Bye o, my ba - by, bye o, my ba - by,

Bye __ o, my ba - by, Bye o ba - by, bye.

Refrain of "Dance to Your Daddy" from record album CB–1, *Golden Slumbers*, Caedmon Records, Inc., New York. Reprinted by permission.

Sandy Land

Characteristics

Every child will be able to sing some portions of this song.
"Sandy Land" is particularly appropriate for the child when he first attempts to sing phrases above a'.

Teaching Suggestions

The child should hear vocal examples of the higher phrase as he learns to sing this song. The teacher may isolate this phrase and present it on melody bells or a recorder-type instrument. The teacher who periodically evaluates individual singing ability will know which child should serve as a singing model for this phrase.

The varied verses shown beneath the song indicate the flexibility of this folk-song melody. The child will invent many other verses if he is encouraged to do so.

The fourth verse is a delightful addition to the small number of birthday songs. It is also an excellent verse to introduce for vocal reasons. Children who hesitate to sing alone for others will find the musical answer to this happy question irresistible and will often sing, although they do not volunteer to sing solos at other times.

How old are you my pret-ty lit-tle miss? How old are you to - day?

She an-swered me with a ha, ha, ha! I am ____ to - day.

The birthday verse of "Sandy Land" will also serve as an opportunity for informal evaluation. The teacher will discover how well the child can sing an upper-range phrase as he sings an answer to the musical question, "How old are you?".

SANDY LAND

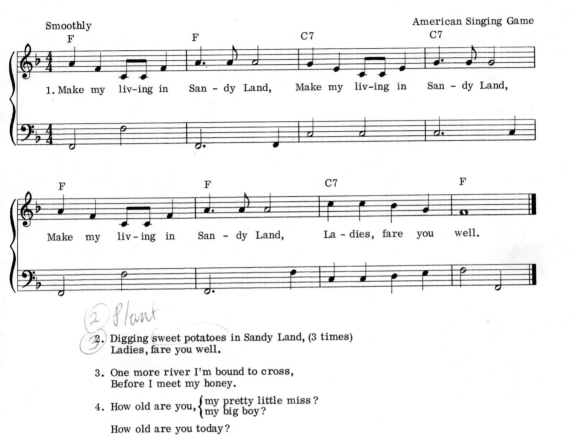

Smoothly   American Singing Game

2. (Plant)
2. Digging sweet potatoes in Sandy Land, (3 times)
   Ladies, fare you well.

3. One more river I'm bound to cross,
   Before I meet my honey.

4. How old are you, { my pretty little miss?
                     { my big boy?

   How old are you today?

   She } answered me with a ha, ha, ha!
   He }

   I am _____ today.

From B. A. Botkin, *The American Play-Party Song* (New York: Frederick Ungar Publishing Co.). Copyright 1937, © 1963 by B. A. Botkin.

Going to Boston

Characteristics

Every child who has developed lower-range tunefulness will enjoy singing the first half of this song.

The refrain is suitable for the child who is developing the ability to sing upper-range tones.

Teaching Suggestions

The child should experiment with different ways to sing the higher refrain. Some children begin to sing higher tones loudly, while others attempt to sing tones in this vocal range with a softer volume. All attempts should be encouraged. The teacher will eventually show the child that a softer sound is appropriate.

The first stanza is obviously intended for girls, while the second is a stanza for boys. The classroom may be divided for these different texts, but *all* should join in singing the refrain.

The child should have many opportunities to hear and to sing the refrain of this song. Finding the first and third phrases on instruments will help him learn to sing this upper-range portion. Three resonator bells may be introduced, and the child will find the pattern as he experiments with them. The teacher will indicate which bell begins the phrase and suggest that he sing the phrase while he finds these melody tones with the three bells.

GOING TO BOSTON

Playfully   American Play-Party Song

1. Come on, girls, we're going to Bos-ton, Come on, girls, we're going to Bos-ton,

Come on, girls, we're going to Bos-ton, Ear-ly in the morn - ing.

Refrain:

Don't we look hap-py when we're sing - ing? Don't we look hap-py when we're sing - ing?

Don't we look hap-py when we're sing - ing? Ear-ly in the morn - ing.

2. Come on, boys, and let's go with them, ...

Courtesy Cooperative Recreation Service, Delaware, Ohio.

Hoosen Johnny

Characteristics

Every child will find at least one pattern he can sing easily in this Illinois folk song. The first melody pattern and others exactly like it will be easy for the beginning singer. The child who has developed lower-range accuracy will also be able to add other tones.

Some preschool children and many primary-grade youngsters with previous singing experience will easily sing the upper-range patterns.

Teaching Suggestions

The first presentation of "Hoosen Johnny" should emphasize a contrast in dynamics as the teacher sings the upper-range tones. This example will show the child two different approaches as he attempts to sing higher phrases.

The child will enjoy singing other verses of this Illinois folk melody. The following are also traditional:

2. First he pawed and then he bellowed. . . .
3. He shook his tail and jarred the river. . . .

HOOSEN JOHNNY

Well accented

Folk Song from Illinois

The lit-tle black bull came down the mea-dow, Hoo-sen John-ny, Hoo-sen John-ny, The

lit-tle black bull came down the mea-dow, Long time a-go.

Refrain:

Long time a-go, Long time a-go, The

lit-tle black bull came down the mea-dow, Long time a-go.

From Carl Sandburg, *The American Songbag* (New York: Harcourt, Brace & World).

Savez-vous?

Characteristics

Children who have developed *upper-range* singing ability will learn to make a smoother transition between lower and higher tones as they sing this song.

"Savez-vous?" is equally appropriate for the child who begins to sing in an extremely *low range*. These children may match tones for the first time as they sing this melody pattern:

Teaching Suggestions

French words will present no problem to the child since he easily repeats new sounds he hears. The teacher may feel more at ease, however, by practicing the song first with this phonetic pronunciation:

Sah - vay-voo plahn - teh deh shoo,
Ah la moe-duh, ah la moe-duh,
Sah - vay-voo plahn - teh deh shoo,
Ah la moe-duh, duh shay noo.

The teacher should use a basic teaching technique in presenting this song if the class has not previously sung a song in another language. Children should be asked to sing the "à la mode" phrases as their part of the song. They will gradually add other phrases as the song is repeated.

This may be the first song the child has heard and sung in 3/4 meter. The teacher may add the following rhythmic activities after the song has been learned: (1) A simple arm conducting pattern may be introduced. The child will hear the stronger first pulse in each measure easily as he makes a large circle with one arm. The first beat in each measure will be indicated by the downward swing of this circle pattern. (2) The child might also clap the rhythmic pattern of "Savez-vous?". He will feel one characteristic triple pattern as he claps the repeated long-short grouping.

SAVEZ-VOUS?

French Folk Song

Smoothly

Sav - vez - vous plan - ter des choux,

A la mode, à la mo - de?

Sav - vez - vous plan - ter des choux,

A la mo - de de chez nous?

Three Pirates

Characteristics

This is another song with a part for every young singer. The child
with a wide vocal range will enjoy "Three Pirates" as much as the
beginning singer.

The higher phrases are appropriate for the child who is learning to
sing upper-range phrases. He will learn to make an easy transition
between lower and higher tones as he sings the second and third
phrases.

Teaching Suggestions

"Three Pirates" should be introduced by a performance in a slower
tempo. The upper-range phrases reverse melodic direction rather
quickly, and the child will hear these changes more clearly as he listens
to a slow performance.

The two-tone pattern that begins and ends this song may be played on
a simple melody instrument. The child will easily find this pattern.
Beginning singers may sing as they play these tones and thus increase
their ability to hear and sing tones.

The first or the final melody pattern may be added to this song as an
introduction. Children should listen to both and decide which is more
appropriate. A few children may then play the introduction on melody
bells before the other children sing. The child should then have the
opportunity to identify this aspect of musical form by listening to several recordings.

This may be the child's first exposure to 6/8 meter. He will begin to
develop an understanding of compound meter as he compares this
type of rhythmic pulse to another. The basic rhythmic patterns of
"Savez-vous?" and "Three Pirates" may be clapped or played on
rhythm instruments. The child will discover that one measure of
"Three Pirates" is similar to two measures of "Savez-vous?". He will
begin to understand that there are two accented pulses in a 6/8 meter
and that the first of these often has a stronger accent than the second:

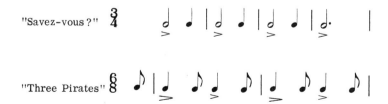

THREE PIRATES

Happily   English Folk Song

Three pi - rates came to Lon - don Town, Yo - ho, _____ yo - ho, _____ Three

pi - rates came to Lon - don Town, Yo - ho, _____ yo - ho, _____ Three

pi - rates came to Lon - don Town to see the King put on his crown, Yo

ho, you lub-bers, yo - ho, you lub-bers, Yo - ho, yo - ho, yo - ho. ____

Riding in a Buggy

Characteristics

The beginning singer will quickly learn to sing the first half of this song. This will be equally true of a three-year-old in nursery school and a second-grade child. Children with more singing experience will enjoy singing the second section.

Teaching Suggestions

The child's singing ability will determine the type of presentation the teacher will introduce. Classes with many beginning singers might be asked to sing just the "Mary Jane" patterns at first. The teacher will introduce the song more informally to children with more singing experience.

The teacher may repeat this song many times with the following variations: (1) The child should be encouraged to think of different word substitutions for "buggy." (2) Names of children in the classroom may be substituted for "Mary Jane." (3) Travel ideas may be substituted for the name in the song. The possibilities are unlimited.

This delightful song has repeated syncopated patterns:

The child will enjoy singing these. He will also enjoy finding them on a drum. Some children might later accompany the singing of this song by playing this pattern each time it occurs. This rhythmic accompaniment will enhance the bouncing quality of "Riding in a Buggy." The experience will also begin to make the child aware of syncopation.

RIDING IN A BUGGY

Well accented   Negro Folk Song

Rid-ing in a bug-gy with Ma-ry Jane, with Ma-ry Jane, with Ma-ry Jane,

Rid-ing in a bug-gy with Ma-ry Jane, We're a long way from home.

Who calls for me? Who calls for me?

Who calls for me, my dar-ling? Who calls for me?

Reprinted by permission of the publishers from Dorothy Scarborough, *On the Trail of Negro Folk Songs.* Cambridge, Mass.: Harvard University Press, Copyright, 1925, by Harvard University Press, 1953 by Mary McDaniel Parker.

When the Train Comes Along

Characteristics

This song has tone patterns that are suitable for any young child. The beginning singer will enjoy singing the three-tone pattern that ends each section. The child who sings lower-range tones easily will be able to sing all phrases that lie between d' and b'. The child with a wider singing range will also be able to sing the upper-range phrases which begin on d".

Teaching Suggestions

The teacher may present this song first with a train whistle introduction and coda effect. Children will thoroughly enjoy their attempts to sing higher tones as they practice the following introductory phrase:

pp   Ooo – ooo – ooo

The teacher should sing this phrase softly as an example for the child to imitate. The song may then be performed by the teacher as a *patrol*. Patrols begin very softly, gradually become louder, and then fade away until the final phrase is pianissimo. The effect is similar to that of a marching band which is heard at first in the distance, draws nearer and passes by, and then marches away until the sounds of music disappear. The child will become aware of dynamic changes as he hears and sings the song in this way. He will also have the opportunity to practice singing upper-range phrases in different ways. The soft train-whistle phrase and the pianissimo beginning and ending will allow him to hear soft examples which he will imitate.

Melody instruments may be added to repetitions of this song. The child will enjoy the challenge of discovering the introductory phrase on resonator or other melody bells. As he plays and sings he will strengthen his visual and aural concept of this melodic outline.

Simple instruments may be added to performances of this song to enhance the musical effects. Sand blocks and guiros are two rhythm instruments that will provide a simple and musically appropriate instrumentation. The child should experiment with other instruments to find those that provide appropriate effects. He will become more intensely aware of musical tone color and instrumental possibilities as he participates in this enrichment activity.

WHEN THE TRAIN COMES ALONG

From Ballanta-Taylor, *Saint Helena Island Spirituals* (New York: G. Schirmer, 1925).

Going Down to Cairo

Characteristics

This Illinois river song also has phrases that every child can sing. The first phrase is suitable for the child who sings higher tones. The child who is just beginning to match a few tones will be able to sing the second measure. The second half of the song is appropriate for the many children who sing lower-range phrases.

Teaching Suggestions

The teacher may present this song in a solo-chorus arrangement. The second measure of each phrase is the "chorus" part which the entire class will sing. As the child sings this answering phrase he has an excellent opportunity to hear the higher beginning pattern he will later sing.

The solo-chorus arrangement provides an ideal setting for vocal evaluation. The teacher may reintroduce this song and have each child sing one melody pattern while a second child sings the alternate melody.

GOING DOWN TO CAIRO

From *Second Fun and Folk Song Proof Book* (Delaware, Ohio: Cooperative Recreation Service).

SONGS FOR OLDER CHILDREN

Blow the Winds Southerly

Characteristics

This song, and others of the same type, should be sung by the older child as he learns to sing easily in the *transition range*.

"Blow the Winds Southerly" is also an ideal first round for children to perform as a part-song.

Teaching Suggestions

The song should be presented first very softly, and the child should imitate this soft example. As he performs softly he will sing from higher to lower tones with an appropriate vocal quality.

The song may also be performed as a round after children have learned to sing the melody. The roman numerals indicate three entrances.

Two chords provide a harmonic accompaniment for this simple melody. Their root tones will provide the child with the opportunity to add an additional harmonic part to this melody:

This added part may also be used as an introduction and coda. As the child arranges the round in this manner he will become more intensely aware of form and structure in music.

BLOW THE WINDS SOUTHERLY

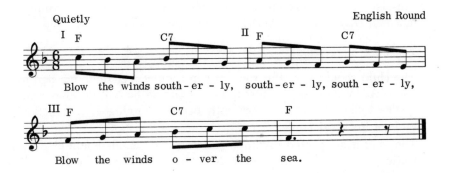

Blow the winds south-er - ly, south-er - ly, south-er - ly,

Blow the winds o - ver the sea.

Ma Bella Bimba

Characteristics

This Italian folk song provides the child with another opportunity to make an easy transition between higher and lower tones.

Teaching Suggestions

The child should hear this song first in a quiet, yet rhythmic performance. As he imitates this first musical example he will develop a vocal quality that will help him sing easily between the higher and the lower parts of his vocal range.

The song has repeated rhythmic patterns. The child should clap these softly and recognize them visually as he gains further understanding of rhythmic notation.

The song is a clear example of ABA form. The B or middle section provides a contrast to the first and third sections. The child will understand musical form more clearly as he hears and identifies repetition and contrast in "Ma Bella Bimba."

The Ash Grove

Characteristics

This quiet and wistful Welsh folk song is appropriate for any older child to sing. The total range is just over an octave, and the middle (B) section emphasizes tones in the transition range.

Teaching Suggestions

The teacher may present this song first as a melody which will help the child solve musical problems involving dynamic change and sequential repetition. Children will discover that crescendo and decrescendo in dynamic level often match the rise and fall of the melodic line. They will also discover as they sing that sequential repetitions (a feature of the B section) are often more interesting when dynamic changes are added. In this particular case each repetition is more effective if it is softer than the preceding pattern.

MA BELLA BIMBA

Italian Folk Song
Accompaniment by A. D. King

Allegretto

Oh, how she dan - ces, bel - la bim - ba, bel - la bim - ba, bel - la bim - ba, Oh, how she dan - ces, bel - la bim - ba, How she dan - ces all the day. Here comes my vil - lage girl, She dan - ces by you; All must ad - mire— her, Grace-ful de - light.

Fine

D.C.

Text and melody from *Work and Sing* (Delaware, Ohio: Cooperative Recreation Service).

This lovely melody is an example of AABA form. The child will understand formal organization in music more fully as he sings and hears the complete contrast of the B section. He will feel the need for the return of the A section as he sings and feels the lack of cadential completion at the end of the B section.

Interpretation possibilities may be studied as children are encouraged to experiment with different ways to sing this song. The class may perform the song in different ways and tape record each version. After they listen to different performances they will select the one that seems to express the melodic outline and text setting most successfully.

The melody has sufficient chord outline and sequential repetition to be introduced as a vocal reading example. The child should not attempt to read this song, however, without previous experience.

THE ASH GROVE

John Oxenford

Welsh Folk Song
Accompaniment by A. D. Ki▮

me. The friends of my child-hood a - gain are be -

fore me, Fond mem-o - ries wak-en as free - ly I roam. With

soft whis - pers la - den, its leaves rus - tle o'er me; The

ash grove, the ash grove that shel - tered my home.

Simple Gifts

Characteristics

This song falls within an easy range for the older child. The text and melodic phrasing are more complicated than the range.

Teaching Suggestions

The melody of this song should be presented to the child as a problem in musical analysis. He will discover that there is no exact repetition of either melody or text. Instead, the musical ideas seem to unfold and to continue without repetition. The child may learn this melody more easily by singing it in four-measure sections. After he has learned the first section, he will compare it to the next and become aware of the changes that take place.

This song melody may also be introduced as another opportunity to solve dynamic and interpretation problems related to the rise and fall of the melodic line. The song may be interpreted quite successfully by adding crescendo and decrescendo to the outline of the melody.

Children will enjoy listening to a recording of "Shaker Tune" from *Appalachian Spring* by Aaron Copland after they have learned this song (see the list of recordings of contemporary music at the end of Chapter 7).

SIMPLE GIFTS

Shaker Song

Kum Ba Yah

Characteristics

This song will help the child make a smooth transition between lower and higher tones.

Teaching Suggestions

The child will easily add a simple harmonic part to this song after he participates in the activities described in Chapter 3 (pages 43-45). The melody has repeated chord outline patterns. Children will recognize these patterns if they have had previous experience with the reading of vocal notation. "Kum Ba Yah" is therefore a suitable song for vocal reading practice.

KUM BA YAH

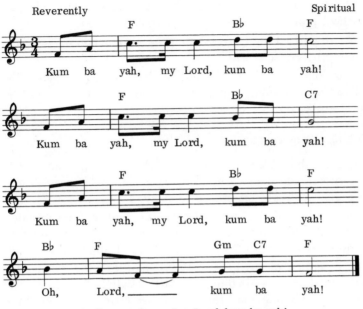

2. Someone's crying, Lord, kum ba yah!
3. Someone's praying, Lord, kum ba yah!

From *Look Away* (Delaware, Ohio: Cooperative Recreation Service).

Masters in This Hall

Characteristics

Children will enjoy performing this effective two-part arrangement for a school program celebrating the Christmas season.

The two-part setting provides an ideal introduction to *chant* as children develop harmonic sensitivity.

The melody of the first half and the chant that accompanies the refrain fall within a five-tone range appropriate for the child with a narrow vocal range.

Teaching Suggestions

The child should sing the melody of this easy part song first. The entire class should then learn to sing each chant. The teacher may decide to present only one chant at a time.

This first half of this joyous Christmas carol may be introduced as a vocal reading example in a minor tonality. The melody moves in a stepwise manner with the exception of one leap of a fifth, from d' to a'.

The repetition of rhythmic patterns may lead the teacher to present the song first as a rhythmic reading activity. The rhythmic patterns offer a clear example of compound meter (two pulses with three eighth notes to each pulse).

Resonator bells will add an effective musical tone color to performances of this song. The bells will highlight the holiday gaiety suggested by the text. The child who is singing harmonic parts for the first time will feel more secure as he sings and also hears an instrument play his part.

MASTERS IN THIS HALL

Brightly

Traditional English Carol

1. Mas - ters in this hall,___ Hear ye news to-
2. Then to Beth - l'em town___ We went two by
3. This is Christ the Lord,___ Mas - ters be ye

No - el, No - el, No - el, No - el, No - el,

day,___ Brought from o - ver-seas, And ev - er I you pray.
two,___ In a sor - ry place, We heard the ox - en low.
glad!___ Christ - mas is come in And no folk should be sad.

No - el, No - el, No - el, No - el, No - el.

Refrain:

No - el, No - el, No - el! No - el, sing we clear! Hol - pen
No - el, No - el, No - el! No - el, sing we loud! God to-

No - el, No - el, No - el, No - el,

are all folk on earth,_ Born_ is God's Son so dear. cast a - down the proud.
day hath all folk raised,_ And_

No - el, No - el,_ Born_ is God's Son so dear. cast a - down the proud.
And_

From *Growing with Music*, Book 5 by Wilson, H. R., et al. © 1966 by Prentice-Hall, Inc., Englewood Cliffs, New Jersey. Reprinted with permission.

Goodnight

Characteristics

The descant that has been added to this lullaby will be sung easily by the older child who is learning to sing simple harmonic parts.

The song falls within a comfortable range for any older child with previous singing experience.

Teaching Suggestions

The child will learn this repeated descant easily after he has become thoroughly familiar with the melody. As every child sings the descant while the teacher plays or sings the melody he may sustain the tones more easily and accurately if he accompanies his performance with hand motions.

Instruments may be added to the descant part. The child who is learning to play a woodwind or string instrument will enjoy adding his instrumental accompaniment to the descant line. Violins, flutes, or clarinets will add an appropriate tone color.

GOODNIGHT

Words by Angela Woods

German Folk Tune

1. Sleep well, sleep well, my fair-est one, Good-night, my loved one true. Sleep well, sleep well, my fair-est one, My dreams are all of you; May an-gels guard your slum-ber deep, And o-ver you a vig-il keep, sleep well, sleep well, my fair-est one, Good-night, my loved one true.

2. Through the night all the earth is peace-ful and still, With moon and stars a-bove. Dear-est one, may your sleep be filled with dreams That tell you of my love; The si-lent stars and moon so bright Will soon give way to morn-ing's light; As I wake with the dawn, my thoughts are of you, On-ly you, my loved one true.

Ah,

From *Growing with Music,* Book 5 by Wilson, H. R., et al. © 1966 by Prentice-Hall, Inc., Englewood Cliffs, New Jersey. Reprinted with permission.

To the Dance (Zum Tanz)

Characteristics

This is an ideal example of the first type of round older children should sing. The melody begins high and moves downward with stepwise motion. Children who are in the second group hear their beginning tone clearly and maintain their part easily because they are singing higher than the group that began the round performance.

The range of this round falls within the child's transition range. As he sings the melody he will practice singing smoothly and easily between higher and lower tones.

Teaching Suggestions

Children should become very familiar with the melody before they sing this round in parts. The song might be introduced as a round by having the entire class begin first while the teacher sings or plays the second entrance to demonstrate the way the melodies are combined. The procedure might then be reversed, with the teacher singing or playing the first entrance and the class beginning one measure later. The beginning tone should be firmly established before this second activity begins.

The round may be extended in several ways and become a more effective choral selection. The child may compose an introduction, perhaps by selecting a phrase from the melody and repeating it several times before the melody is sung. A chord-root accompaniment might be added to a unison performance of the melody. The entire round may be harmonized with one chord, the F Major I chord, and the chord root, F, will provide a suitable drone harmonization. The class may also experiment with different ways to end the round. The first group might hold their final tone. The second group might end at the same time as the first group by omitting the seventh measure.

The child might later analyze the round to discover why the two entrances are effective when they are sung together. As he sees the round written as a two-part example he will understand that the pleasing harmonic effects are due to the fact that the two lines combine in thirds:

TO THE DANCE

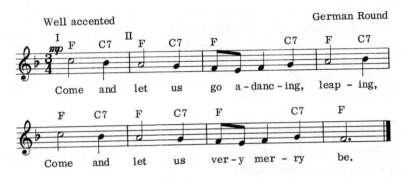

From *This Is Music*, Book 4, by William R. Sur, Mary R. Tolbert, William R. Fisher, and Gladys Pitcher. Copyright © 1967 by Allyn and Bacon, Inc. Used by permission.

Come Follow Me

Characteristics

This 17th-century canon will provide a successful harmonic singing experience for older children. The first phrase begins high and gradually moves down. The child will hear his entrance easily because of the high beginning tone.

The song may be used as an example of counterpoint and as an introduction to polyphonic music.

Teaching Suggestions

Children should learn this longer melody thoroughly before singing it as a two- or three-part canon.

Several teaching techniques may be added before singing the canon in parts if the class has never sung a song of this type before. (1) The class might be divided into groups and perform the canon as a rhythmic canon. Each group will chant the words in rhythm and clap the rhythmic pattern. Later the words may be omitted, and the divided class will clap the canon. The child learns to listen attentively to his own section of the canon as he chants and claps in this way. (2) The child may analyze the melodic structure before he begins to sing. He will discover that the first phrase consists of descending scale motion with a strong final cadence. The second phrase has two similar patterns. An ascending scale-step pattern is followed once by descending thirds and the second time by a simple cadence. The third phrase features three sequential repetitions and ends with the same cadence as the second. These two activities, feeling the rhythmic pulse and analyzing melodic structure, will be very helpful as children later sing the canon in parts.

The teacher may introduce the study of counterpoint, polyphony, and the baroque period after this canon has been learned. Suggestions will be found in Chapter 7 (pages 144–47). The contrapuntal characteristics of "Come Follow Me" may be shown to the child by presenting the different phrases as they look when they are performed together. The class will discover that the pleasing harmonic effects are more complex than those that occur in the simple rounds they have sung previously:

COME FOLLOW ME

Come fol - low, fol - low, fol - low, fol - low, fol - low, fol - low me. Whith - er shall I fol - low, fol - low, fol - low, Whith - er shall I fol - low, fol - low thee? To the green - wood, to the green - wood, To the green - wood, green - wood tree.

I Love the Mountains

Characteristics

This charming song has something to offer every child in the classroom. The "Boom-ti-a-da" phrases are ideal for the inexperienced singer and for the child with a lower voice.

Teaching Suggestions

"I Love the Mountains" is one of those delightful songs that sounds more difficult than it is. The child will learn to sing the melody easily because of the constant sequential repetition. He will begin to sing his own part in a three-part round easily since the entrances are three different tones of the I chord in F Major.

The teacher may help the groups singing the second and third entrances if this is the first time they have sung an entrance lower than the group that begins to sing the round. All children may sing the first phrase together. The first group continues with the second phrase as groups two and three repeat the first entrance.

Additional teaching suggestions may be found in Chapter 3 (pages 48–49).

The song is an excellent choice for classroom performances and an effective addition to the repertoire chosen for special choirs.

I LOVE THE MOUNTAINS

Expressively

Traditional Song

I love the moun-tains, I love the roll-ing hills, I love the foun-tains,

I love the daf-fo-dils. I love the fire-side when the lights are low.

Boom - ti - a - da, Boom - ti - a - da, Boom - ti - a - da, Boom - ti - ay!

Boom-ti-a-da, Boom-ti-a-da, Boom-ti-a-da, Boom-ti-ay! Boom, boom, boom!

There's a Meeting Here Tonight

Characteristics

This delightful song will captivate the child because of the bouncing, syncopated rhythmic patterns.

The added thirds (small notes) at the ends of some phrases are an ideal way to introduce children to this type of harmonization.

Teaching Suggestions

This may be the first song the child has learned that features a syncopated rhythmic pattern. The teacher may isolate this pattern by placing it on the board. The child will feel and understand the pattern by clapping and then adding the words as he continues to clap:

there's a   meet - ing   here   to-night

The harmonic part may be added to this song quite easily after the class has learned to sing the melody. Every child should learn this higher ending phrase and later alternate in singing either the melody or the harmonic part. The teacher may use two simple techniques in teaching this added part: (1) The teacher may play the melody and then the harmonic part and help the child discover that the harmonic part sounds very similar to the melody. He will also discover that it is higher. (2) The class should then hear and see the relationship of the added harmonic part to the previous melodic phrase. They will find that this part is delightfully easy to begin since they simply sing one step higher than the final tone of the previous phrase:

dai - ly   walk; There's a   meet-ing   here   to-night

A rhythmic accompaniment adds to the effect of this song. The child might experiment with different ways of clapping as he sings. A steady pattern of clapping the second eighth note of each beat is effective.

THERE'S A MEETING HERE TONIGHT

Negro Folk Song

From *Music for Young Americans*, Book 6 (New York: American Book Co., 1966).

Sleigh Bells (Minka)

Characteristics

The child will sing a harmonic part in sixths easily as he learns this exciting Russian folk song.

The added harmonic line will be particularly appropriate for the child with a lower vocal range.

Teaching Suggestions

Children will learn to sing this melody without difficulty. They should then hear and see the similar melodic outline of the lower harmonic part. They will discover as they look and listen that the part a sixth lower has the same outline as the melody, with two short exceptions. After the child has learned this harmonic phrase ending (measures 7–8 and 15–16) he will sing the lower part easily as the teacher plays or sings the melody. Every child should have repeated opportunities to sing the lower part.

The melody may be used as a vocal reading activity. The child should have had previous experience with the reading of melodic patterns in minor tonalities or be introduced to this aspect of vocal reading before he attempts to read this melody. Children will be able to read most of the melody easily after they have practiced reading and singing a I-chord outline in A minor. The teacher should prepare them to read measures seven and fifteen in the following manner: The class should find the tones of the V chord in this key. They should be placed on the board as a basic chord outline and as an outline in the first inversion. After reading and singing the chord outline in the root position the class should sing the inversion to become familiar with this different arrangement of the chord tones. Children will then recognize this inversion in the melody of "Sleigh Bells":

This song is an effective choice for winter-holiday special programs. The class may decide that instruments should be added to the performance. Wrist bells will provide a sleigh-bell effect.

SLEIGH BELLS

May Sarson

Russian Folk Tune

Light and fast

1. Mer – ry bells go ting – a – lin – gle, Toes and fin – gers freeze and tin – gle,
2. As we ride our song goes ring – ing, Through the air its ech – oes wing – ing,

With our friends we gai – ly min – gle, While the snow – flakes fall.
Till the world seems full of sing – ing: So we speed a – long.

Boys and girls, come out to – geth – er, Clad in coats of fur and leath – er
Through the town and by the riv – er Where the birch – es sigh and shiv – er

Made to brave the cold – est weath – er, When the sleigh bells ring.
And the birds are si – lent nev – er, Join – ing in our song.

From *Discovering Music Together*, Book 6, by Leonhard, Krone, Wolfe, and Fuller-
ton. Copyright © 1970, Follett Educational Corp., Chicago, Illinois. Reprinted by
permission of the publisher.

Sarasponda

Characteristics

The child will begin to read vocal notation easily as he learns to recognize and sing the repeated melodic patterns in this song.

"Sarasponda" is an easy song to sing. The three phrases emphasizing tones between c' and a' are particularly appropriate for the child who sings lower tones more easily.

Teaching Suggestions

The song should be introduced as a vocal reading activity. The teacher will prepare children for reading by explaining the key signature and by placing the I-chord outline and a scale-step melodic pattern on the board:

The child will read the first half of this melody easily after he has practiced reading and singing these examples. He should not attempt to read the second half. The intervals are more difficult, and this portion of the song should be learned in a rote manner.

A simple chant may be added to the first half of the song to provide a harmonic effect. This chant is also appropriate as an introduction:

Boom-da, boom-da, boom-da, boom-da

SARASPONDA

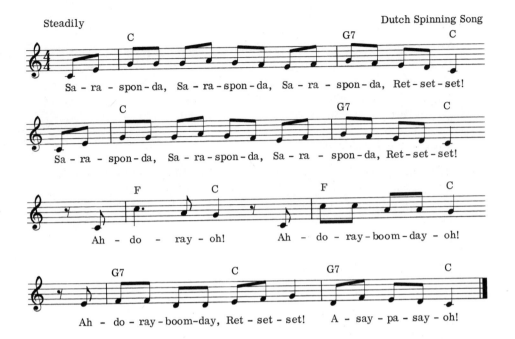

From *Chansons de notre chalet* (Delaware, Ohio: Cooperative Recreation Service, 1962).

The Deaf Woman's Courtship

Characteristics

This English folk song will provide ideal beginning practice in reading vocal notation.

The song melody consists almost entirely of tones in the easiest singing range. The child who has had little experience with singing will benefit greatly from the opportunity to sing these simple phrases.

Teaching Suggestions

The teacher should present this song as a reading activity if the child has been previously introduced to vocal reading. Three melodic patterns are featured:

Children may practice singing these patterns first by reading and singing them after they have been placed on the chalk board. They should then identify and sing them in this song.

This is also an ideal song for introducing the reading of rhythmic notation. The class will understand that there are two metrical pulses to each measure. They may then clap and chant the words rhythmically as the teacher or other children clap the meter.

The dialogue between boys and girls provides the teacher with an excellent opportunity to use this song for evaluation of the child's singing ability. The humorous questions and answers will prove irresistible to any older child.

THE DEAF WOMAN'S COURTSHIP

English Folk Song

With humor

Boys: 1. Old wom - an, old wom - an, Will you do my clean - ing?
2. Old wom - an, old wom - an, Will you do my wash - ing?
3. Old wom - an, old wom - an, Do you want to marry me?
(Whisper)

Old wom - an, old wom - an, Will you do my clean - ing?
Old wom - an, old wom - an, Will you do my wash - ing?
Old wom - an, old wom - an, Do you want to marry me?

Girls: 1. Speak a lit - tle loud - er, sir! I'm ver - y hard of hear - ing.
2. Speak a lit - tle loud - er, sir! I'm ver - y hard of hear - ing.
3. Oh my good-ness gra-cious, sir! I hear you ver - y clear - ly.

I've Been to Haarlem

Characteristics

This lighthearted chantey is ideal for a vocal reading activity. It is also a delightful song to sing.

The child who is an inexperienced singer will hear some limited-range patterns which are easy to sing. The child who sings well will also enjoy singing this American folk song.

Teaching Suggestions

This melody will provide ideal reading practice for children who have had previous vocal reading experience. Two melodic patterns involving chord outlines are repeated several times. One of these will be familiar to the child who has previously read and sung the ascending I-chord outline:

The pattern involving the chord root and the lower fifth may be new to the class. They should practice this interval and then learn to hear and add the sixth scale step as it appears in this phrase:

"I've Been to Haarlem" is also an ideal song for practicing the reading of rhythmic notation. As some members of the class clap four even pulses in each measure, others will easily find and clap the repeated rhythmic patterns involving eighth notes, quarter notes, and half notes.

The teacher may introduce the *alla breve* meter signature at this point. The child will be thoroughly familiar with 4/4 meter. He will notice that the meter of this song seems to be the same. The teacher should have the class find the number of pulses in each measure by tapping, clapping, or conducting while they sing. The child will discover, after he has experimented with the pulse of the meter in this way, that each measure has two strong pulses rather than four. The *alla breve* signature will become meaningful after this exploration.

I'VE BEEN TO HAARLEM

American Singing Game
Accompaniment by A. D. King

Find me an-oth - er job when this trip is o - ver. Sail - ing east,

sail - ing west, Sail - ing o - ver the o - cean, Bet-ter watch out when the

boat be-gins to rock, Or you'll fall off the deck in the o - cean.

Early One Morning

Characteristics

The child with vocal reading experience will learn more about vocal notation as he reads this challenging song.

The child will respond to the beauty of this English song and enjoy experimenting with appropriate dynamic changes as he interprets the rise and fall of the melody.

Teaching Suggestions

The child should analyze the melodic outline of this song by finding the chord outlines presented in Chapter 3 (page 56). Vocal reading problems will be solved through this analysis and by the practice of these patterns.

The child should apply dynamic contrast to the rise and fall of the melody. The most obvious dynamic changes will involve crescendo and decrescendo in direct relation to the shape of each phrase. The child should also consider the text as he interprets this song. He may decide that the second verse should be interpreted in a different manner from the first, since there is a distinct difference in mood.

EARLY ONE MORNING

English Folk Song
Accompaniment by A. D. King

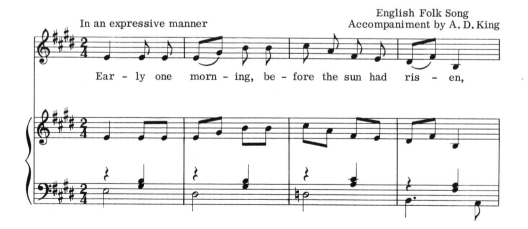

I heard a blue-bird in the fields— gai-ly sing,

"South winds are blow — ing, Green grass is grow — ing,

We— came to her - ald the mer - ry— spring."

2. One autumn afternoon, just as the sun was setting,
   I heard a bluebird on a tree pipe a song,
   "Farewell! We're going,
   Cold winds are blowing,
   But we'll be back when the days grow long."

Tum Balalaika

Characteristics

The first eight measures of this song may be used to introduce the child to vocal reading in a minor key. The first two phrases may be harmonized easily with lower thirds.

Teaching Suggestions

Suggestions for presenting this song as a vocal reading activity are presented in Chapter 3 (pages 56–57).

Children who have not had previous experience with adding original harmonic parts to a melody may be helped to discover the harmonic possibilities of "Tum Balalaika" in the following ways. The teacher may remind them that they have sung harmonizations at the interval of the third before and ask them to try to find a harmonizing part as they listen to the melody. If the children do not discover a harmonizing part after this experiment, the teacher may have them sing an f′ and then suggest that they begin on this tone and sing the melodic outline a third lower:

The child will easily sing this lower part. He will discover that a c-sharp′ sounds better at the end of the first line. He will also discover that the melody and the lower part should join in a unison ending to complete the second melodic line.

The song may also be harmonized by adding an autoharp accompaniment. Two children might cooperate in playing the accompaniment. One might press the chord bars while the other plays a tympani–roll effect by using two soft mallets.

TUM BALALAIKA

Jewish Riddle Song

Tum-ba - la, tum-ba-la, tum ba-la-lai - ka, Tum-ba - la, tum-ba - la, tum ba-la-lai - ka, Tum ba-la-lai - ka, tum ba-la-lai - ka, Tum ba-la-lai - ka, let us be gay.

Accompaniment by Walter Ehret, from *Growing with Music,* Book 5 by Wilson, H. R., et al. © 1966 by Prentice-Hall, Inc., Englewood Cliffs, New Jersey. Reprinted with permission.

Hush, My Babe

Characteristics

This lovely French lullaby has many musical possibilities. The melody lies in the child's transition range; the repeated phrases provide ideal vocal reading practice; and the quiet mood provides an effective contrast to other songs the child sings.

Teaching Suggestions

This song is described in Chapter 3 (pages 58–59) as a way of introducing the child to vocal and rhythmic dictation.

The melody may also be presented as a vocal reading example. The child who is familiar with the key of F Major, the I-chord outline, and scale-step motion will read this song without difficulty.

Children should make decisions concerning the appropriate dynamic level and type of accent as they sing this lullaby.

The teacher may underline the importance of phrasing and breathing as the child learns this song. The musical phrases are often repeated in exactly the same way. The text, however, contains phrases of different lengths.

HUSH, MY BABE

Isaac Watts

Jean–Jacques Rousseau

Gently

Hush, my — babe, lie
Heav'n - ly — bless - ings

still and slum - ber, Ho - ly — an - gels guard — thy — bed,
with - out num - ber, Gent - ly — fall - ing on — thy — head.

How much__ bet - ter thou'rt at - tend - ed Than the__

Son of God could be, When from__ heav - en

He de - scend - ed And be - came a child__ like__ thee.

From *Discovering Music Together,* Book 5, by Leonhard, Krone, Wolfe, and Fuller-
ton. Copyright © 1966 by Follett Publishing Company, Chicago, Illinois. Used by
permission.

Die Musici (Music Alone Shall Live)

Characteristics

The child who has maintained his part while the class has sung several easy rounds will be able to sing this simple German canon.

"Die Musici" is also appropriate as a beginning song for the special school chorus.

Teaching Suggestions

The teacher should present this melody first as a unison song. The child should learn to sing the melody well and then be made aware of several additional musical elements. He should compare the text to the musical phrases. He will discover that the three phrases are similar and that the first and third are identical. The word phrases are more varied. He must sing the entire first line without taking a breath. The word phrases that accompany the second and third lines of music suggest breathing in the middle of each line. As the child becomes aware of these differences and practices phrasing and breathing, he will develop sensitivity to this important expressive element of music.

"Die Musici" may be sung as a two-part canon. Children will discover, however, that it is much too short if it is performed only one time. This canon may be extended in several ways. The melody should be sung first in unison. The canon might then be repeated as a part song. Other possibilities will occur to the child who has discovered different ways to repeat a round or canon. The class may want to add one or more of the following possible changes: (1) An instrumental performance might alternate with a choral performance. Brass, string, or woodwind instruments will play a simple duet. (2) Instruments and voices may be combined in a two-part version. (3) The class may repeat the unison or two-part performance by substituting a neutral syllable, "la" or "ah," for the text.

This song may also be introduced as a rhythmic reading activity. The rhythmic patterns are simple and repeated. Children will understand dotted note patterns after they clap the rhythm of this song against the meter:

DIE MUSICI

German Canon

All things shall per - ish from un - der the sky;

Mu - sic a - lone shall live, mu - sic a - lone shall live,

Mu - sic a - lone shall live, nev - er to die.

Ah, Robin

Characteristics

This song may be presented to introduce older children to early music. While the child will hear some unfamiliar melodic sounds, the unusual effects are not difficult to sing.

The song has parts that will be appropriate for any level of singing ability. The boy with a deepening voice and the inexperienced singer will sing one part easily. The child with an unusually acute ear and a wide range will find another part quite challenging.

Teaching Suggestions

This canon may be extended by singing the lines in reverse order at the completion of the three-part arrangement. "Robin" is pronounced "Ro-bean."

Although the child should learn to sing each part and in this way become thoroughly familiar with the total effect, "Ah, Robin" may be performed in a way that will permit the child to sing the part best suited to his vocal ability and range. A few fifth- and sixth-grade boys begin to develop a lower singing range. They will sing the alto part easily. Children who sing easily over a wider range but who place extremely high tones with difficulty will enjoy singing the soprano part. The uncertain singer will also find this five-tone part (e'–b') easy to sing. The child who has developed a wide and accurate range will enjoy the musical challenge of the descant part.

A simple accompaniment will add to the musical effect of this three-part arrangement. The child who plays the recorder or other simple woodwind instrument may play the soprano part. Finger cymbals or a tambourine will add colorful rhythmic accents.

AH, ROBIN

Gently

William Cornyshe
(? -1523)

Soprano

Ah, Ro - bin,   gen - tle Ro-bin,   tell me how thy lay - man doth and

Soprano

thou shalt know of mine;   Ah, Ro - bin,   gen - tle Ro - bin,

Alto

Descant

Ah, Ro - bin,

Soprano

tell me how thy lay - man doth and thou shalt know of mine;

Alto

gen - tle Ro-bin,   tell me how thy lay-man doth and thou shalt know of mine.

Hosanna to the Living Lord
(Von Himmel kam der Engel Schar)

Characteristics

This two-part chorale will introduce the child to another style of early music.

The arrangement is suitable for a special choir and for classrooms in which soprano and alto tessituras are dominant.

Teaching Suggestions

Every child should learn to sing the soprano part of this chorale first. The alto part is more difficult and should be learned as a special part by children with lower voices and by outstanding singers with a wide range and an excellent rhythmic sense.

Chorale melodies are extremely effective when they are sung in unison. The full beauty of both the chorale and the lower harmonic part will be revealed to the child if each verse is performed first in unison and then in two parts.

Children should be aware of phrasing as they perform each verse. The melodies are identical, but the texts have word phrases of different lengths.

HOSANNA TO THE LIVING LORD

Caspar Othmayr
(1515-1553)
Arr. A. D. King

Majestically

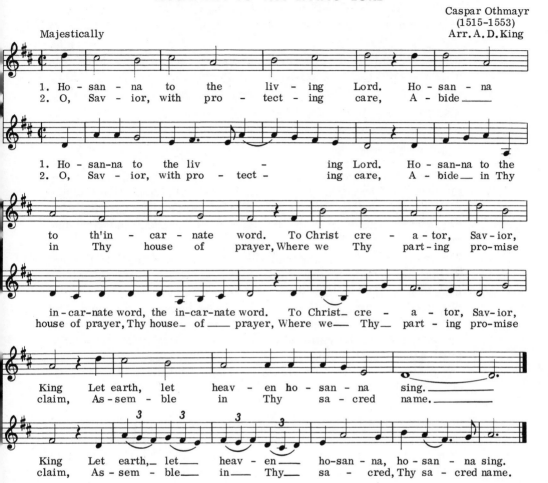

1. Ho - san - na to the liv - ing Lord. Ho - san - na
2. O, Sav - ior, with pro - tect - ing care, A - bide____

1. Ho - san-na to the liv - ing Lord. Ho - san-na to the
2. O, Sav - ior, with pro - tect - ing care, A - bide__ in Thy

to th'in - car - nate word. To Christ cre - a - tor, Sav - ior,
in Thy house of prayer, Where we Thy part - ing pro - mise

in - car-nate word, the in-car-nate word. To Christ__ cre - a - tor, Sav-ior,
house of prayer, Thy house__ of ____ prayer, Where we__ Thy__ part - ing pro-mise

King Let earth, let heav - en ho - san - na sing.____
claim, As - sem - ble in Thy sa - cred name._____

King Let earth,__ let__ heav - en__ ho-san - na, ho - san - na sing.
claim, As - sem - ble__ in__ Thy__ sa - cred, Thy sa - cred name.

He's Got the Whole World in His Hands

Characteristics

This spiritual will appeal to any child. The rhythmic effects are captivating, and the overall effect is both simple and musically moving.

The melody lies within a small vocal range of six tones. The child who needs additional opportunities to sing in the transition range will benefit vocally from repetitions of this spiritual.

Children are introduced to three-part choral music as they learn to sing this easy and effective arrangement.

Teaching Suggestions

Children should learn to sing this melody well before they learn to sing either of the accompanying chants. They will enjoy clapping the rhythm softly as they sing. They will also become more aware of the syncopated changes as they participate in this singing and rhythmic experience.

The chants should be introduced separately after the child has learned to sing the melody of this spiritual and the higher chant should be learned first. The child will find that this is an easy harmonic part to sing for the following reasons: (1) The chant begins on the same tone as the end of the unison melody which introduces this three-part arrangement. (2) The entire chant consists of repeated intervals of a third, either repeated exactly in the same place or sequentially repeated one tone lower. (3) There are no rhythmic problems to solve as children sing this chant. The rhythmic pattern is exactly the same as the meter.

The lower chant is also easy to sing after children have found the tone that actually introduces this pattern. The lower chant harmonizes with the higher chant at the interval of the sixth. The child who has previously sung the lower part of "Sleigh Bells" or other songs with lower sixths will easily maintain his part.

HE'S GOT THE WHOLE WORLD IN HIS HANDS

Well accented   Spiritual

1. He's got the whole ____ world ____ in His ____ hands, He's got the
2. He's got the wind and the rain ____ in His ____ hands, He's got the

whole wide ____ world ____ in His ____ hands, He's got the whole ____ world ____
wind and the rain ____ in His ____ hands, He's got the wind and the rain ____

in His ____ hands, He's got the whole world in His hands.

From *Making Music Your Own*, Book 6 (Morristown, N.J.: Silver Burdett Co., 1968).

Vesper Hymn

Characteristics

This quiet hymn will be simple for older children to sing. The first eight measures contain only those tones that are the easiest for children of any age to sing. The "Jubilate" refrain features two upper-range tone patterns which children will perform without difficulty.

Teaching Suggestions

"Vesper Hymn" is presented as a rhythmic reading example in Chapter 5 (page 104).

The hymn is appropriate for any school occasion when a solemn or reverent atmosphere may be enhanced with music. The text may be adapted to help children celebrate Thanksgiving and other special days.

VESPER HYMN

Thomas Moore

D. S. Bortniansky

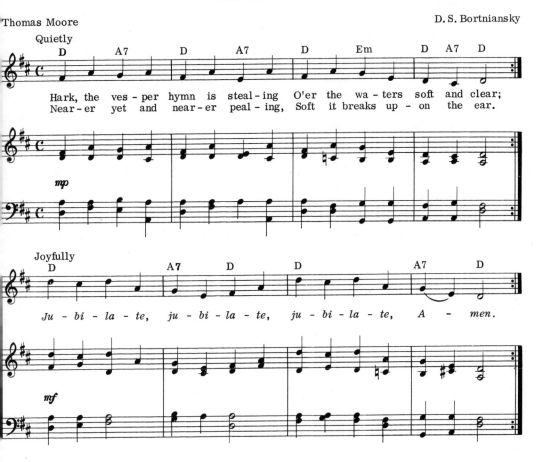

Hark, the ves - per hymn is steal - ing O'er the wa - ters soft and clear;
Near - er yet and near - er peal - ing, Soft it breaks up - on the ear.

Ju - bi - la - te, ju - bi - la - te, ju - bi - la - te, A - men.

From *Growing with Music*, Book 3 by Wilson, H. R., et al. © 1966 by Prentice-Hall, Inc., Englewood Cliffs, New Jersey. Reprinted with permission.

Sweet Betsy from Pike

Characteristics

Four of the six phrases in this song lie between c′ and g′. The child who sings higher phrases with difficulty will find these repeated lower phrases extremely easy to sing.

Teaching Suggestions

This song is an excellent example of repeated metrical patterns. The teacher may introduce the song as the child begins to read rhythmic notation. The activities described in Chapter 5 (pages 104–05) will help the child understand triple meters.

"Sweet Betsy from Pike" may also be used for melodic reading practice. The first, fourth, fifth, and sixth lines are particularly appropriate.

SWEET BETSY FROM PIKE

With spirit

American Folk Song

Oh, have you heard tales of sweet Bet - sy from Pike,

Who crossed the wide prai - rie with her hus - band Ike,

With two head of ox - en and one spot - ted hog,

Ver - y few hens and roost - ers, an old yel - low dog?

Refrain:

Sing-ing too - ra - li, too - ra - li, too - ra - li - ay,

Sing-ing too - ra - li, too - ra - li, too - ra - li - ay.

An American Vow

Characteristics

This song will provide the child with additional opportunities to practice transition range phrases. The first and third phrases feature tones in this range.

Teaching Suggestions

"An American Vow" is described as a song for a rhythmic reading activity in Chapter 5 (page 106).

This song should be added to the child's repertoire of patriotic songs. A performance of "An American Vow" will heighten the child's feeling about his country as children gather to celebrate a patriotic holiday.

The melodic outline may be used by the teacher to provide children with additional opportunities to add dynamic changes and expressive effects to the singing of this melody. Crescendos and decrescendos may accompany the rise and fall of the melody. Children should also help make decisions concerning the general dynamic level and the strength of rhythmic accents.

AN AMERICAN VOW

Claire Goodall

Scandinavian Folk Tune

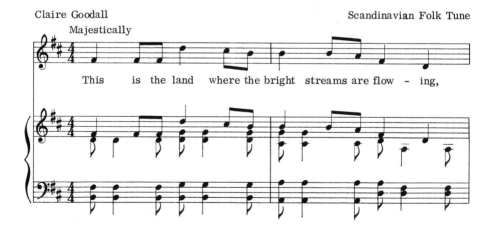

This is the land where the bright streams are flow - ing,

Sun - light is gold - en and soft winds are blow - ing,

Land where the mea - dows are rich with their sow - ing, Oh,

may it ev - er be Beau - ti - ful and free.

2. Then to the hills where the sun in its burning,
Blesses the land with a last crimson turning,
I breathe the vow in my heart, ever yearning,
To keep it, sea to sea,
Beautiful and free.

From *The Treble Ensemble.* Used by permission of the publishers, Schmitt, Hall & McCreary Company, Minneapolis, Minn.

Jesu, Joy of Man's Desiring

Characteristics

This song may be introduced to make the child aware of one type of religious music. He will learn to sing the melody easily and at the same time experience the simplicity and solemnity of an early German chorale.

Teaching Suggestions

The chorale is presented as a rhythmic reading activity in Chapter 5 (page 107).

The child will become more intensely aware of the beauty of religious music of the baroque period as he participates in the expressive listening activities described in Chapter 5, pages 101–02.

The teacher should emphasize the importance of phrasing as children sing this song. The melody phrases are very similar, and the child may conclude at first that each should be performed in a similar manner. The word phrases, however, demand greater variety in performance. The child should become conscious of the commas that separate portions of the text. It is often appropriate to breathe or hesitate slightly at these places.

JESU, JOY OF MAN'S DESIRING

Melody attributed to
Johann Schop

Word of God, our flesh _____ that fash-ioned,

With the fire of life _____ im-pas-sioned.

Striv - ing still to truth un - known,

Soar - ing, dy - ing round _____ Thy throne.

Blow the Wind

Characteristics

This folk song has a haunting, lonely quality. The child will respond to this in an expressive manner.

The range is appropriate for the child who sings well. The lowest and highest tones represent the extreme tones older children sing easily after they have developed their potential range.

Teaching Suggestions

"Blow the Wind" is included as a rhythmic reading activity in Chapter 5 (pages 107–08).

The song may be repeated several times as an example requiring an awareness of expressive performance and careful phrasing.

BLOW THE WIND

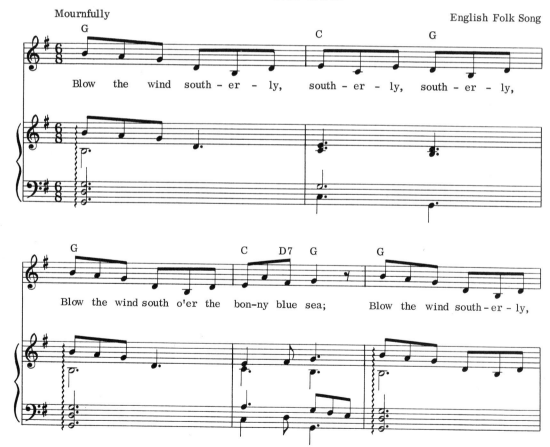

English Folk Song

Blow the wind south - er - ly, south - er - ly, south - er - ly,

Blow the wind south o'er the bon-ny blue sea; Blow the wind south - er - ly,

south-er-ly, south-er-ly, Blow, bon-ny breez-es, my dear ones to me.

They told me last night there were ships in the off - ing, And

I hur-ried down to the deep roll-ing sea; But my eyes could not see it, wher-

ev-er might be it, The bark that is bear-ing my dear ones to me.

D.C. al Fine

From *Growing with Music,* Book 6 by Wilson, H. R., et al. © 1966 by Prentice-Hall, Inc., Englewood Cliffs, New Jersey. Reprinted with permission.

Tirra-lirra-lirra

Characteristics

The child who sings extreme lower tones more easily will find melody patterns that are extremely comfortable. Other children with wider vocal ranges will learn this German melody with equal ease.

Teaching Suggestions

"Tirra-lirra-lirra" is described as a rhythmic reading example in Chapter 5 (pages 108–09).

This engaging folk song expresses the joyous feeling that accompanies the beginning of the spring season.

TIRRA-LIRRA-LIRRA

From *Growing with Music,* Book 5 by Wilson, H. R., et al. © 1966 by Prentice-Hall, Inc., Englewood Cliffs, New Jersey. Reprinted with permission.

A Murmuring Brook

Characteristics

The child will be introduced to an example of the German art song as he learns to sing this simple melody. He will sing easily in the range from b to b'.

Teaching Suggestions

This melody by Schubert is presented as an example (Chapter 5, page 109) to help the child learn to read and sing repeated uneven rhythmic patterns.

Several related activities are suggested in the same chapter. They will help children discover more about the nineteenth-century German art song.

A MURMURING BROOK

Madeleine A. Dufay

Franz Schubert

A mur - mur-ing brook sings a song of spring, A
song of de - light to be wan - der - ing, To

rip - ple and run with a gen - tle breeze, Tell - ing mea - dows in bloom of the bud - ding trees.

From *Growing with Music*, Book 5 by Wilson, H. R., et al. © 1966 by Prentice-Hall, Inc., Englewood Cliffs, New Jersey. Reprinted with permission.

Eliza Jane

Characteristics

This is another song in which lower-range phrases predominate. The child who has had little previous singing experience will have repeated opportunities to practice lower tones as he learns to sing "Eliza Jane."

Teaching Suggestions

The child will learn to recognize and to sing the syncopated patterns featured in this song as he participates in the activities described in Chapter 5 (page 110).

The engaging, rhythmic qualities in this song will make children want to sing other spirituals and Southern songs with similar characteristics.

ELIZA JANE

Well accented   American Folk Song

There's a girl in Bal-ti-more, E - li - za Jane,

She's the one that I a - dore, E - li - za Jane.

Oh, E - li - za, E - li - za Jane,

Oh, E - li - za, E - li - za Jane.

GLOSSARY

accelerando   Gradually becoming faster.

accent   A stress of one tone more than others.

alla breve   A tempo marking (₵) indicating the half note (rather than the quarter note) as the basic metrical unit; 2/2 rather than 4/4 meter.

allegretto   Moderately fast; slower than *allegro.*

allegro   Fast tempo, lively, quick.

Alberti bass   An accompaniment featuring alternating chord tones.

arpeggio   Sounding the tones of a chord in succession instead of simultaneously.

art song   A composed song in which the text, melody, and accompaniment are of equal importance in contributing to the expressive effects.

atonal   A compositional style of this century. Atonal music does not have a traditional tonal center.

baroque   A term used to describe music, art, and architecture of the period roughly between 1600 and 1750.

binary form   A basic two-part form.

cadence   A partial or complete melodic and harmonic resolution. A cadence may occur at the end of a phrase or a section, or in the final measures of a complete composition.

canon   A composition in which one part imitates another part at any pitch or time interval.

chorale   A religious melody composed for congregational singing at the time of the German Reformation.

chorale prelude   An organ composition based on a Protestant chorale to be played before the chorale is sung by the congregation.

classical period   While the term "classical" has several definitions, the reference in this text is to the Viennese classical period and the compositions of Haydn, Mozart, and Beethoven.

consonance   A combination of tones that produces repose and a lack of tension.

coda   A concluding section, often extending and reinforcing the final cadence.

counterpoint   A combination of two or more melodies to provide harmonic textures as well as melodic effects.

crescendo   Increasing in loudness (————).

da capo, D.C.   Return to the beginning.

dal segno, D.S.   Return to the sign (𝄋).

decrescendo   Decreasing in loudness (————).

diminuendo   Gradually softer (————).

dissonance   A combination of tones that produces an effect of tension.

embellishment   Ornamenting a tone with other tones.

fermata   Hold or pause; a sign placed over a note or rest (⌢).

fine   End; the final cadence.

forte   Loud (*f*).

fortissimo   Very loud (*ff*).

fugue   A musical form based on imitative counterpoint; from Italian
fuga, "flight."

glissando   Consecutive tones played rapidly by sliding the hand over
piano keys or the strings of an instrument such as the autoharp.

harmony   Vertical groupings of tones played together. Combinations
of these groupings—chord progressions—form the harmonic element in musical compositions.

   Basic chords   The most commonly used chords in traditional
harmony, also called *primary chords*, are triads (three-tone chords)
built on the first, fourth, and fifth tones of the diatonic scale:

A four-tone chord, the V₇, is traditionally substituted for the V
chord to provide added tone color:

   Chord inversions   Chords may be arranged in as many positions
as there are tones in the chord. The following example shows the
inversions of the I chord in C Major:

Root   First   Second
position inversion inversion

Chord progressions Traditional progressions of chords are often used in simple harmonizations. The progression I–IV–V₇–I is presented below in the tonalities most often found in the collection of songs in the Appendix:

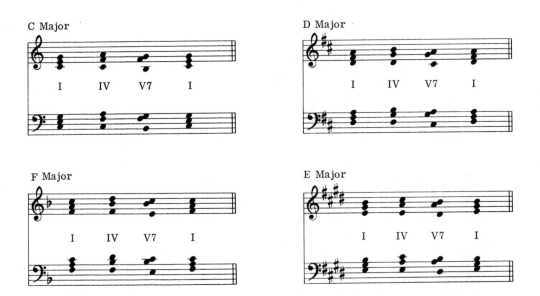

C Major

I   IV   V7   I

D Major

I   IV   V7   I

F Major

I   IV   V7   I

E Major

I   IV   V7   I

This chord progression also includes inversions of chords. The IV chord in each of the above examples is a second inversion. The V₇ chord is further simplified by the deletion of one tone:

Chord root The basic tone of a chord. Chord symbols (I, IV, V₇, etc.) are derived from the position of the chord root tone in a diatonic scale.

impressionism A style of musical composition developed in the late nineteenth and early twentieth centuries. The works of Debussy and Ravel are characteristic examples. Pentatonic, chromatic, and whole-tone scales provide some of the tone colors representative of this style.

interval The harmonic or melodic relationship of two tones:

minor   major   minor   major
second   second   third   third

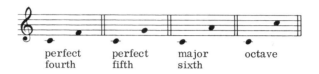

perfect   perfect   major   octave
fourth   fifth   sixth

Other intervals may be found in more complicated melodic or harmonic examples. Those above appear most frequently in the music examples included in this book.

inversion See *harmony.*

key See *tonality.*

legato Smooth and connected.

major See *harmony, scale.*

measure The smallest complete metrical unit; enclosed by bar lines.

melody The horizontal outline of a combination of tones; consists of varied combinations of scale-step motion, chord-outline motion, and exact repetition of tones.

meter The regular pulsations that occur throughout a musical work. Metrical groupings are generally duple (in twos), triple (in threes), or compound (a combination of duple and triple). The most common metrical designations are as follows:

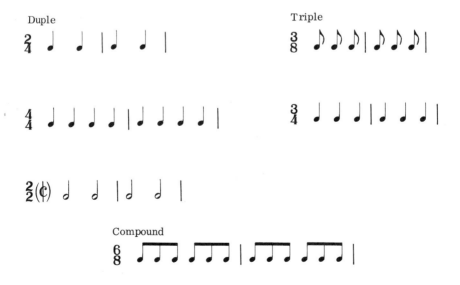

minor See *harmony, scale.*

minuet A dance form in triple meter; often incorporated in earlier symphonies as a third movement.

notation The written language of music (see *harmony, meter, scale*).

opera A staged drama performed by singers with an orchestral accompaniment.

oratorio A religious musical drama performed by soloists, chorus, and orchestra without scenery or costumes.

ostinato A short melody pattern repeated throughout a section or complete composition as an accompaniment.

phrase The smallest complete unit in a melodic line; often compared to a sentence in speech.

pitch A specific, continuous vibration.

polyphony Several melodic lines that combine in a pleasing harmonic manner; from Greek *polyphōnia,* "many voices."

polytonality A technique used by composers of this century. Several tonalities (more often two, *bitonality*) are heard at the same time.

resolution Progression from a moving or dissonant tone or chord to another (usually consonant) that provides a feeling of relaxation or completion.

rhythm That element of music pertaining to the temporal quality or duration of musical sounds.

romanticism Many nineteenth century composers rejected the characteristics of the earlier Viennese *classical style.* Romantic music is subjective and emotional, programmatic ideas are often featured, and rich sonorities are characteristic.

rondo A musical form featuring the alternation of different sections. The main theme or section (A) alternates with subsidiary themes or sections (e.g. A B A C A D A).

round A canon in which the melody is repeated at the same pitch level (see *canon*).

scale A horizontal (melodic) combination of tones in ascending or descending order through the interval (q.v.) of an octave. The following scales are most prevalent in traditional music:

   Diatonic scales A combination of half steps and whole steps:

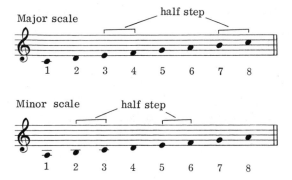

The second example is a *natural minor scale*. Two other minor scales are used in creating melodies. The *harmonic minor scale* has a raised seventh scale-step. The *melodic minor scale,* which raises both the sixth and seventh scale-steps ascending but is the same as the natural minor scale descending, is seldom found in music for children.

Pentatonic scale   Technically, sounding any five tones within the octave in succession produces a pentatonic scale. However, the term nearly always refers to a diatonic (major) scale with either (1) the third and the seventh or (2) the fourth and the seventh tones omitted. The former scale, which corresponds to the intervals between the black keys on the piano, is the more common, at least in children's song literature, and is the one referred to whenever the term is used in this book:

Pentatonic scale

Chromatic scale

Chromatic scale

sequence   Repetition of a melodic phrase or pattern at a higher or lower pitch level.

scherzo   A fast composition in triple meter with a feeling of one pulse per measure; often used as the third movement in a symphony.

sonata-allegro form   A three-part form consisting of exposition, development, and recapitulation.

staccato   Detached; short. Indicated by a dot over or under a note.

syncopation   Rhythmic patterns with tones of unequal lengths, often with a jazz or Latin-American anticipation.

tempo   The speed at which a composition is to be performed.

ternary form   A three-part form, with the third part a repetition of the first (A B A).

theme   A complete melodic musical statement, generally consisting of several phrases with a final cadence or resolution.

timbre   The characteristic sound of an instrument or a voice. The sound of an oboe is easily distinguishable from the sound of a flute. The tenor voice has a timbre quite different from that of a baritone.

tonality   Traditional compositions have a tonal center. In a musical work in the tonality (key) of C Major, all tones are related to the tone C as a resolution point.

tone color   See *timbre.*

transposition   Placing a composition in a different tonality.

trill   The rapid alternation of two adjacent tones.

twelve-tone   A technique of melodic composition developed by *atonal* composers. Melodies consist of an arbitrary arrangement of the twelve chromatic tones within an octave (*tone row* or *series*).

variation form   A flexible compositional form in which melodic, rhythmic, and harmonic elements may be varied. There are two related but distinct types of variation form: *sectional* (theme and variations) and *continuous* (chaconne, passacaglia, ground).

SONG INDEX

GENERAL INDEX